Plato on
Knowledge and Reality

Plato
on
Knowledge and Reality

Nicholas P. White

Hackett Publishing Company
Indianapolis • Cambridge

Cover design by Richard L. Listenberger
Interior design by Jared Carter
Printed in the United States of America
Fourth Printing 1993

For further information address Hackett Publishing Company, Inc.,
   Box 44937, Indianapolis, Indiana 46244-0937

Library of Congress Cataloging in Publication Data

White, Nicholas P.   1942-
    Plato on knowledge and reality.

    Bibliography: p.
    Includes indexes.
    1.   Plato—Knowledge, Theory of.   I.   Title.
    B398.K7W48   121   76-10993
    ISBN 0-915144-22-0, pbk
        0-915144-21-2, cloth

The paper used in this publication meets the minimum requirements of
the American National Standard for Information Sciences—Permanence
of Paper for Printed Library Materials, ANSI Z39.48-1984.
∞

for P. D.W.

Contents

Preface

This book is an account of a part of Plato's thought that was crucial to his philosophy and is no less important now. That there is a reality about which we may know or fail to know is an idea that all of us, even philosophers, almost always believe. But what this idea means still eludes us. For all their antiquity, Plato's reflections on this idea are deeper and more direct than any since, and they can help us to understand it in some degree.

My intention is that this book be of interest to the members of different groups. First there are those who, both as philosophers and as students of the Classics, have a primary concern with Plato's work. But in addition to them, I aim my exposition both at philosophers and at Classicists who count Plato's philosophy among their interests. I have not written quite as I would have if I had intended my account for any single one of these groups of readers, and I do not think that I can have satisfied them all. In extenuation of my failure in this respect, the best that I can do is to cite what Plato says at *Republic* 420b about the happiness of the three classes within his ideal city.

Thanks are due to the Rackham School of Graduate Studies at the University of Michigan, to the National Endowment for the Humanities, and to the Center for Hellenic Studies, all of which have, in their various ways, greatly aided my work. I am grateful to the Loeb Classical Library Foundation for support of its publication. In addition, I thank the *Review of Metaphysics* and its editor for permission to reprint a few paragraphs of an article that appeared there in 1974.

I am indebted to the many people who have helped me with this work. My debt to numerous authors who have written on pertinent subjects is greater than the footnotes can show. Moreover, the debt to scholars whom I happen to cite in disagreement is often by far the greatest.

Among those who have made helpful suggestions, I am particularly grateful to John M. Cooper, John McDowell, and Morton White, all of whom read the book at earlier stages and provided me with very valuable comments. And I am especially indebted to my teacher, G. E. L. Owen, for the very great help that he has given me in my work over the years.

N.B. The references by line number to Plato's text are to the Oxford edition of Burnet. In the notes accompanying each chapter, a numeral in boldface type following the author's name refers the reader to the complete bibliographic data for that reference, carried under List of Works Cited. This List begins on page 235.

Introduction

There is a reason why the aspect of Plato's thought that I am about to discuss should be important at this stage of the history of philosophy. I have in mind two pertinent facts. One is that there are abroad a great many signs of the relativistic, subjectivistic, and sceptical tendencies that Plato deplored in his own time and endeavored to combat. The other is that developments in contemporary Anglo-American philosophy have led to a point at which the central ideas of Plato's theory of knowledge, as I see it, are becoming a possible and even inevitable topic of philosophical reflection and debate. Exactly what causal relations hold between these two facts is difficult to say, but their consequences are important, both for Platonic scholarship and for philosophy in general.

As I shall present it here, the fundamental fact about Plato's theory of knowledge, from the beginning of his career to the end, is his conviction that there are matters of fact in the world, in some sense independent of our ideas and judgments, about which these ideas and judgments may be correct or incorrect. Plato's effort throughout his career was to expound this conviction, to explain what it seemed to him to mean and entail, and to defend it. The conviction as I have stated it is unclear, as is the term "realism" which seems to me appropriate to apply to it. It is an unspoken force within the mind that we endeavor, still (I think) without success, to articulate. Though he has had his followers, Plato's attempt to articulate it surpasses, in its force and directness, all that have been made since.

In a philosophical effort that has been of great import, and that still has a very great deal to be said in its favor, certain Logical Positivists made claims which, if carried through, would have proscribed this idea almost completely. Under the influence of the early Wittgenstein, they became convinced, for example, that intelligible talk about a relation between language and something called "reality" was impossible, and this conviction led to various attempts to do without this idea while still retaining the notion that our cognitive efforts are capable somehow of both success and failure. One thinks in particular of various accounts of truth that employ the notion of "coherence," so as to avoid a notion of "reality" which is viewed as not respectable. The attempts faltered rather quickly, by the end of the 1930s in many quarters but in a curious way the effect of the original impulse persisted, and was augmented by parallel forces operating in British philosophy, with its emphasis on ordinary language, which also worked against sustained examination of the notion. Outside of the philosophy of mathematics (it is no accident that this part of philosophy should have stayed closer than any other to Platonic preoccupations) realism and the notion of reality were topics that philosophers tended to treat in a gingerly fashion, rarely asking directly and squarely what they amounted to. By now the impulse is waning rapidly, as is also the instrumentalist and pragmatist view of science which was often combined with the positivist outlook. As a result, certain questions are coming out into the open which have previously been submerged, and questions surrounding realism are among them. Perhaps this development is in part a result of the increasing prominence, which I have just mentioned, of relativistic and other antirealistic ideas. But in any case, the appropriateness of an examination of this particular aspect of Plato's philosophy seems to me evident.

The appropriateness is all the greater because, for whatever reason, the epistemological side of Plato's doctrine is often slighted. This situation goes back a long way. Aristotle, it seems to me, did rather poorly by Plato's theory of knowledge. He concentrated his attention and fire instead on other features of Plato's thought, and most prominently on the metaphysics that had grown up in Plato's works as both support for and coequal part with his epistemological convictions. And when the Academy turned long after Plato's death to more epistemological concerns under the headship of Arcesilaus, it appears also to have turned away from Plato's own views. Moreover, as in earlier times, much of the critical and thoroughgoing examination of Plato's thought in modern days (and not only in the English-speaking world) has been inspired by

Aristotle and designed from his perspective. This fact has produced much work of high value, but it has had its drawbacks on the epistemological side of things and has left a gap which needs to be filled.

I treat Plato's ideas on these matters both because they are of such power and subtlety as to be intrinsically interesting, and because I take his position with utmost seriousness. The realistic view that he developed and defended is one that all of us feel must have something, and perhaps even everything, right about it. I also take his opponents seriously, as did he. Sometimes their views are unclearly or unstably defined by Plato (this defect was no doubt in large part their fault); at other times, as in the *Theaetetus*, their case is stated with more clarity and in more detail, as represented by the figure of Protagoras. Apart from various historical formulations of them, the different antirealistic philosophical impulses are as difficult to articulate clearly as the realistic impulse which they oppose, and certainly most modern formulations of relativistic, subjectivistic, and sceptical views leave many questions about their meaning still to be asked. (This latter point is true even of various sorts of scepticism, which has generally been framed with more care and treated with greater respect than the other two.) But the impulse or impulses themselves are by no means easy to contend with and must be treated with respect. Moreover, the opposition itself, between realistic and antirealistic viewpoints, is one that seems to me impossible for a philosopher to ignore. No one who believes it unfruitful will have much interest in the main line of thought in this book.

In my account of Plato's views I speak as the partisan neither of him nor of any of his direct opponents. In fact, my own view is that something at the core of Plato's realism is correct, something at the core of a certain kind of Protagorean relativism is correct, and that when these two things are properly understood, it can be seen that they do not in fact conflict. But I do not propose to argue this view here nor systematically to discuss the notion of reality which is at issue.

What I do propose to do is to examine critically Plato's views on the relevant issues, pressing his conception of the nature of human inquiry, and of the connection between that of which we may have knowledge and that knowledge itself. What we find is that through the various turns of his doctrine, he is pressing these conceptions himself and revealing, or more probably discovering, the problems that are latent in them. In this way he rewards the pressure that we put on his ideas. At times he shows himself to be in difficulty. The difficulties are of two kinds. Those of the former are nugatory, sometimes merely signs that certain rather technical points (though sometimes quite useful ones), which we now can see clearly after more than two millenia since his time, were unknown or not vivid to him. I remark on them occasionally, not to end argument but to show the lines which it may take, and to enable the reader less familiar with Plato than with contemporary philosophy to get his bearings. More important are the points at which I urge the difficulties affecting Plato's basic position, for example over the nature of inquiry in the *Meno*, or over the relationship, unclear in many works, between the effort to establish definitions and the effort to gain a sort of mental apprehension of Platonic Forms. These difficulties are not nugatory, and it is Plato's response to them that constitutes a central part of his epistemological enterprise. It is only by pressing them, and by endeavoring to understand the truths that they reveal, that due respect can be paid to the philosopher who discovered them, and proper sympathy be shown for his philosophical undertaking.

As the reader will by now have recognized, I do not intend to treat all aspects of Plato's philosophy, or even of that part of it that might, with one degree of latitude or another, be labeled epistemological. I am concerned with a particular problem, central to Plato's work, and I expound only so much of his related doctrines as seem to me essential to the understanding of his response to it. For this reason, I ignore much that is conventionally and correctly regarded as central to the Platonic theory of Forms. That theory had many philosophical purposes, of which I am here concerned chiefly with one. Plato was convinced that there must be more to believing truly than simply believing what comes to one's mind or the minds of those around one; he was convinced that there must be facts somehow independent for us to be right or wrong about. For a variety of reasons, he believed that those facts must be facts about Forms. But not every feature that he ascribes to Forms or to reality is central, or even necessary, to their role as that of which we may know or fail to know. Other features are attributed to Forms for other, equally important, philosophical reasons. But those other features are not the focus of attention here.

The focus of attention, as the reader will see, has two parts which are closely bound together. For I have treated Plato's response to the issues surrounding his realistic viewpoint in tandem with the viewpoint and issues themselves. There is a reason for this procedure. It is easy to confuse a philosopher's fundamental impulse with the various different formulations of it. To help avoid this confusion, it is best to show the philosopher working at the articulation of the idea. In this way, one gains understanding of, and sympathy for, what he is trying to do in abstraction from whatever difficulties he may encounter in actually doing it. It is only in the last chapter of the book, after a brief summary of the course of Plato's thought, that I give a more extended treatment of the issues that he faced and of his reaction to them. The treatment is not simply an appendix to the discussion of Plato but an essential completion of the exegesis. It of course falls far short of what the philosophical issues themselves require, but it will have to serve for the present.

Of the many issues that I have had to leave aside in this way, I have tried to indicate some in the footnotes that cater to various—some more philosophical and some more philological—different interests. I hope that these are consulted by readers interested in seeing matters pursued further than they sometimes are in the text. I only regret that because the line of thought in this book cuts across so many others, I have been unable to mention all of the issues that might be raised, and all of the pertinent things that have been said about them.

I believe that whereas his basic philosophical aims and impulses remained the same throughout his life, some of his views and approaches changed. I take it that as far as concerns his epistemology, Plato was from the start preoccupied with certain problems and a rough conception of how they were to be attacked. As time went on, it appears that this conception became progressively elaborated and refined and in certain respects altered. Still, it would be possible to suppose in certain cases that instead of changing or refining his views, Plato merely revealed them more and more clearly; and someone who accepts this supposition could accept, *mutatis mutandis*, a fairly large portion of my account. In other cases, however, this accommodation is not possible, even though I would tend to emphasize the continuity and stability of Plato's ultimate philosophical purposes.

It is from this picture of adaptation to new problems in the pursuit of unchanging goals that I think we can derive the most plausible and coherent account of Plato's thought. On some matters the interpretations that I offer are novel, but the reason is that, holding the view that the coherence of the whole picture is one consideration in favor of particular interpretations which are its parts, I follow a line of his thought which, as I have remarked, is usually left unexplored. The result, I think, is that we can begin to see Plato's works less as isolated attacks on separate problems, carried out in no very clearly intelligible sequence, than as stages in the systematic and rational response to a deep and complicated philosophical problem, of which he inaugurated the discussion and which he can help us to comprehend.

CHAPTER I

Early Dialogues:
The Setting of the Scene

We know something of the sources of Plato's philosophy, but not a great deal. For although we know that certain of his predecessors must have had some influence on him—the Pythagoreans, Heraclitus, the Sophists, Socrates—we cannot be sure which force was the strongest.[1] We know the figure to whom he acknowledged the greatest debt: it was Socrates. But we do not know precisely how this debt was incurred, because we do not know precisely what Socrates believed or said.[2] We also know that the intellectual figures to whom Plato paid the greatest attention—much of it hostile—were the Sophists, but again the lines of both opposition and affiliation are blurred by our ignorance of much of what they thought.

When we think specifically of Plato's theory of Forms, we still find problems of origins and authorship. Some have speculated, for example, that this theory was Plato's inheritance, and not, as is usually thought, his invention.[3] Although this speculation is not now popular, we shall never know for sure how much truth there was in it.[4]

Philosophically, the most important questions about the origin of the theory of Forms concern the philosophical problems that gave rise to it, and how it was supposed to help solve them. Quite apart, that is, from the identification of the authors of various parts of the theory, we need to know what sorts of philosophical tasks the theory was supposed to perform. For the discovery of the originator or originators of the theory, although it might give us clues as to intended theoretical purposes, could never by itself constitute a full account of the matter. For example, even if we suppose that Socrates had already possessed a substantial portion of the theory, it would not follow that his reasons for holding it were the same as Plato's. We need as much to know what the theory was intended to achieve as to know who fashioned it, and it is on the former sort of question that I shall be concentrating here. What are the philosophical problems broached in Plato's dialogues? What measures are taken against these problems? Precisely how were these measures supposed to be able to disarm the problems? What philosophical difficulties can be raised against the use of these measures against these problems? Which of these difficulties did Plato see? How did his response to these difficulties affect his views? It is questions of this sort (with a restriction of subject matter, of course) that will dominate the pages to follow.

It is noncontroversial that what there is of epistemological importance in the early dialogues can be associated with one or both of the following two issues: the nature of the search for definitions which these works typically pursue, and the nature of the entities which the search is generally made to involve. Although everyone agrees that these works are concerned with definitions, in some sense of that term,[5] the problem is to say what these definitions are supposed to be like and what they are for. Part of this problem, in turn, is to say what sorts of objects or entities Plato's definitions require, or seem to him to require. We shall now begin to focus on these problems.

We shall begin to focus on them, however, by taking a broad look at the intellectual and philosophical concerns that were working on Plato from the start, and that affected his outlook from then on. It is a commonplace, though a crucial one, that Plato's philosophical activity was directed toward finding something that could be taken to be certain and reliable knowledge, toward discovering judgments[6] which could be in some manner counted on. This description of his aim is of course rough, but it will do for present purposes. A likewise rough characterization of the sort of view that he particularly opposed can be constructed with such terms as "relativism," "scepticism," "anti-objectivism," and the like. These labels are not precise, and they can be confused with one another in obfuscatory ways, but we can still say that they fit, in one degree or another, various targets of Plato's philosophical attack. Another common label for that target is the term "Sophist," but we must be careful here, because the tendencies of the Sophistic movement were too complicated to permit simple description, and there were many trends in Sophistic thought that were not sceptical or relativist or anything of the kind.[7] But some Sophistic trends were indeed of that kind, and Plato took them to be such.[8] And even when he did not blame them exclusively on the Sophists, he deplored them and took pains to try to counteract them. In so doing, he fixed the form of his philosophical reflections.[9]

The role of Socrates in this debate is a fascinating and unanswered question. He has himself been pictured as a sort of sceptic,[10] and as such would paradoxically be the sort of philosopher against whom Plato was reacting most vigorously.[11] More plausibly, however, it has been thought that his scepticism was, as it were, a first step toward ridding oneself of a false conceit of knowledge, so that genuine knowledge might, somehow, be put in its place.[12] Plato, so this view continues, went beyond Socrates in developing a view about how such knowledge might be gained.[13] This account is, on the whole, believable, and I think that it is correct. But I shall not rest much on it, and I mention it primarily to point out one of the more important questions surrounding Socratic philosophizing.

But however it may have been with Socrates, Plato certainly opposed the tendencies that he sometimes associated with the Sophists. He thus opposed the various suggestions that were abroad, that in spite of man's ordinary unreflective convictions, questions that one might hope to settle are in fact not settleable, disagreements that one might hope to resolve are not resolvable, and that the truth of statements is somehow relative to the individual, or that there is no determining the truth about the facts with any certainty, or that there are no facts about which to determine the truth anyway. These suggestions are distinct from each other (though they were not, and are not, always kept apart), and Plato opposed them all.[14]

But—and this fact is crucial—there is one attitude that was held by Plato and (in all probability) Socrates in common with those Sophistic or quasi-Sophistic thinkers whom they attacked. This attitude was one of—as I shall frequently put it—distrust of hearsay, and, as a sort of corollary, refusal to accept anything simply because it was believed by the majority, or particularly by anyone who did not have some demonstrable claim to expertise or knowledge about the matter at hand. The idea is expressed in Socrates' professions of ignorance, which obviously show him unwilling to take for granted the testimony of others claiming to be purveyors of knowledge.[15] It is also expressed in the conviction of both Socrates and Plato that credence can only be given to—if one can only find out for certain who he is—the expert in whatever it is about which one is inquiring, including questions of government.[16] And most importantly and typically, it is expressed in the insistence, often repeated in Plato's works, that one should not trust the testimony of others (even putative experts) in place of one's own firsthand inspection or examination.[17] In Plato's view, the person who trusts another is settling for something less than the best grounds for making a judgment, or for confidence about any cognitive matter. Moreover, Plato thinks that this point holds even when it is a question of holding out against the universal agreement of all others.[18] (We shall see, furthermore, that this applies even to those issues which, according to some contemporary views, are *par excellence* proper issues on which to accept the pronouncements of the community; cf. secs. 3, 4.) That a judgment *should* be made never follows, Plato thinks, from the fact that it *is* made—no matter who makes it—nor will he allow that unanimity can confer authority.[19]

In adopting this view, Plato was taking a step that must have seemed nearly unavoidable. For clearly there was one important factor that fed the contemporary tendency to think (at least on occasion) that there is no settling disputes or disagreements and even to think that there are no "objective" matters of fact which those disputes and disagreements concern. That factor was simply, as has often been remarked, the realization of the extent to which there *was* disagreement, and the difficulty that was to be found in eliminating it. The rapid broadening of knowledge in this period led people to see differences in belief and attitude that had not previously been anticipated, and as is constantly pointed out, this fact led people, particularly in cosmopolitan centers such as Athens, to reflect that there was no telling *what* you might find people believing if you looked hard enough.[20] This is not the place to recount the story of this phenomenon, but its effect on Plato, given his frame of mind, is obvious. Appeals to the views of the majority at hand, or of some somehow sanctified authority, were unlikely to have much force, because one might, for all one knew, find somewhere else a larger group or a more august personage holding precisely the opposite opinion. All the more reason, then, for hearsay to seem an unattractive source of secure information.

It is in this situation that Plato found himself, wishing to discover some secure basis for judgment and firm claim to knowledge. Or at any rate so I shall picture him, because there seems to me little way otherwise of making sense of the line of thought that he followed. Thus, it will be his effort, starting from this point, to find such a basis for judgment, which will be the primary concern of this essay.

1 Forms in the Early Dialogues and Considerations for Their Existence

We have already glanced briefly at the philosophical tools that Plato used in constructing his epistemology: the definitions that many of his works try to find, and the Forms that are somehow involved in those searches. We shall ultimately be trying to see how the two are connected with one another, and some problems about their interconnection will emerge by the end of this chapter (sec. 5). Before we link them, however, let us look at them separately, to see in part what was expected of each of them. First, the Forms. For it is important to see that initially they appeared on the scene in a modest way, without fanfare, and that the reasons for their introduction were not, in Plato's mind, fully distinguished from each other or fully spelled out. Seeing these facts will later help us to understand why their epistemological role is, in certain respects, incompletely fixed.

First, however, we must satisfy ourselves that the objects that Plato tends to call "Forms" (εἴδη)[21] do indeed appear in the early dialogues.[22] For their initial entrance is so quiet that one finds it often, and understandably, denied that they are there at all, particularly by those who claim that the philosophical discussion of the early dialogues involves no entities other than, say, concrete sensible objects.[23] Others, however, see objects there beyond the concrete and the sensible and believe that Plato is dealing with them more or less consciously.[24] Still others are inclined to think that Plato already held in his mind a full-blown theory of Forms, such as we shall see in the later *Phaedo* and *Republic*.[25]

Even those who think that Plato had already formulated the bulk of his later theory rightly refrain from contending that very much of it is actually put to use in the earlier works. At best, what they can point to are hints of it. The importance of these hints, however, is magnified by their connection with the question of the authorship of the theory. For some who have seen the theory in the early works have doubtless done so because they were ready to attribute it, in basic outline at least, to Socrates.[26] Our present purposes, however, are served by saying that although we may admit that these hints might conceivably be signs of more elaborate views, inherited or already originated by the early Plato, such speculations are best left aside so that we may concentrate on what the early works give us explicitly and on what its philosophical import is.[27]

Our present question, then, is whether or not the early Plato thought that his philosophical investigations involved entities other than con-

crete sensible objects—quite regardless of whether he had a fully developed theory of what these entities were like.

There seems to me no doubt that in these works Plato *talks as if* he
believed in such entities.[28] When, for example, he asks in the *Euthyphro*
"What is *holiness*?" he takes no pains whatsoever to say that this manner
of searching for definitions (and it is his typical manner, early and
late)[29] is a mere *façon de parler*. Nor does any of the other early
dialogues, when indulging in such locutions, show any effort to soften
their force.

If objects such as holiness, bravery, and the like are to be denied a
place in these writings, it must be because one thinks that whatever
Plato's wording may have been, the use to which he puts his talk of such
objects may perfectly well be carried out in the absence of any reference
to them. In other words, as one would continue in this vein, Plato could
have said all that he wanted to say while still ignoring holiness and its ilk
altogether. Thus spelled out, however, the view provides an unappeal-
ing interpretation.[30] For whatever *we* may think of the possibility of
ignoring such entities in discussions such as Plato's, it is clear that this
possibility did not occur to him. He gives no hint of it. Accordingly,
even if we can admit that some parts of his early views and procedures
are in fact independent of the need to recognize such entities, we had
better suppose that he himself thought that he had them on his hands,
and that they are liable to play a genuine role in his cogitations. This is
not to say that at this point Plato had developed much of a theory about
what these entities are like, or that he had yet attributed to them very
many of the characteristics that later come to seem so characteristic of
Platonic Forms and serve to distinguish them from other non-sensible
entities that philosophers have from time to time hypostatized.[31] But if
we keep this fact in mind, then there is no harm in employing the
expression "Forms" in the description of even this early stage of Plato's
thought.

The reason why some have doubted the presence of the Forms, as I
have said, is that they are never formally introduced. Indeed, the
surprising fact is that nowhere in Plato's works—and, most notably,
nowhere in his earliest works—does one find what could be called a
full-fledged argument for the existence of Forms fully spelled out.[32]
There are fragments of such arguments in, for example, *Phaedo* 73-74
and the much later *Parmenides* 132a and 135b-c, but Plato never sets
them out with any explicitness.[33] Thus, if we are asking for his reasons
for believing in their existence, we have to go on somewhat rough
evidence.

When we follow up that evidence, the chief results are two. First, Plato had several reasons for believing in Forms, which can be expressed by saying that he thought that their existence would explain certain facts which would otherwise go unexplained.[34] Second, however, he did not express these considerations for the existence of Forms as openly and meticulously as one might wish, nor did he keep them fully distinct from one another. Still, he plainly has several considerations for the existence of Forms, and not all of them are epistemological in any very strict sense. Let me now sketch three of these considerations—not an exhaustive list[35]—to show something of their variety and something of their interplay.

The first consideration is epistemological. It is to the effect that one must suppose that the Forms exist in order to explain how we can know, or at least have grounds for believing, certain things to be true. The claim is that in order for us to know, e.g., that a certain action is just, there must be such an entity as Justice, whose existence helps to explain how it is that we can know that the action in question is just. The next step, of course, is to try to show *how* the existence of Justice helps to explain the knowing, or the having of grounds for believing, and the details of the explanation will depend on, and in turn have an effect on, the other views that the philosopher holds about such entities. What all of these explanations have in common, however, is that they all purport to be ways of accounting for the assumed fact that we do or can know, or have grounds for believing. One common way to try to start the explanation, of course, is to say that we somehow "know" or "apprehend" the object Justice, and then in some way use our apprehension of it to gain grounds for judging whether or not a particular action is just. But I anticipate.

That is the first consideration, roughly sketched. Let me distinguish from it two others, labelling them the "semantic" and the "metaphysical" considerations.

The semantic consideration that is pertinent here is the notion that the existence of an entity such as, for example, Justice can explain, not how it is possible to know something or have reason for believing it, but how it is that certain words make sense or are significant. The idea is that we could not explain, for example, how it is that a singular statement of the form "*a* is just" makes sense, or can be understood, unless we suppose that there is such a thing as Justice, which somehow confers meaningfulness on the word "just" and thus contributes to the meaningfulness of the whole statement. As before, the details of the explanation will vary from thinker to thinker, but what is ostensibly being explained is understanding rather than, as in the previous case, knowing or having grounds for belief.

The epistemological and semantic considerations are closely related inasmuch as their explananda, knowing and understanding, are so. For example, an explanation of knowing might be thought necessarily to include an explanation of some sort of understanding. Thus, the two sorts of consideration can easily be confused, and confusion is made all the easier by the fact that a theory of how statements can be meaningful can easily seem dull and useless, if not nonsensical, without a theory of how one can have grounds for believing some of them. But that does not show that the two considerations may not be distinguished.

The third, metaphysical, consideration is a view or family of views purporting to use talk of Forms or the like to explain in some general manner how things are, rather than simply how we understand or know about how they are. Consider, for example, the view that the objects in the world somehow fall out into "natural kinds," and that certain ways of collecting things together yield genuine groups and others do not, quite independently of the way in which we ourselves happen to classify things.[36] Thus, the class of tigers might be thought of as a genuine or natural class or kind, whereas the class of all of the things in Australia might be thought of as somehow artificial or lacking in standing. Of course, the mere claim that there is such a distinction between natural and artificial classes is independent of any particular way of drawing the line between them, and thus of the particular example just given. But however the distinction be drawn, it can be claimed that the putative fact that certain things somehow "go together" to form a natural group is to be explained by invoking Forms or similar objects corresponding to such groups. As before, the details of the proffered explanation may vary.[37]

All three of these considerations entered to some extent into Plato's work.[38] The first, epistemological, view appears, for example, in *Euthyphro* 6d-e, in which "looking to"[39] the Form or *eidos* of holiness is supposed to help us tell which things are holy:

> ... for you said, I think, that it is by one character (ἰδέα) that unholy things are unholy and holy things are holy. ... Then teach me what this character is so that I may look to (ἀποβλέπων) it and, using it as a paradigm (παράδειγμα), assert to be holy those things which are of the same sort, whether done by you or someone else, and assert not to be holy those things which are not of the same sort.

Other passages, too, betray much the same idea (cf. sec. 2).

The second, semantic, consideration does not find a wholly explicit enunciation until much later, when Plato says in the *Parmenides* that to deny the existence of Forms is to "destroy utterly the significance of discourse" (135b-c).[40] But the same view is present before that, though less openly espoused. It is at work in *Meno* 72-74, for example, in the tacit assumption that if one can say informatively that a number of things are virtues, there must exist some additional entity, Virtue (72c1-8; cf. b3-c2, d4-el).[41] It is also lurking in *Euthyphro* 5c8-d5, in a similar context. In the passage from the *Meno*, part of the explanation of the intelligibility of the statements in question appears to include the claim that the word "Virtue" is the "name" of this additional entity.[42] This sort of terminology is not raised to prominence in that dialogue, but we shall see it emerging again in the *Phaedo* and afterward (Ch. III, sec. 5, and Ch. VI).

The semantic consideration is connected with a related, but for our purposes tangential, issue of exegesis. The confusion has been shown by centuries of philosophy to be such an easy one that it is no denigration of Plato to note, as many have, that his writings exhibit a tendency to confuse meaning and reference and in particular to assimilate the claim that a term is meaningful or significant with the claim that there is an entity in the universe that it in some sense stands for or picks out.[43] The tendency appears in connection with both singular terms like "Socrates" or "the teacher of Plato" and general terms like "man" or "wise" or "large." It is shown particularly by the ease with which some can assume, without argument, that in order to be meaningful and to function as an intelligible part of discourse, a general term such as "wise" must, in contexts such as "Socrates is wise," pick out or refer to some piece of the contents of the world (such as, say, wisdom) in the way in which the name "Socrates" refers to Socrates. Of course to hold this view is not *ipso facto* to be subject to that confusion; but confusion may be suspected when a philosopher sees no need to support the view with argument. By this standard, Plato may have been confused. Certainly the *Sophist*, a relatively late work, has been interpreted as making a strenuous effort to avoid the confusion as applied to singular terms (e.g., the unargued assumption that in order to be usable in discourse, the word "Medusa" must refer to Medusa, notwithstanding our well-grounded desire to say that there is no such thing as Medusa).[44] But even if this interpretation is correct, it is not clear that the effort is successful, and it is thus even more unlikely that Plato has achieved great clarity on this matter in the period that we are now reviewing. Fortunately, however, this matter will not much affect our discussion.

The metaphysical consideration, finally, also arises at various stages of Plato's thought. Of his dialogues, the *Phaedrus* and the *Statesman* most clearly exhibit the belief that the things in the world can be divided into natural kinds, and they plainly tie this view to the theory of Forms (see Ch. V, sec. 1). The earlier dialogues also tacitly adopt something like a belief in natural kinds, as is shown by the fact that Plato clearly assumes that only certain groupings of things are important enough to take account of by postulating Forms for them, though he may not have realized explicitly that he was making this assumption or have seen its importance. He did, however, put the Forms to another task which can be seen as related to the metaphysical consideration. For he thinks in general the Form of *F* can be used to explain why each of the *F* objects is *F*. Thus *Euthyphro* 6d-e says that it is "by a character (εἶδος) that holy things are holy" (d10-11), and "by one character (ἰδέα) that unholy things are unholy" (d11-e1). Similarly, the *Meno* says that various virtues are virtues "because of" (διά) one character, virtue (72c7-8), and that if a woman is strong she is so "by" strength. The same view, more fully developed, appears in the *Phaedo*, in which we see the doctrine that the Forms are "causes" (αἰτίαι). No need to wonder how closely this notion of "cause" approximates our own;[45] it suffices to realize that in all of these places Plato wants somehow to use the Forms in order to explain why certain things are thus-and-so (e.g., just, holy).[46]

As I have said, Plato does not distinguish these various considerations from one another or separate the epistemological consideration from the rest. There is accordingly no place in which he announces the epistemological questions that concern him and tells in so many words how he expects the Forms to figure in the answers to them. Thus, the introduction of the Forms is not a meticulously planned affair, and not all of the details are settled and taken care of from the start. An awareness of this fact on our part will help us to be less surprised when we see some of the difficulties that arise as soon as we come to his application of the Forms to epistemological matters.

2 A Preliminary Look at the Roles of Definitions in the Early Works

Turning away from Forms for the time being, let us now examine Plato's purposes in seeking definitions. A survey of the early dialogues shows two aims that he has primarily in view. Once we have glanced at them we shall return to the Forms again.

Not surprisingly, one of Plato's most important purposes in looking for definitions is to help him determine what terms may be truly applied to sensible objects, including actions and events. In trying in the *Euthyphro* to say what Holiness is, for example, the interlocutors are trying to determine whether or not a particular action, the prosecution by Euthyphro of his father, is holy or not, and at the end of the dialogue Socrates says that he has been disappointed in his expectation of learning which things are holy and which are not (μαθὼν τὰ ὅσια καὶ μή, 15e6-7). Similarly, the last sentence of the *Lysis* ("though we think of each other as friends we are not yet able to discover what a friend is," 223b) shows that one of the main purposes of the effort to say "what a friend is" has been to become better able to tell who one's friends are, and the dialogue abounds with efforts to do just that. In *Charmides* 176a-b, and *Hippias Major* 286c-d (the latter, of course, being relevant only if the work is genuine)[47] an analogous purpose is evident, as perhaps also at *Gorgias* 448e, where we seem to need an account of the skill practiced by Gorgias in order to know "what to call him." In the *Meno* furthermore, although the conversation is drawn away from the question, what is virtue (86c4ff., 100b4-6), it is suggested that if we had a clear account of virtue we might have a different view from our present one about who the genuinely good men are.[48] Let "*F*" represent a predicate or general term; then the view is that the answer to a question like "What is *F*-ness?" (we shall see that there are other forms of this question) will somehow aid us in telling which things are *F*.[49]

There is another sort of motivation behind questions of the type "What is *F*-ness?" beside the effort to determine the extension of the corresponding general term "*F*." For example, the *Meno* asks not only what virtue is, but also how one acquires it and whether or not it is teachable (70a1-4); the *Lysis* is concerned not only with what it is to be a friend, but also with "how (ὄντινα τρόπον) one man becomes the friend of another" (212a5-6); the *Laches* asks what bravery is and also how one may acquire it (189e-190c); *Republic* I—and indeed the whole of the *Republic*[50]—reveals an effort to discover both what justice is and whether or not it is (in some sense) profitable (354c, etc.). In all these cases, answering the "What is it?" question is supposed to be helpful for, and indeed a *sine qua non* of, getting a particular sort of information about something beyond the mere extension of the pertinent general term. To modern eyes, the information sought appears, at least at first sight, to be of causal or quasi-causal nature: the *Meno* seems to be asking what procedures will cause a man to become virtuous or good; the *Lysis* seems to be asking what causes one man to be a friend of another; and the *Republic* seems to be asking whether or not being just will cause a man gain or happiness.[51] But whether or not this initial impression is correct (and there are reasons for doubting it), we must acknowledge that Plato does not attempt to give an explicit general characterization of the sort of information that he expects to be provided by answers to "What is it?" questions. The brevity with which he treats the point (*Meno* 71a-b, 100b; cf. *Laches* 189e-190c) suggests that he thinks it immediately obvious that one cannot know whether virtue is teachable until one knows what it is, and he may be relying on what he takes to be the plainest common sense. But we should try to push the matter further, to see how he thinks that answers to "What is it?" questions might yield this additional information.

The *Meno* gives us a possible clue. In 86ff. Plato "hypothesizes" that virtue is a sort of knowledge and concludes from this hypothesis that it must be teachable, on the ground that every sort of knowledge is teachable. What this procedure might suggest is that in Plato's view the answers to further questions such as "Is virtue teachable?" may be deduced from the definition.[52] If so, would he apply the same model to bravery, e.g., and say that given its definition (and perhaps some auxiliary premises as well), we could deduce correct statements about how people come to be brave? Do we see here a general way in which he thinks that definitions give us additional information, by serving as premises from which the information may be derived?[53] Plato does not make the matter clear, and we shall see that there is a competing possibility arising from things that he says in the *Meno* (see Ch. II, sec. 1). Simply note for now that his theory starts out, not surprisingly, in an undeveloped or at least unexpounded state.

Let us return now to that other matter on which definitions are supposed to be of help, namely the effort to determine the extensions of predicates. Answering the question "What is holiness?" is supposed to tell us which things are holy. But we have already seen Plato saying in the previous section that the same enterprise would be furthered by "looking to" (ἀποβλέπειν πρός) the Form, Holiness (*Euthyphro* 6d-e). So the determination of what things are holy is to be aided both by getting a definition in answer to the question "What is Holiness?" and by (in some sense) "looking to" the Form. And this fact, though in and of itself not problematical, should stimulate us to ask what the connection is between these two projects—getting a definition and looking to the Form—and just how the conjunction of the two of them should help us to tell the holy from the unholy. With this question in mind, and also the ends for which Plato intended definitions to be used, let us consider what resources he thought were available for discovering them. That considered, we shall return (sec. 5) to the question just raised.

3 The Quest for Definitions

Why did Plato conceive an interest in definitions? Of course it answers no philosophical questions simply to reply with Aristotle that he inherited the interest from Socrates (*Metaphysics* 987b1-4, 1078b17-30). For the question would then still be why he thought that interest worth inheriting. It is of extreme importance in understanding the line of his thought to realize that in the early dialogues he does not attack this question directly. If we think that he does, then we shall both underestimate the complexity of the philosophical issues involved and also fail to appreciate properly the moves that he makes in later works toward answering precisely those questions that arise out of the earlier ones.

The beginning of the answer to this question is a simple one, though we shall see that it gives way to something much more complicated. We have seen that one of Plato's aims is to determine the extensions of general terms. But there is a natural link, with which all of us are familiar, between this aim and things that we think of as definitions. For we are often enough confronted with words which, as it turns out, are common and unproblematical, but which we do not (yet) understand. People in such predicaments often repair to dictionaries, parents, or the nearest speaker of the language, and are given some expression or string of expressions that they understand (or at least think that they understand), and that purports to provide an explanation, in some sense, of the word or phrase that was causing the problem. We need not trouble ourselves over exactly what is happening, philosophically considered, in situations such as this, or over what other procedures we may also employ in mastering language. What is important here is that often, having previously been uncertain what a general term is true of, say, we come to be able to use it with confidence and in accord with our neighbors, believing henceforth that—if the term in question be represented by "F"—our singular statements of the form "a is F" are at least usually true, and that when they are false our mistakes are not due to any misunderstanding of the term, as we look at the matter, but by our failure to take proper account of some facts not directly relevant to the meaning of the term itself. For example, we incorrectly call something in the grass a spider, not—as it may seem— because we do not understand the word "spider," but because we cannot see the thing very well and do not realize that it is a lizard.

Whatever philosophical problems this view may engender,[54] the view itself is in one form or another both widespread and tempting, even in nonphilosophical circles. Thus, we think of ourselves as mastering the term "bachelor" by means of some such expression as "unmarried male adult." There is no reason not to think that this sort of view influenced Plato. It is not that he need already have invented or imbibed some *theory* about how these linguistic explanations work. It is simply that, like the rest of us, he learned a good many words by receiving such explanations of them. There is no reason not to see the influence of this fact in his quest for definitions.

We must digress briefly to take up one obvious point arising out of this account. It is that not all of our terms can be learned in this way, because unless we want to move in circles, we need to start our explanations somewhere with expressions that are taken to be understood. Some have taken this fact to show that some terms must be thought to be primitive or undefined, whether absolutely or relative to some particular program of explanation. (Others think that undefined terms are explained by ostension, but we shall put off ostension until later; see Ch. VIII, sec. 3, and n. IX-14). We must raise this matter here in order to remark that although the idea of the primitive and undefined creeps later into Plato's thought,[55] it seems to play no role in his early discussions.[56] The dialogues now before us show no sign of any explicit belief that some terms simply need no definition, or of an attempt to try to mark off such terms in a general way from others. Nor is there any hint of the notion that some terms may be unsusceptible of definition for other reasons. It has been suggested by philosophers, for example, that ethical and other evaluative terms may be terms of this sort, at least in some cases.[57] Likewise, it has been suggested that we cannot gain fully justified confidence in the correctness of our use of them because they encapsulate expressions of *pro* or *con* "attitudes" or feelings, disagreement in which we can find no court of appeal in facts about the world.[58] This latter sort of noncognitivist or emotivist view of evaluative terms is, as is generally recognized,[59] foreign to Plato, and moreover there is no trace in his works of the idea that such terms are improper subjects for definition, or importantly different from others. The *Meno*, for example, suggests that we use a definition of "shape" as a model in our search for a definition of "virtue" (74b*sqq.*), without ever warning us that the two words might differ in such a crucial manner. None of this is to say that Plato actively held the view that every term needs a definition; but it is to say that he did not, at this stage at least, wish explicitly to exempt some particular terms from his definitory efforts.

But the foregoing facts should not mislead one into thinking that our ordinary use of words is itself the subject matter, or the ultimate testing ground, of the Platonic investigation into definitions. For it is of the first importance in understanding Plato to realize that this is not the case.

For although we have so far seen nothing extraordinary about Plato's interest in definitions, because he simply takes his cue from one of our ordinary procedures for mastering words, his attitude toward those procedures engenders something quite different. The crucial twist comes when we realize that Plato does not accept what can be seen, from certain viewpoints at least, as a basic presupposition underlying this way of acquiring confidence about one's judgments and use of language. For the account roughly sketched of how we learn words *seems* to require that when one asks for the definition of a term, or for samples of its correct application, there be some authoritative source—whether people who "know the language," or dictionaries written by them, or whatever—to which one can go for authoritative answers.[60] And one's picture changes radically if one starts to wonder whether these sources are really reliable, and whether the definitions and applications supplied by them are correct or to be trusted. Why is their testimony not the merest hearsay—unless, of course, one can find some grounds for being sure that they know whereof they speak? Why could not their definitions or applications of words, in any particular case or cases, be quite mistaken? Why should their reports be accepted, unless some way of corroborating them can be found?

These rhetorical questions set the scene for some of the more important epistemological moves in Plato's work and deeply affect his reflections from start to finish. One of the most important functions of the Forms, from the beginning of his career, was to solve the problems that these questions attempt to pose, because we shall see that it is the Forms that are supposed by him to fill the gap left by the supposed lack, in the community of speakers of language, of authoritative sources of reliable information about the proper explanation and application of the sorts of terms with which he was concerned.

It is not that Plato exhibits, in his earliest works, a fully refined and elaborated position on these matters. But he does have certain fixed attitudes which are pertinent to them. Chief among them, in simple form, is the view that somehow one is not simply to trust what people say, about more or less anything, and in particular about which terms are true of which things, and about how terms are properly explained or defined.[61] Now whatever Plato's actual practice may be (more on this point shortly), nothing could be clearer than that his official attitude is not to trust people's unreflective definitions, and that he does not think that the currency of a definition ensures its correctness or reliability. A number of definitions proposed in the early dialogues are meant to represent common or influential opinions, but they receive no particular respect on that account. Thus, for example, the view of Cephalus in *Republic* 330-331, that justice is telling the truth and paying one's debts, is not regarded as being any the better for being current; and the vaguely Simonidean position that justice is helping one's friends and harming one's enemies fares no better (331ff.). What is particularly important here is not that these positions are rejected, or even that they are rejected briskly. It is that there is not even the faintest suggestion that whatever faults they might have, they are owed some real credence by virtue of having a wide following. And indeed in examining a definition, or any claim at all, Plato never claims that an advantage lies in its jibing with ordinary usage or opinion.

Nor does Plato believe that ordinary opinion or usage is a reliable guide on questions of particular application of terms to objects. There is no sign of the view that the mere fact that a particular action is *called* "just," say, is by itself sufficient ground for saying that it is just or that the term "just" is in fact true of it.[62] Rather, we have him making the well-known claim that, for example, one cannot know for certain that a thing is just until we know what justice is.[63] The pertinent passages were cited earlier to illustrate his view that definitions help us to determine extensions of terms (sec. 2), but the point now to be drawn from those passages is a stronger one. The same outlook is at work in his disapproving attitude toward attempts to supply a definition for a term by giving examples of things to which the term is supposed to apply. For instance Euthyphro and Meno are both scolded for this transgression in the respective dialogues bearing their names, and the namesake of the *Theaetetus* is similarly rebuked in that work.[64] For Plato seems to hold that the examples that they give cannot be trusted to be correct until a general definition has been established.

But the two foregoing paragraphs raise obvious difficulties. For if we cannot know what things are just until we have a definition of justice and cannot have any confidence in any accounts of justice handed down to us by those who have taught us our language, then we may be at an *impasse* if we can find no way to gain a definition other than from what is handed down to us. But even worse for Plato, the fact is that an important part of his own procedure for testing definitions, a procedure known as *elenchus*, involves the presentation of particular cases which are counterexamples to definitions which have been proposed, in order to refute them.[65] But if this procedure were disallowed, then many important arguments in the early dialogues would apparently have to go by the board.

In reflecting on these difficulties, one may be tempted to try to extricate Plato from them by supposing that in fact he does not disallow, as initial data for the investigation, *both* definitions suggested by common usage *and* particular applications of terms to agreed-upon cases. In fact, the temptation becomes greater when one notices a possible alternative construal of Plato's objections to attempts to give definitions by citing examples of things to which a term applies. The alternative account is that such definitions are useless, and that their uselessness is due to the fact that even though we *can* establish correct and trustworthy examples of the application of a general term (e.g., as *Republic* 331a-d plainly supposes that there are clear cases of injustice, antecedent to the final establishment of a definition), there is nevertheless no way, merely by citing such cases, satisfactorily to settle those cases over which there is dispute or uncertainty. The problem—this account continues—is one of how to *extend agreement* from clear cases to unclear cases, and Plato can quite reasonably believe that this extending of agreement will require the enunciation of, and agreement on, a general boundary between what the term is true of and what it is not true of.[66]

But this alternative account is unattractive as an interpretation of Plato's intent, primarily because it requires a distinction between clear and unclear cases which he nowhere explicitly recognizes, but which any explicit belief on his part in this methodological view would certainly have required to be discussed. Indeed, he might object to the distinction anyway, on the ground that one man's clear cases are often enough another man's disputed or unclear cases.[67] That this is so is strongly suggested by the fact that in his early ruminations on the so-called method of hypothesis in the *Meno* and the *Phaedo* (Ch. III, sec. 7), he seems to treat this method of reaching agreement—which involves *inter alia* the testing of claims against particular cases—as a strictly *ad hominem* procedure, in which the parties to a discussion can seek only to resolve disagreements among themselves but cannot guarantee themselves against all likely or well-grounded objections.[68] This method does indeed allow us to begin by forming and proposing hypotheses which accord with our own opinions (*Phaedo* 100a3-4, with Ch. III, sec. 7), but the point of this procedure is never said to be that these opinions are in accord with, or are indices of, some sort of general or common opinion. Moreover, when Plato later amplifies the method in the *Republic* (Ch. IV, sec. 4), he does so in a manner that involves appeal neither to common opinion nor to the notion of antecedently clear and agreed-upon cases.[69] Furthermore, passages in which definitions by example are rejected, or in which doubt is expressed about particular cases (see esp. *Euthyphro* 5dsqq., *Theaetetus* 147b, *Lysis* 223b, *Charmides* 176a-b), hardly seem to be hinting that there are firm and reliable examples to be found somewhere else.[70]

But can we in our interpretation allow Plato to fall prey to such a disabling predicament, from which the alternative account tried to rescue him?[71] The answer is twofold. In the first place, by describing it succinctly we have highlighted it far more than is ever done in Plato's own texts. In fact, Plato's own methodological views are not at this stage sufficiently fixed for the difficulty to have presented itself to him explicitly. But there is a much more important reason why he would not have felt pressure to focus on it. For even though he does rely on examples which have not yet been endorsed by an established definition and uses such examples to test definitions which have been proposed,[72] his own actual principles of method, to the extent that he has adopted any, are different from what might be suggested by these facts. For as we shall see in the next and succeeding sections (Ch.III, sec. 4; Ch. IV, sec. 1), what Plato has in view is that the subject matter of definitions will in fact be, not the particular cases by which definitions are tested in *elenchus*, but the Forms themselves, and that it is ultimately by their faithfulness to the facts about Forms, and not to unreflectively accepted cases or usage, that definitions have to be tested.

It is this fact that engenders the problems and issues that are so characteristic of Platonic theory of knowledge, in contrast to what is familiar from some contemporary philosophical discussion.[73] As a matter of official method, Plato never aims ultimately to be true to ordinary usage, or to our unreflective inclinations about what our language, or customary belief, prescribes.[74] Nor does he imagine that what one could gain from examining usage is, rather than facts about the world on which one needs expertise to pronounce authoritatively, information about the rules or conventions of our language, which one must abide by if one is to speak the language at all, which are the common property of everyone in the linguistic community, and to which a general distrust of hearsay would be argued not to apply. But Plato never suggests that definitions are conventions or stipulations or that they are part of language in a way that would allow any competent speaker to present data or adjudicate their correctness.[75] Nor does he see the problem of saying what a satisfactory definition is as a task of answering metalinguistic questions about what relation ought to obtain,[76] in a satisfactory definition, between the expression which is the definiens and the expression which is the definiendum.[77] For him, philosophical questions have a subject matter that neither is the data of usage nor is tied to reflecting it or giving it credence.[78]

One important stimulus to the reliance on the data of a linguistic community has been, quite obviously, the fact that it can seem to be a starting point from which philosophical investigation, so subject to doubt and scepticism, can begin, and also to be a test for its conclusions.[79] The question must therefore arise, concerning Plato's views, what are his data and ultimate tests? Viewed from one point of view, this is precisely the chief question that his theory of knowledge both asks and must have asked about it. We have seen both that it is uncertain what is granted to us at the start of a search for a definition, and that Plato's attitude, not yet hardened into theory, is that one cannot trust hearsay but must discover for oneself. We have been well prepared to see this attitude on his part by our reflections on what he held in common with the Sophists (Ch. I, introd.). It is easy to see, therefore, that it would have been entirely uncharacteristic of him to accept the verdict of people at large on how words are properly to be used, or to rely on them without some sort of independent support. His problem is to find, and to explain how he can begin to find, this independent support—for he is convinced that it exists.

4   Enter the Forms Again

In Plato's view, then, if we were to accept the testimony of our neighbors in matters concerned with Forms and definitions, we would have to have gained some assurance that their expertise is more than simply that of a native speaker of the language, and that they know whereof they speak. But whereof *do* they speak? As we have already seen reason to expect, Plato's answer is, in a word, Forms. This answer is at first given without much fanfare, and the reason is in large part that he did not initially mark off from each other the various different functions that he assigned to Forms, or the reasons he had for believing in them, so that the epistemological consideration for their existence, being only one of those competing for his attention, did not press itself on him explicitly from the start. But once the Forms were on the scene, it was natural for him to think that because we could not automatically accept what others tell us about what things are just, holy, brave, and so on, we might nevertheless gain grounds for confidence in our judgments by acquiring knowledge of or about Forms.

This reflection now allows us to begin making the connection that we earlier anticipated, between definitions and Forms. For one idea that it suggests is that if we cannot look to current linguistic practices to settle the explanations or extension of terms, then we should look to Forms. And in fact he at times makes this suggestion. We have already observed him maintaining, for example, that if we want to tell whether or not a given action is holy, we should "look to" the Form of the Holy and use it, in a certain manner, to settle the issue (sec. 1). As for definitions, Plato also maintains that it is by "looking to" the Form that one should pass upon the correctness of a definition. In *Meno* 72c6-d1 we read:

> ... even if (the virtues) are many and various, they at least have the same character (εἶδος) because of which they are virtues, to which it is well for the answerer to look (ἀποβλέψαντα) in explaining to the questioner what virtue is.

In a similar vein, *Laches* 190c (speaking of courage) tells us that "if we know a thing, we can presumably say what it is" (see also *Laches* 194a7-b4 and *Charmides* 159a1-7).

But this is not the only way in which Plato depicts the situation. For recall *Euthyphro* 6d-e, already cited (sec. 1):

> ... for you said, I think, that it is by one character (ἰδέα) that unholy things are unholy and holy things are holy .... Then teach me what this character is in order that I may look to (ἀποβλέπων) it and, using it as a paradigm (παράδειγμα) assert to be holy those things which are of the same sort, whether done by you or by someone else, and assert not to be holy those things which are not of the same sort ....

This passage expounds the relation between looking to a Form and ascertaining a definition quite differently. The answer to the question

"What is holiness?" is requested "in order that" (ἵνα) one may look to the Form, so the suggestion is that somehow it is with the help of the definition that one looks to the Form, rather than the other way around, as the *Meno* passage indicates. Moreover, it is natural enough to take these lines from the *Euthyphro* as suggesting, to the extent that they suggest anything very explicit, that by telling one "what holiness is" one is giving a person some sort of directions enabling him to turn his mind, as it were, to holiness, and thus to use it as a paradigm.

But however exactly we press these lines, it is easy to see that the two portrayals of the situation threaten to lead us up a circular path, on which we are required both to look to the Form in order to determine the correctness of any putative definition and also to find the definition first, in order to look to the Form. So we have a point—and an important one—on which Plato's method needs clarification with regard to the connection between the search for definitions and the attempt to look to Forms. And it is a point that cannot be handled by the manoeuvre of supposing that in Plato's view, to apprehend or look to a form *simply* is to gain a definition.[80] This expedient would eliminate this problem (though it would leave others in its place), but it would make nonsense of the passages just quoted, in which the two things are treated as clearly distinct, if closely linked (cf. Ch. IV, sec. 1).

Moreover, the problem is not a trivial one. At bottom, it is a question of what, if anything, Plato regards as the starting-point, or the data, in this crucial phase of his epistemological enterprise. We have already seen this question seeking an answer, in the light of Plato's attitude toward ordinary usage and untutored or inexpert opinion and hearsay. In the previous section it appeared in the guise of a problem concerning how Plato could (as he seemed inclined to do) both demand that we have definitions for terms before we allow ourselves confidence over their applications, and at the same time employ antecedently accepted applications in the testing of proposed definitions. This problem, we saw, was not attended to by Plato, in large part because he was inclined to view the crucial test of a definition not as its faithfulness to our beliefs about particular cases, but, in principle, as its truth, in some sense, to the facts about Forms. What we now see, however, is that the problem is a more general one, having to do not merely with one's attitude toward the testing of definitions against instances. For even if we try somehow to ignore instances and say instead that definitions are in some relevant sense about Forms, there remains the question what means we have of knowing about definitions and the Forms of which they treat, and what data we may exploit in our efforts to do so.

The data in the quest for definitions, we saw, were not simply the deliverances of custom and usage. Rather the tendency of Plato's view, though not yet solidified, was that the applications and definitions that common opinions afforded were in fact susceptible of scrutiny and independent check, and that there were matters of fact, evidently concerning Forms, for definitions and other statements to be right or wrong about. The question next arises what our access to that subject matter is, and if the answer is that it is a kind of apprehension or mental viewing, then the further question arises how this is to be accomplished, and what pitfalls and possibilities of mistake must be guarded against in attempting it. And of course the overarching question, which Plato is the first to have raised clearly, is the question how, once we become critical of the unreflective opinions of ourselves and others, we may hope to make a start toward something better.

Notes

N.B. The numeral in boldface type following an author's name refers the reader to the complete bibliographic data for that reference, which is carried under List of Works Cited beginning on page 235.

1. There is no need for our purposes to discuss the nature and relative strength of these influences. In some cases the matter is unclear in the extreme (cf. next note, and Shorey **5**, vol. II, p. 189, n. *g*: "... the student of Plato will do well to turn the page when he meets the name Pythagoras in a commentator."). Aristotle attests to Heraclitean influence (*Met.* I.6), but it is difficult to be sure how pronounced it was (and the evidence of the *Tht.*, in particular, is unclear; cf. *infra*, n. VII-16). Against substantial Eleatic influence, see Ross **2**, pp. 163-164; for it, see Prauss, esp. pp. 27ff.

2. For a survey of the evidence, see Lacey.

3. For this debate, which has not been carried on much recently, see e.g., Burnet **2**, Chs. VIII-IX; Taylor **4**, Ch. IV; and on the other side G. C. Field **1**, esp. Appendices II and III; Ross **1**, vol. I, pp. xxxiii-xlviii; and (2), pp. 157-160. Notice that the problem is not just how much Plato owed to Socrates, but also how much each of them owed to Pythagorean thought; cf. Ross **2**, pp. 160-163, and Shorey, *ibid*.

4. For a brief statement of the likeliest view, see Raven, pp. 86-87.

5. See Robinson **1**, esp. Chap. V.

6. I shall not use much precision in employing, or distinguishing among, such terms as "judgment," "statement," and even "sentence" (except at certain

points when care is required), because the text usually will not permit it. For some pertinent observations, however, see Hintikka **2**, pp. 1-14, esp. 3.

7. Some scholars emphasize the areas of inquiry that were opened by the Sophists, even while generally admitting that they were not in any sense a systematically scientific movement. See for example Jaeger, vol. I, pp. 286ff., with pp. 295, 328. Jaeger tends to minimize the sceptical and relativistic tendencies of the Sophistic movement (though see pp. 299, 323ff.).

8. See Zeller **1**, pp. 1283ff., 1307, 1368ff., along with an admission that there were very different types of Sophist (pp. 1334ff., 1368ff.). (Jaeger notes, however, in vol. I, p. 305, that Plato saw a real family resemblance among them.) See also Guthrie, pp. 44-48, 50-51, 164-175. Unfortunately, the tendency to assimilate relativistic and sceptical views is strong in Zeller's characterization (see pp. 1289, 1355-56), as in others.

9. Even if we think that Aristotle was right not to include the Sophists in his account of previous philosophy (*Metaphysics* I), that does not mean that they could not have been a crucial influence on Plato, if only in creating the intellectual climate within which he operated and in determining which problems seemed most pressing to him. See Shorey **4**, pp. 12-16. This sort of phenomenon is not at all unusual. The logical positivists, for example, hardly counted Hegelian idealists as important philosophers, but nonetheless were certainly influenced by them—in the same negative way in which Plato was influenced by certain Sophistic ideas.

10. For a discussion of this issue see Gulley **3**, pp. 62-74.

11. For various indications of other ways of assimilating Socrates and the Sophists, see Guthrie, pp. 33-34, 370ff.

12. Thus see Zeller **1**, p. 1290, and also Zeller **2**, pp. 118-120; Guthrie, pp. 431-433, 466-467; Grote, vol. I, pp. 291ff.

13. Thus Zeller **2**, pp. 559ff., and the bulk of the tradition since his time, with exceptions such as Burnet and Taylor (cf. n. 3 *supra*).

14. With due qualification to allow for certain of Plato's views about the sensible world and its epistemic pitfalls (cf. Ch. III, sec. 2, and Ch. IV, sec. 1), this point is presumably uncontroversial and rarely goes unsupported in a stretch of Platonic text of more than a few pages. See, e.g., *Rep.* 538c*sqq.*, along with Zeller **2**, pp. 559ff.; Field **1**, pp. 195-196, **2**, pp. 21-27; Bluck **1**, pp. 7, 10.

15. On Socratic ignorance, as it appears in Plato, see *Apol.* 21b, d; *Gorg.* 506a, 508e-509a; *Charm.* 165d, 166c-d; *Prot.* 348c; *Euthyd.* 307a-c; as well as Aristotle, *S.E.* 183b8, Gulley **3**, pp. 62-64; Zeller **1**, p. 118, n. 1, pp. 118-120 p. 121, n. 1, p. 116, n. 1, with Xenophon, *Mem.* IV.6.15; Jaeger, vol. II, pp. 60-62, 85; Sidgwick **2**, p. 24.

16. Jaeger, vol. II, p. 29 with *Gorg.* 454e*sqq.*, 459c*sqq.*; Sidgwick **2**, p. 26. For those who believe *Alcibiades I* to be genuine (as I am inclined to do), there is also 106ff., esp. 109d-112d, from it.

17. *Meno* 92b-c, 97b1-2; *Phaedo* 82e3-4, 83a-b; *Rep.* 479d, 488a*sqq.*, 492c, 493a-c, 506b-c; *Phdr.* 270c, 275c1-2; *Crat.* 437d, 440c-d; *Tht.* 145a-b, 201a-c, with Robinson **1**, p. 79.

18. *Rep.* 488a*sqq.*, 492c, 493a-c; *Gorg.* 472b-c, 474a-b, 475e-476a; *Laches* 184e; *Crito* 47a-d. Such passages in the *Rep.* as 538c-539a do not show Plato relying on ordinary opinions, because the scene there is set in the ideal city, in which people have been properly educated and informed (see 541a1-3). The passages from the *Gorgias* and the *Crito*, at least, may well reflect the views of Socrates. But note that for our purposes here, what matters is not the historical views of Socrates, but the way in which they are presented by Plato. (Cf. also Gulley **3**, p. 207, n. 52 with Xenophon, *Mem.* IV.6.13-15, and Grote, pp. 246ff., 307-309.) For this reason we need not concern ourselves with the possible (though invalid) argument that since according to Aristotle Plato got his scepticism about judgments concerning the sensible world from Cratylus (*Met.* 987a32ff.), it is unlikely that he was subject to a similar influence from Socrates; clearly, the two influences can have complemented each other.

19. In this respect, and also with regard to the ideas discussed in sec. 3, Plato is firmly in the tradition of Greek philosophers who think of themselves as superior to the multitude in their insight into the nature of things. See Kapp, pp. 71-72; and von Fritz **1**, esp. pp. 68-71. The Sophists' general stance seems to have been quite different, at least in some cases, as is observed by Jaeger, vol. I, pp. 296 (with *Protag.* 320c*sqq.*), 305, 324; but not always, to judge by Thrasymachus in *Rep.* I. (The case of Callicles in the *Gorg.* is a bit different, because he does not label himself a Sophist; see Dodds, pp. 12-15, 367. But the situation is complicated; see Adkins **1**, p. 242, n. 20, and Ch. X.) For data on the notion of expertise in ethics (though not, to my mind, entirely rightly interpreted), see Gould, Ch. II.

20. For this commonplace, as well as a caution against accepting it without qualification, see Guthrie, pp. 16-17.

21. Plato also uses the term "ἰδέα," as well as others. On his terminology, see Ross **2**, pp. 12-21, Gillespie, and Baldry. It is important to be aware that Plato does not have a fixed technical terminology; see Baldry with *Tht.* 184c, and Campbell, pp. 267ff.

22. The chronological ordering of Plato's works presents difficult problems. The order that I adopt (of those works with which I am chiefly concerned) would not, in most respects, be very unusual nowadays. Fortunately the *Tim.*, which has been the subject of perhaps the sharpest disagreement recently (see Owen **1** and Cherniss **7**), is not crucial for the topics that primarily concern me. Stylometric criteria, which seem to me at their present stage of development to be somewhat shaky (mainly because until more data are brought to bear from other writers, we cannot securely determine what the various stylistic variations in Plato really prove, because we will not know in general what degree of fluctuation can be produced by what factors, including even random and insignificant changes of linguistic mood), seem compatible with—though I do not claim that they positively demonstrate—the present ordering (for some discussion, see *ibid.*). But that ordering is supported mainly to the extent that it helps to give a coherent picture of Plato's manner of dealing with the issues that face him. I believe that it does so for the matters with which I am not concerned,

and I believe that it does so especially for those with which I am. Certain special problems of chronology are dealt with in the notes *infra* (esp. nn. I-50, IV-3 and 6, V-5, and VI-1, and Ch. V, introd. and sec. 1 *passim*). I am well aware that much more remains to be said on these problems than I can present here.

23. I oversimplify here. There is also the view that the early dialogues involve Forms, but only "immanent" Forms and not the "transcendent" Forms of later works. Although the use of this terminology was understandably provoked by the compressed and obscure manner in which Aristotle characterized the difference between Socrates' and Plato's views about ἰδέαι (e.g., at *Met*. 987a1-14, 1086b2-13), its continuation is inimical to understanding, because these terms do nothing but obscure the questions that need to be answered. At any rate, for efforts to deny that Forms are fully in play in the earlier dialogues, see e.g., Grube, p. 9 and the reff. there in n. 1, as well as Ross **1** Ch. II.

24. For example Friedländer, pp. 85-86.

25. Thus for example Burnet **3**, on *Euthyphro*, 5d3, 5d6; Shorey **2**, p. 32; Cherniss **2**, pp. 497-500.

26. Burnet is one such; see *ibid*.

27. This contention certainly holds for such works as the *Charmides*, the *Laches*, the *Lysis*, the *Euthyphro*, the *Gorgias*, the *Euthydemus*, and the *Protagoras*. The *Meno* can be claimed to have more substantial traces of developed doctrine, but I defer full discussion of it until Ch. II.

28. For a clear appreciation of this fact, see Allen **4**, pp. 105ff. (though it is hard to see how Allen is entitled to the philosophical moral that he draws there, namely that (p. 110) "a commitment to essence is . . . latent in our ordinary use of words").

29. See Robinson **1**, Ch. V.

30. See Allen, *ibid*.

31. I have in mind such features as are described in Ch. III, sec. 2, and Ch. IV, sec. 2, as well as "self-predication" (cf. Vlastos **2**.)

32. See Taylor **2**, *ad* 51c5-d3, and Grube, p. 7. See n. IX-12 for remarks pertinent to the claim that Plato thinks of his theory of Forms as a "postulate."

33. One might also cite *Hipp. Mai*. 287b-d and *Tim*. 51b-52a, though there is little real argument in the former, and the latter is more like a statement of the conclusion of an argument than the argument itself. More substantial is *Rep*. 477ff. (cf. n. IV-9).

34. For this line of thought, though differently applied, see Cherniss **1**.

35. Without pursuing an elaborate exercise in typology, let me mention two further uses which may or may not be assimilable to those which I am exploring. In one case, we have the notion that our ability to think (or to think certain sorts of thoughts; cf. Aristotle, *Met*. 990b14-15) is best explained by invoking Forms. In another case, we have the considerations which lead Plato to claim in the *Phaedo* that Forms are αἰτίαι. (Note that it is highly dubious that this word is best translated by "cause" in this context: see Owen **6**, p. 82,

and Vlastos, **10**, pp. 291-325.) In both cases, it would be both difficult and controversial to say what, if anything, these uses share with those which I am emphasizing. For example, Vlastos' account of αἰτίαι in the *Phaedo* sometimes suggests what I call the "linguistic" consideration (e.g., p. 306; cf. *Phaedo* 102b2), but at other times suggests the "metaphysical" consideration (e.g., p. 301). To my knowledge, no one has attempted a thorough-going classification of these considerations, but some of the requisite distinctions have been made. For example, Staniland, p. 17, marks off pretty much the three sorts of considerations which I emphasize. Butchvarov, pp. *ix-x* does likewise, and adds what may be another, having to do with "abstract thinking." Russell **1** uses several different considerations without distinguishing among them (compare pp. 91-92, where he attributes to Plato what seems to be the metaphysical consideration, with pp. 90, 94, apparently broaching the linguistic consideration, and pp. 93, 101ff., which contain epistemological considerations). Notice that on pp. 101ff., Russell uses universals to account not simply for knowledge, but rather for *a priori* knowledge, while Frege used his *Sinne* to account for the distinction between *a priori* and *a posteriori* knowledge, in his **2**, pp. 56-78. In general, it seems fair to say that philosophers arguing for the existence of universals have not always been as clear as one might hope in explaining just what sort of considerations they are starting from. (Butchvarov rightly emphasizes [introd. and *passim*] that it is one thing to think that there are abstract entities that fill these various explanatory roles, but yet another thing to say that these entities are in any sense "universals." Plato, however, passes without much ado to supposing that they are "shared" by distinct particulars, and has little to say about alternative possibilities [see, however, n. III-2].

36. The idea of natural kinds is usually associated with Aristotle, but it goes back at least to Plato's *Phaedrus* in an explicit form (Ch. V, sec. 1).

37. It is not easy to say for certain, but I think it likely that this consideration plays an important role in the notion that Plato is dealing with "real definitions" rather than "nominal definitions," e.g., as the idea appears in Allen **4**, pp. 79-105, 110-113 (and note esp. pp. 118-120, 82), and Nakhnikian, p. 145. Although this contrast between types of definition is frequently invoked in an incidental way in modern discussions, it needs more clarification before it can be of much use. To see that widely differing versions of the distinction are abroad nowadays, compare Allen's with Nakhnikian's, and see also Robinson **2** which, while it claims that Plato and Aristotle were concerned with "real" definition (pp. 7, 149), leaves the import of the claim obscure, at least to my mind. For more traditional discussions, see Mill, bk. I, Ch. 8, and Joseph, pp. 91ff. For more that is pertinent to this matter, see Ch. IX, sec. 2.

38. Aristotle of course knew that Plato (or Platonists) had offered a variety of arguments for the existence of Forms, but he did not classify them, or their premises, in any systematic way. On the variety of considerations reported by him, see e.g., *Met.* 987b2-7, 31-33 (semantic?), 990b11-13, 26-27 (epistemologi-

cal), 990b14-15, 25 (having to do with "thinking"; cf. n. I-35, and his remarks about *aitiai* in 990a34ff., 991a8ff. (cf. again n. I-35)). (Note the philosophical point that one cannot simply assume that the entities called on to do the various jobs outlined by these and other considerations must be the same entities; see Austin **2**.)

39. The verb is "ἀποβλέπειν." For the use of other terms of this sort in this context, see Ch. IV, sec. 1, as well as Snell, pp. 13-14, and von Fritz **1**.

40. Cf. Ch. III, sec. 6. The same consideration may perhaps be in evidence in *Phileb.* 15d, at least if we accept the view of Mills, p. 166, n. 27. *Rep.* 596a5-8 might be thought to contain the same idea, but it only says *that* we posit a Form for each ὄνομα which is applied to many things, not *why* we should do so.

41. Note that Plato is not here talking about "virtuous things" (e.g., virtuous people) over which virtue might be said to stand; rather, virtue here stands over virtues. For related complications, see nn. I-66 and V-17.

42. "Name" translates "ὄνομα": 74d5-6, 8, e11. Of course many would not now employ "name" in this way, but its Greek counterpart is well established in this sort of usage, so it is better not to disturb it, or try to inflict too much modern semantic theory or terminology upon the passages in question. See further Ch. VI, sec. 2.

43. On the confusion, see Quine **2** and **6**.

44. Whether the interpretation is quite correct is another question. See Owen **11**.

45. Cf. n. I-35.

46. Also, perhaps, to explain why certain things *exist*; but this issue lies to the side of our path.

47. For a defense of its authenticity see Ross **2**, pp. 3-4.

48. See esp. 100a1-2, along with Taylor **3** pp. 144-145, and Bluck **4**, *ad* 100a1.

49. I say "*the* answer" to the question, but although Plato generally gives the impression that he thinks that such answers are unique, he does not always do so; see Nakhnikian, esp. pp. 130ff.

50. The bulk of the *Republic* certainly does not come from the period of Plato's activity that we are now examining. Nor, I think, does its first book, but numerous scholars have been ready to see *Rep.* I as an early work which was later tacked on to the rest of the *Rep.* as an introduction. For a survey of some of the literature on the question, see Friedländer, pp. 305-306. The most that has ever been shown is that this book *could* have been an early dialogue, not that it must have been. Friedländer, *ibid.*, accuses those who dispute its separate status of neglecting the "formal element," saying that "Book I of the *Republic* has in all essentials the form of a dialogue of the aporetic group." But this fact—and it *is* a fact—has no probative force at all on the question at issue. For it has long been recognized that this book is meant, by reaching an impasse, to set the stage for the development of theory by which Plato in the rest of the work hopes to solve the problems raised at the start. What could be

less surprising, then, that he should cast the introduction in the form of an aporetic discussion like those of the early dialogues? That he should have done so, moreover, is made all the more natural if we suppose that in the *Republic* Plato means to show certain limitations of his own earlier, or of Socrates', methods, by giving them a run for their money in bk. I, and then showing in the rest of the work what he now thinks are the necessary further steps to be taken. Still, it must be admitted that these considerations do not *dis*prove that bk. I was originally a separate work. Shorey **5**, vol. I, p. *x*, is right in calling the view an "idle and unverifiable conjecture". *However* the case may be, though, *Rep.* I is an appropriate work to cite in the present context. For it is either an early work itself or—more likely—an effort to imitate and represent the methods and procedures of early works.

51. Whether "cause" is correct here is a difficult and controversial question. Cf. n. I-35, as well as Sachs and Mabbott.

52. Actually, there are difficulties regarding what Plato in this passage intends his hypothesis strictly to be; see Robinson **1**, pp. 117ff. If this interpretation of the passage (which Robinson upholds) should be incorrect, then a much more cumbersome version of the point that I want to make could still be defended.

53. This seems to be the view of, e.g., Vlastos **9** pp. 155-156 (though perhaps p. 157 suggests otherwise). See also Robinson **1**, pp. 100, 105ff., and Moravcsik **2**, pp. 60-61 (but see p. 67). It is also suggested, perhaps, by such Aristotelian passages as *Met.* 1078b23-25. Robinson **1**, pp. 100-101, 120, considers and rejects the view.

54. It is of course a nice problem to determine what is "directly relevant to the meaning of" a term and what is not, and whether it is possible to make the distinction. Thus see, e.g., Quine **3**.

55. According to some views, it is present in *Rep.* VI-VII, and in *Tht.* 200-202. See, for example, Shorey **5**, vol. II, p. *xxvii*, and Morrow. Cf. Ch. IV, sec. 4; Ch. VII, sec. 5.

56. Nakhnikian (pp. 138, 141-142) sees a trace of the notion in *Charm.* 160e, but *a*) it is not clear that Plato would acknowledge the passage as containing a definition in any strict sense, and *b*) Nakhnikian's hypothesis rests heavily on the unargued supposition expressed by his "*If* modesty is not analyzable . . . " (p. 141, my emph.).

57. E.g., by Moore **1**, in the case of "good."

58. E.g., by Stevenson.

59. For observations on this point see Adkins **2**, p. 157, as well as the remarks of Cross and Woozley, pp. 117-119, on the related point that Plato does not draw a distinction of the Humean sort between reason and passion or desire. It has been held by Geach **2** that in *Euthyphro* 7b-8b Plato is indeed distinguishing between "factual" and "moral" questions (p. 373), but this is neither Plato's intent nor what he says. Rather, he is contrasting those disputes which, when they are not settled, provoke fights, and those which do not (note the wording of 7b6-7, c10-12, d3-5, e3-4, 8a1-2). Although there is,

to be sure, the suggestion that certain disputes can be settled by measuring and weighing (c3-8), the implication is not drawn that there is anything in principle unsettlable about the disputes about justice and goodness and fairness which are contrasted with them. Indeed, what Socrates is pictured as trying to do at this point in the work is to try to find a procedure for settling an issue of just this sort (see 6d9-e6).

60. For expressions of this and importantly related views, see for example, Ayer **1**, Ch. IV; Wittgenstein **3**, sec. 381; Ryle **2**, pp. 167-186; Austin **3**, pp. 82-83.

61. Note that this scepticism does not lead, in Plato's hands, to a scepticism about the external world, or the existence of other minds, or the like. (An analogous point holds for the view that is attributed in the *Tht.* to "Protagoras"; cf. n. VII-16.) The world is assumed to be there, and the other people talking about it. What is questioned is what they say about it. It is interesting to speculate on why really thoroughgoing scepticism, and solipsism, were so late in taking hold in Greek philosophy (cf., however, Gorgias— if it is he—*apud* Sext. Emp., *Adv. Math.* VII.65-87).

62. Thus there is nothing in Plato of the idea, approved by some logical positivists and some others, that there are cases of the application of general terms that are somehow ensured or sanctified by convention—e.g., the case of the "standard pound" or the "standard yard." (Cf. Strang, esp. the section "Self-Predication, Paradigmatism, and the Standard Yard.") Similarly, Plato in his early works has nothing to do with the notion of "ostensive definition," particularly in the version under which, when a term is explained by ostending samples of things that fall under it, those particular samples become somehow tied to the meaning of the term, so that if they are later denied to fall under it, then the term has changed its meaning. (But I here leave aside consideration of Forms; cf. n. IX-14.) Positive evidence against this view in Plato is forthcoming if we accept the authenticity of *Alcibiades I*; for in 111a*sqq.* it is made clear that Plato does not regard teaching a person Greek as including teaching him the extensions of general terms in Greek.

63. See sec. 2 *init.*, with the passages cited there, as well as Ross **2**, p. 16, and Robinson **1**, pp. 50ff. Robinson says that there is no argument for this attitude; it is best to suppose that it seemed an obvious consequence of the general distrust of hearsay and ordinary opinion (Ch. I, introd.).

64. See Robinson **1**, pp. 50-51.

65. For the problem see Geach **2**, esp. pp. 371-372. For the procedure, see Robinson **1**, pp. 7-32. For a criticism of Geach, see Santas, who rightly observes that Plato's procedure does not jibe with what I am claiming to be his official position, but who fails to disarm the evidence for attributing that official position to Plato. The same point was noted by Sidgwick, *à propos* of what he took (probably rightly) to be Socrates' own actual procedure, which, he says, is destructive of, but relies on, common sense (**2** p. 29).

66. We should notice, in passing, one point of obscurity that arises on

either account. When Plato objects to definition by example, the rejected example can seem to be either a particular object or action (such as Euthyphro's particular act of prosecuting his father on that particular occasion), but it can also seem to be some relatively restricted class or type of actions (such as the general type of act of prosecuting one's father under such-and-such sorts of circumstances). What is rebuked in *Meno* 71ff. is fairly clearly an example of the latter sort; what receives censure in *Euthyphro* 5d*sqq.* might be the one or the other (notice the type/token ambiguity of "what I am doing" in 5d8-9). This ambiguity is extremely important in some connections, but we can afford to leave it aside here, since Plato makes nothing of it, and shows no sign, in these contexts, of noticing it. Let me adopt the former interpretation for the sake of convenience; what I shall say will apply *mutatis mutandis* to the other.

67. See Allen **4**, pp. 117-118.

68. See Robinson **1**, pp. 136-141, 146-147, 172-177. For a discussion of Socrates in this connection, see Vlastos **3**, pp. *xxx-xxxi*.

69. Robinson **1**, pp. 169-179.

70. Robinson notes that in the *Phaedo* Plato holds the curious belief that when a hypothesis is overthrown, it is overthrown by showing that it contradicts *itself*, even though it must actually be that it contradicts some other, more firmly held belief (**1**, pp. 110, 29-32, 131-132). Perhaps an explanation of this mistake is that Plato was loath to think that his method required taking something antecedently for granted, because that would involve taking for granted one's unreflected on, unexamined convictions. Cf. n. IV-46.

71. The desire to rescue him seems to motivate Santas, and also Nakhnikian, pp. 144-145, 146-148. *Rep.* 442e, cited by the latter, p. 148, does not seem to support his point. Ordinary usage is brought in only to finish up the job of establishing the account of justice envisioned there, and is given no importance beyond allaying lingering doubts (note esp. e1-2, 443c4-5).

72. See Geach **2** and Sidgwick **1**.

73. In this respect, the difference between Plato and Aristotle is deep: see Owen **5**, esp. pp. 83-92.

74. Thus, he is not prone to such ideas as are pursued, e.g., by Carnap. (Injunctions to candor, as at *Meno* 83d and *Tht.* 154c, are no evidence to the contrary.)

75. This point, which I take to be noncontroversial, is rightly emphasized by Allen **4**, *passim*. Even in the *Crat.*, which discusses the notion of convention in language, it is a quite different notion of convention that is treated (cf. n. VI-8). In addition, it is notable that Plato's works nowhere suggest a contrast between statements that are true *by* convention and statements that are true in some other way, or between analytic and synthetic statements, or the like (although of course he is not without a distinction of a sort between the necessary and the contingent). Aristotle does not have such a contrast—see Sorabji—and his not having it would be a surprise if Plato had had it. Nor is it shown by such casual remarks as *Meno* 82b4 and *Tht.* 163b-c.

76. Another reason for this fact is that he was not likely to talk in an explicitly metalinguistic way at all, largely because, as is now a commonplace, he did not have the use of a convenient system of quotation, because the Greeks had not developed one (on what they did develop see Kühner-Gerth, p. 31).

77. Thus he does not speak of two expressions as being synonymous, or analytically equivalent, or the like. It is instructive, however, to see just what hints he does give about the relationship between definiens and definiendum (I shall here use these expressions in their metalinguistic senses). For doing so makes us realize that although there are such hints, there is only the most meager evidence on the basis of which we might try to fasten a view about this relationship on him, and why we do better to look elsewhere for elucidation of his views about definitions.

First of all, we can observe that when Plato asks what justice is, or the like, he expects the thing referred to by the definiens to be identical with what is referred to by the definiendum (taking "referred to" here in a loose and nontechnical sense). Thus, *Euthyphro* 10d12-13 rejects a proposed definition of the holy as what is loved by the gods, by saying that the two are "different" (ἕτερον), and in the *Tht.*, Plato speaks unmistakably in the same vein (146d2, 7, 151e1-3). (Cf. Goodman **1**, esp. p. 1.) The same thing, moreover, is fairly plain from the "What is . . ." locutions themselves. (See also Nakhinikian, who rightly observes, p. 131, that Plato does not stress the point, and occasionally— but only occasionally—shows signs of moving in a different direction; the attempt by Sharvy to uphold a different position is unsuccessful, and the alternative that he propounds is obscure, and has little basis in the text besides his very debatable interpretation of *Euthyphro* 9-11). To say this much, how-ever, does not get us far, since we need to know whether Plato has any requirements in turn for two expressions of the relevant sort to refer to the same thing. Apparently he does. When Euthyphro proposes that holiness is god-lovedness (τὸ θεοφιλές), he is answered with an argument which shows that this identification cannot be accepted even on the assumption that "holy" and "god-loved" are coextensional (see esp. 11b3-4). Mere coextensiveness of general terms "*F*" and "*G*,," then, is not *sufficient* for "*F*-ness" and "*G*-ness" to stand to one another as definiendum and definiens, though as the use of counterexamples to rebut definitions shows, coextensiveness is taken to be *necessary*.

What specifiable relation, if any, between the terms "*F*-ness" and "*G*-ness" is sufficient to make "*F*-ness is *G*-ness" a proper definition? Plato does not try to say in general, but he does make certain moves which allow us to conjecture what his view might be if he worked it out. In *Euthyphro* 10-11 his argument against the identification of holiness and god-lovedness is, in part, that whereas (1) "What is holy is loved by the gods because it is holy" is true, (2) "What is god-loved is loved by the gods because it is god-loved" is false. However, Plato says, if the holy and the god-loved were the same, then (2), which is derived from (1) merely by replacing "holy" by "god-loved", ought to be true if (1) is. A companion argument in the same passage is analogous.

Although some of the details of the two arguments raise puzzles, it is clear that each of them relies on the supposition that if holiness and god-lovedness were identical, then it would be possible to replace the general term "holy" by the general term "god-loved" within a context governed by the word "because" (ὅτι). Now for such replaceability, as is well-known, mere coextensiveness of the two general terms does not suffice. For example, from the trivial though presumably true sentence "People are subject to spinal fractures in part because they have spines," along with the coextensiveness of the terms "has a spine" and "has kidneys," we get no license to infer "People are subject to spinal fractures in part because they have kidneys." This illustration involves a use of "because" which is causal in sense. Plato's use of the word, on the other hand, is ambiguous and has given rise to debate. It might be a causal "because"—though here we might have to choose among different causal senses—or it might be the sort of "because" that gives a person's reason or justification for something—in this case, the gods' reason for loving certain things and not others. Because of this ambiguity, and also because the different senses of "because" are not fully understood in their own respective rights, it is difficult to say just what relationship must hold between two predicates for them to be interchangeable *salva veritate* within the sort of context that Plato has in mind. Some might nowadays say that they must be, in some sense of "causal," *causally* equivalent (that is to say, it must be in one way or another a causal law that they are equivalent), but Plato's view of causes is so different from the pertinent modern one that such an interpretation cannot be firmly fastened on the text. Let it suffice to say, then, that "*F*" and "*G*" must be something more than merely coextensional, and that that something more is tied up in Plato's mind with some sort of notion of "because."

Another passage gives us more information, though again we must be careful not to press it too far. In *Meno* 74d-e, Socrates is arguing that shape (σχῆμα) is different both from straight and from round (τὸ στρογγύλον and τὸ εὐθύ). His argument begins with the observation that we call both straight and round by the term "shape" (i.e., we say that both are shapes). He then goes on, "You do not say that round is more a shape than straight is" (el-2) and receives assent from Meno. "Then in saying this," Socrates continues, "are you saying that round is no more round than straight is, and that straight is no more straight than round is?" and he receives a negative reply. To take one half of the argument (the other half is analogous), the point is this: consider the two sentences

(3) Meno says that round is no more a shape than straight is

and

(4) Meno says that round is no more round than straight is

of which the first, as the quoted passage makes clear, is supposed to be true and the second is supposed to be false. The burden of the argument is that this difference in truth-value shows that shape is not identical with round (the other half of the argument shows likewise that shape is not identical with straight). This argument is based on the claim that if the two were identical, then (4) would have to be true as long as (3) is, because (4) is derived from (3) by a replacement of "shape" by "round" (the indefinite article in (3) being irrelevant; cf. Vlastos, cited in n. III-7). At this point a problem is thrown in the path of further interpretation by the fact that we cannot be sure whether to take the interchanged "shape" and "round" as singular or as general terms. In either case, however, we can safely conclude that Plato is imposing a very strong requirement for the identity of "*F*-ness" and "*G*-ness," namely that "*F*" and "*G*" (or perhaps "*F*-ness" and "*G*-ness" themselves) be interchangeable within a context governed by "says that." Some would claim that this requirement is, in effect, that the terms be not only somehow causally equivalent, as the *Euthyphro* suggested, but that they have just the same meaning in some quite strong sense. Once again, however, Plato does not indicate what conclusion is to be drawn, and of course he is not posing the problem in the terms that we are employing. It is safe to say, however, that again we have evidence that the sort of identifications that are made in definitions require, in Plato's view, some very close connection—to put the matter vaguely and uncontroversially—between the definiendum and the definiens, and between the corresponding general terms. Perhaps we should say that this connection is sameness of meaning, but that would be our way of expressing the point, not Plato's. Luckily, we need be no more precise than this, since nothing to come will hinge on any more meticulous characterization of the situation. Indeed, as I have maintained, such a characterization is bound to go beyond any firm evidence in the texts, and is best avoided. Rather than pressing this matter further, then let us return to issues which actually engage Plato's explicit attention.

78. Hence the well-known fact that Plato consistently views the dialectician as the person who is expert in the matter of definitions. See *Rep.* VI-VII, *passim*, esp. 531*csqq.*, and *Phdr.* 266b-c. (It should not be forgotten, in this connection, that it is only in this century that we have seen, in any developed form, the idea that philosophy, or even logic, has no subject matter of its own except language.)

79. See esp. Austin **3**, and, in a somewhat different connection, Quine **8**, pp. 3-5.

80. A contrary view was argued for by Cross, (see esp. pp. 27-30), but it was effectively answered by Bluck **2**. See also Ch. IV, sec. 1, and, for references to views related to Cross's, Cherniss **3**, p. 207, n. 124.

CHAPTER II

The Meno:
Inquiry and Its Goals

In spite of the large amount of attention devoted in the *Meno* to problems concerning knowledge, some have thought that its main topics are ethics and the philosophy of education. In fact, the choice is illusory; the dialogue is given over to both sorts of topic, without any line of demarcation between them. This lack of compartmentalization is not surprising from a philosopher who, as we have seen (Ch. I, sec. 2), does not distinguish between evaluative and non-evaluative notions. It is in general misguided to try to classify a Platonic dialogue as "ethical" or "nonethical," and the *Meno*, like most others, is both.[1] That said, I am going to continue to concentrate on epistemological issues, without making any claim that they are all that the *Meno* deals with. For it makes significant advances over earlier dialogues in the subtlety with which it approaches problems about knowledge and comes closer to presenting the full doctrine of Forms which appears in the *Phaedo* and afterwards. The *Meno* can and should be seen as approaching the problems that Plato had begun to see in the quest for definitions, and in the general epistemological picture of which it is a part.

1 "Τί and Ποῖον"

At the beginning of the *Meno*, Socrates is asked by Meno how virtue is acquired, and in particular whether or not it is teachable. Socrates is made to ask in return how he could possibly answer the question, it being the case that he does not know at all what virtue is (ὅτι ποτ' ἐστίν). And he puts the question more generally (71b3-4; cf. 86e1, 100b): "If I don't know *what* something is, how would I know *what sort of thing* it is?" (ὃ δὲ μὴ οἶδα τί ἐστιν, πῶς ἂν ὁποῖόν γέ τι εἰδείην). For, he continues,

35

could it be that someone who did not know at all *who* Meno is (Μένωνα μὴ γιγνώσκει τὸ παράπαν ὅστις ἐστίν) could know whether he is handsome or wealthy or well-born, or the opposite? Evidently Plato has in mind some distinction between two sorts of things which, so to speak, one might know about an object. But just what is that distinction?

At first sight—though only at first sight—it is tempting to assimilate this distinction to later distinctions drawn in what might seem to be related terms, such as Aristotle's distinction between what belongs to a thing *per se* (καθ᾽ αὑτό) and what belongs to it *per accidens* (κατὰ συμβεβηκός), or to other similar contrasts between essence and accident or the like. This temptation arises partly because of another contrast that Plato draws, in *Euthyphro* 11a-b, between the "essence" or "nature"—as translators variously render "οὐσία"—of holiness, and an "affection" (πάθος) of it, in which it is the "showing" (δηλῶσαι, a8) of the οὐσία of holiness which Plato there regards as the proper response to a request for a definition, i.e., to the question "What is holiness?" (see a11, b1, 4-5).[2]

To be told this much, however, is not to be told much, because a distinction between essence and accident can be drawn in importantly different ways.[3] Another unfortunate fact is that Plato does not say enough about the τί/ποῖον contrast for us to get a firm grip on it. He alludes to it occasionally elsewhere (e.g., perhaps *Rep.* 429c1-2, 8; cf. *Rep.* 354e; *Laches* 189c-190c; *Protag.* 360e-361c), but he never tries to explain exactly what it amounts to, and he occasionally uses the words "τί" and "ποῖον" in a way that suggests that he is ignoring it, or at least that his terminology is not consistent.[4] Such meager evidence as this is not going to give us a very solid connection between what Plato here has in mind and later, more elaborately worked-out views.

A more promising line of interpretation is to turn away from the distinction between essence and accident, and to see precisely what use Plato makes of the τί/ποῖον distinction, and discover thereby what his reason might have been for introducing it. Consider it, then, as it appears in *Meno* 71a-b. Plato says that we cannot answer the latter sort of question until we have answered the former and claims that similarly we cannot know whether Meno is handsome until we know who (τίς) he is. Now what could be the justification for these claims? The latter is offered as an elucidation of the former, and is itself not argued for, so we can reasonably suppose that Plato took it to be fairly obvious, and we should look for an explanation of it in ideas that he would have thought to lie ready at hand. And an explanation of it does in fact appear when one considers a question that one might naturally raise as an objection against it. The objection emerges in the following question: Why should one not be told on excellent authority (e.g., by Plato) that Meno is handsome, without being given an answer to the question "Who is Meno?", and why should one then not know that Meno is handsome without knowing who he is?

The answer to this question arises naturally out of what we have already seen (Ch. I, introd. and sec. 4). For, we can ask, if someone tells us that Meno is handsome, what reason do we have for believing his report, and how could we claim, simply on the basis of that testimony, to have knowledge of the fact? Rather, the reply runs, we should eschew such reliance on hearsay and try to put ourselves in the best possible position to determine the matter for ourselves. Given what we have observed, we can see that this is a natural reply for Plato to make, and we can thus naturally link the τί/ποῖον distinction to lines of thought which we know he was already following.[5]

We must investigate the matter for ourselves rather than relying on hearsay. What does this require? In the present case it seems reasonable to say that we must go and examine Meno. How do we do this? It seems reasonable to say that we must find him, and that to do this, in turn, we must in some sense know who he is—i.e., whom we are to find. The cash value, accordingly, of the contention that we must know who Meno is should be that we must know whatever can be said that will enable us to find him and to examine him. The claim, then, is that certain statements about the object answer to this need whereas others do not.[6] This is not, of course, to give a clear way of picking out proper answers to "What is it?" questions, but it is to begin to explain what the proper sort of answer is supposed to do.

Applied to an entity such as virtue instead of an entity such as Meno, the idea is that knowing the definition (the answer to the question "What is virtue?") enables us to "find" virtue, or in the terminology that we have already observed, to "look to" it. And, once again, we want to do this because we do not want to have to rely on hearsay for our information about virtue; rather, we want to acquire that information by examining the thing ourselves. Once again we see an application of the quasi-sceptical attitude dwelt on in Chapter I. It is only by "finding" and "examining" Forms that one is supposed to be able to tell certain things about them; e.g., whether virtue can be instilled by teaching. Thus, the general claim that we must know what *F*-ness[7] is before we can know other things about it arises out of the view that one must be able in some fashion to examine that object oneself on one's own behalf.[8]

It is important to observe that the distinction in *Euthyphro* 11a-b between *ousia* and *pathos* is introduced in a context in which this sort of issue is not in play at all. Socrates there maintains that being god-loved is not the *ousia* of holiness but rather a *pathos* of it, but he does not contend that knowledge of *ousia* must precede knowledge of *pathos*. On the contrary, he seems there to be quite ready to say with confidence that holiness is god-loved (though not as a matter of definition), without any caveat to the effect that we ought to suspend judgment on the matter until we have provided a definition of holiness (see esp. 11b3-4). The remarks in *Meno* 71a-b would indicate that, in his view at the time of the *Meno*, such confidence was unjustified, and that he would now wish such a caveat to be inserted in the *Euthyphro*. The moral to be drawn is both that at the time of the *Euthyphro* Plato had not thought through the τί/ποῖον distinction as he drew it in the *Meno*, and that in the earlier dialogue the *ousia/pathos* distinction was not being asked to bear the same epistemological freight that was subsequently placed on the τί/ποῖον distinction. Instead, the *ousia/pathos* distinction was probably introduced as a more or less *ad hoc* device to deal with the matter at hand in the *Euthyphro*, and was then turned in the *Meno* into a working part of Plato's developing epistemological scheme.[9]

These reflections yield a view about one of the Platonic uses of definitions that is importantly different from one that suggested itself earlier (Ch. I, sec. 2). It was then proposed that Plato might regard definitions of Forms as premises from which further statements about those respective Forms could be deduced, and that it was in this way, for example, that one might, given a definition of virtue, tell that it is or is not teachable. The competing view, on the other hand, is that the definition enables us to look to and examine the Form, and that by this examination we somehow observe certain features of the Form which are neither given to us in, nor are in any way inferable from, the definition itself. Very roughly put, the difference is like the one between telling that Socrates is a teacher by learning that he is the teacher of Plato and therefrom inferring that he is a teacher, and learning that he is the most snub-nosed man in the market place, finding him on the basis of that description, observing his behavior, and telling from that observation that he is a teacher. Plato does not give us any clear indication of which alternative he has in mind. Thus we have another case in which his views about definitions and Forms, and their interconnections, have not crystallized.

2 The Univocality of
General Terms in the Early Dialogues

Commentators have noticed that Plato often seems oblivious to the possibility that many of the predicates that concern him might plausibly be claimed to be in one way or another ambiguous and not susceptible of any single definition.[10] For Plato, this possibility would naturally be linked to the possibility that a predicate might correspond to more than one Form. On the other hand, at certain points there are signs of awareness of just this danger, as in the relatively early *Euthydemus*, and it might seem that the concern with ambiguity shown in the *Cratylus* and the *Phaedrus* should be equally in evidence in the earliest works.[11] Now although Plato is in fact sometimes aware of the danger of ambiguity (we shall see in a moment plain evidence of this fact), there is no sign yet of the vivid appreciation of it that the *Cratylus* demonstrates, and the fact is that he sometimes shows notable neglect of it. A good example of this neglect appears in the *Lysis*, in which Plato holds on with remarkable tenacity, in the face of numerous contrary indications, to the idea that the term "φίλος" can be provided with a single explanation covering all of its uses. Likewise, there are important passages in the *Phaedo* in which the threat of ambiguity seems to be ignored altogether.[12]

There is a passage in the *Meno*, however, that does show Plato giving heed to, and trying to argue against, a claim that a certain term is in some sense ambiguous. The term is "virtue" ("ἀρετή") and the passage is *Meno* 73a-c.[13] Just before this point Socrates has induced Meno to agree that everything that is truly labeled "strong" is so by virtue of the same thing, strength. This is in effect an admission that the term "strong" always corresponds, in some sense, to the same object or Form. (The reader will note that we have so far not discussed the question what such "correspondence" might consist in; but see Ch. III, sec. 5, and Ch. VI.) Meno jibs, however, at the suggestion that the same holds for "virtue" and that all people who are virtuous are so because of one and the same thing (73a4-5). There follows an attempt to prove precisely this contention. Although the argument is not compelling and although it embraces only applications of the word "virtuous" or "good" to human beings and not to other sorts of thing as well, it nevertheless does show that Plato is here aware of the issue that confronts him.[14] Briefly expounded, the argument depends on the principle that if all people who are good (virtuous) are so "in the same way" (τῷ αὐτῷ τρόπῳ) then their virtue is one and the same thing in all cases (c3-4), along with the claim that all people who are good are indeed so "in the same way." What is problematical about the argument is, among other things, the lack of clarity of the phrase "in the same way." To judge by 73b1-c1, the point of the argument is that because for any person justice and self-control are necessary conditions of virtue, anyone who is virtuous must be so "in the same way" as anyone else. Now even if we accepted the contention that justice and self-control are always, in the case of people, necessary conditions of virtue, this fact by itself would not show that "virtue" always carries the same meaning or corresponds in the requisite way to the same Form. So Plato's argument will not establish what he wishes it to.

Still, it is what he wishes that is important to us here, and the passage shows an explicit awareness on his part of the need, at least in this case, to show that a term is not ambiguous. But at this stage of his career the awareness stops short of a desire to treat the topic of ambiguity in a systematic manner, and the present passage remains isolated for the time being. It is in the *Phaedrus* and the *Cratylus* that the whole matter comes to the forefront of his mind (see Ch. V, sec. 1, and Ch. VI, sec. 2).[15]

3   The Paradox of Inquiry: Its Setting and Function

It is easy to underestimate the importance of the little paradox that Plato unveils in *Meno* 80d-e, but it is a mistake to do so, because his treatment of it is indicative of some central features of his philosophical program.[16] One reason why his interpreters have failed to assess the paradox properly is that they have paid insufficient attention to the fact that it is inextricably tied up with his theory of recollection, which is presented in 81-86 immediately after the paradox itself.[17] In fact, it is crystal clear that it is as a solution of the paradox that the theory of recollection is presented,[18] and each must be interpreted in the light of the other. It would thus be wrong, for example, to think that the reason for introducing the theory of recollection is *simply* to explain the fact that the slave-boy is able, without being explicitly "taught" by Socrates, to arrive at the answer to a problem of geometry. The theory is supposed to explain that fact, to be sure, but this is not its sole function.[19] The place of the conversation between Socrates and the slave-boy in the structure of the argument is as follows. Socrates has given Meno a good deal of trouble over the sorts of definition of virtue that he has proposed; Meno responds in 80d-e with the paradox, intended to be a general obstacle to the project of "inquiring after what one does not know"; Socrates then suggests that the paradox can be disarmed if we suppose that we do not learn anything new but instead recollect (esp. 81c-e); Socrates then initiates the conversation with the slave-boy to show that it is plausible to maintain that we do in fact recollect. The theory of recollection is there to disarm the paradox, and the conversation is there to provide support for the theory. Because the theory of recollection is rightly thought to be of some importance in Plato's doctrine, it behooves us to attach importance also to the paradox that motivates it.[20]

It is sometimes thought that the paradox is a mere interlude prior to the main business of the theory of recollection,[21] and part of the reason for this view is the notion that the paradox is dismissed by Plato and regarded by him as a mere "trick" argument. But this view is a serious mistake. In the first place, the word "ἐριστικός," that is used to describe the paradox in 80e2 and that is often translated by "trick" or the like, is equally renderable by "contentious" or "obstructionist," and consequently this word by itself shows nothing about the point at issue.[22] Secondly, although Socrates is made to respond negatively to the question "Does this argument seem to you to be well taken (καλῶς λέγεσθαι)?" this does not mean that he thinks that the argument is trivial or foolish, but only that he does not think that it establishes what it tries to, namely that there is no possibility of fruitful inquiry.

Seeing the structure of Plato's argument helps to explain an otherwise puzzling fact, that Plato so very easily accepts the idea that the conversation is evidence for recollection. Obviously, the slave's behavior might be accounted for otherwise than by the hypothesis of recollection. Why does Plato not make a serious effort to develop alternative accounts? Simply because by attacking the possibility of successful *de novo* inquiry, the paradox has encouraged him to think that only if recollection occurs is *any* sort of fruitful inquiry possible—and he is very anxious indeed to show that it *is* possible. The hypothesis of recollection seems to him attractive, therefore, because he thinks that it will allow him to cope with both the paradox and the slave's behavior at once.

What does the argument employing the paradox purport to show? To put it roughly, it purports to show that there is no such thing as fruitful inquiry (ζήτησις), because *a*) it is impossible to search for or inquire after (ζητεῖν) what you do not know, and *b*) it is impossible—or perhaps pointless—to search for or inquire after what you do know.[23] And what is Plato's response to this argument? To accept a large part of it. As the theory of recollection has it, our inquiries in fact concern things that we do know (but that we somehow need to recollect), and Plato has clearly granted the part of the argument that says that we cannot inquire about what we do not know (cf. sec. 5). The part that he has rejected, on the other hand, is the part that says that we cannot inquire about what we already know, and it is by rejecting this part of the argument that he tries to save the possibility of fruitful inquiry, by construing inquiry as the attempt to recollect. Accordingly, if he is to show that we sometimes do fruitfully inquire, he must show that we sometimes do succeed in recollecting, and it is to show this that the conversation with the slave-boy is portrayed. In Plato's view, therefore, there is nothing merely "eristic" about the paradox; on the contrary, he treats it with all seriousness.

4 The Paradox of Inquiry: The Main Issues

In fact, the problems arising out of his epistemological views dictate that he should take the paradox seriously, because it is intimately connected with what he has said about definitions and Forms. Both his treatment of the paradox and his attempt to solve it illustrate, in their respective ways, some of the difficulties with which he is faced, and the tendencies on his part that make those difficulties hard for him to avoid.

Plato's setting of the paradox is obscure enough to require close examination. I therefore display it (80d5-e5):

> MENO: But in what way will you inquire after (ζητήσεις) something such that you do not know what it is? What sort of thing, among those things which you do not know, will you set up beforehand as the object of your inquiry? Or to put it otherwise, even if you happen to come right upon it, how will you know that it is that which you did not know?
>
> SOCRATES: I understand what you mean, Meno. Do you see how contentious the argument is which you are introducing, that it is not possible to inquire either after that which one knows or that which one does not know? He would not need to inquire after that which he knows, since he knows it and there is no need of inquiry for such a thing, nor after what he does not know since he does not know what he is inquiring after.[24]

We must now ask just what the problem is which concerns Plato here.

The crucial fact about the paradox is that although it is often called the "learner's paradox," it is not in fact a paradox about *learning* as such but a paradox about *inquiry* and the successful completion thereof, and about only such learning as is directed toward fulfilling a project of inquiry set up in advance. That this is so is shown by the crucial sentence (80d7-8): ". . . even if you happen to come right upon it [i.e., what you are inquiring after] how will you know that it is that which you did not know?" The paradox would collapse completely if it were not for this allegation that there is something problematical about *recognizing* the successful but hitherto unknown outcome of an inquiry already framed and undertaken. Thus, the paradox says nothing whatsoever against the possibility of coming upon an object or piece of information previously unsought.[25] Nor is this fact at all surprising, in the light of the fact that the paradox has been presented explicitly as an obstacle to a project of inquiry already enunciated, namely the effort to gain knowledge of virtue.

The effect of this crucial piece of the argument is to maintain that if you do not already know the thing that you are endeavoring in your inquiry to discover, then you will be unable to recognize it if it appears, or in other words— to take the contrapositive of this claim, which is logically equivalent to it—if you can recognize it, then you already know it. It is not too difficult to see why this claim should appear plausible. In the typical case, one's ability to recognize the object of an inquiry (whether it be an object in some narrow sense, or something more like the answer to a question that frames the inquiry) involves one's having a specification or description which is to be satisfied by what one is seeking. One may "have" this specification in only a relatively weak sense, because one may not even be able to formulate it without considerable effort. Still, there must be circumstances imaginable under which one could produce it, because otherwise there would be no distinguishing purposive, directed inquiries from a random interest in notable facts or objects which happen to present themselves to one's scrutiny.[26]

But it is the idea that one might already possess a specification of what is sought that can make it seem, under certain circumstances, that one already has attained what one is striving for. There are various reasons for this fact. One of them is somewhat special to Plato's position, arising from some of the things that we have seen him saying (Ch. I, sec. 4). We have seen him engaging in both the effort to establish definitions and the effort to apprehend Forms corresponding thereto. We have also seen him suggesting, in separate places, both that the

Form should be apprehended in order to allow us to establish the correct definition, and that the definition might itself be a specification by which one could recognize the desired Forms when it was apprehended. A hasty combination of these two suggestions, however, might easily lead to the idea that if, for example, one proposed to use an already established definition as a means of recognizing the corresponding Form, then one must somehow already have apprehended the Form in order to have established the definition. A person who had never apprehended the Form, on the other hand, might seem to be without any way of recognizing it.

But the attitude that leads to this problem need not have arisen from this sort of hasty combination of separate suggestions, because the root of it is independent of Plato's own special situation. For suppose that you are searching for something, armed with a single specification of what it is that you are to find. Thus, you might search for something under the specification "my left glove." But now suppose that you attempt to adopt a sceptical attitude toward your specification, and that you conceive it doubtful that this specification actually applies to the object of your search; and suppose that you go so far as to think it necessary for you to examine the object of your search in order to tell whether the specification actually applies to it. You are obviously in a *cul-de-sac* . You have put yourself in the position of supposing that you must find the object before you can be confident that the specification actually applies to it, while at the same time you lack any specification by which you may recognize it. If you begin with a number of specifications of what it is that you are seeking, then the situation becomes more complicated.[27] But you will be equally in a bind if you decide that you may trust none of them until you have examined the object to which they are supposed to apply. For once again there will be no way of recognizing it.[28]

However much difficulty they raise, the attitude described by these reflections is not an unnatural one, and the fact that it enables us to see is no trivial one. For the upshot is that when one begins an inquiry, one must in some sense have a specification of its object which is unquestioned, in a certain sense, and which serves to *define* what the inquiry is. That is, the inquiry must be taken to be directed to *whatever* it is that satisfies the specification. But it is all too easy to think that this is to say that one is, at the start of an inquiry, taking for granted something about what it is searching for, as though there were something about an object that one could tell without any investigation of it. For it seems as though one were, simply by forming a wish to find something, somehow mysteriously rendering it certain that that object has a particular property, namely the property expressed in one's specification. And it is thus not at all difficult to understand why the paradox of inquiry should seem thus to arise, and that it should seem that the initiator of an inquiry must already have, inexplicably, a certain important piece of information about what he may never have seen. Moreover, the force of the paradox seems even greater—to return now to the special features of Plato's circumstances—if one thinks of the specification as the sort of definition at which Plato has been aiming. For clearly the definition is not something that Plato would want to be taking for granted at the start of an inquiry. Nevertheless, the fact is that there is no possibility of genuine *de novo* inquiry without an ability to recognize its consummation, and thus without some prior idea of what would count as such. Inquiries do not begin *in vacuo*, but only with a background that allows one to say what it is that they are seeking, and with the possibility of distinguishing between the ability to say what they are seeking on the one hand, and their successful completion on the other.

What allows the paradox to gain a foothold in Plato's early reflections is the fact that in his early epistemological efforts he has begun without a clear vision of their goals and of the points from which they start. This fact was plain in our observations of his different accounts of the relation between the project of apprehending a Form and the project of establishing a definition (Ch. I, sec. 4). It is also plain in the fact that he tends to describe his epistemological efforts quite indifferently as being efforts to "know *X*" and also being efforts to "know what *X* is," without signaling any difference between these two manners of speaking. Thus, *Euthyphro* 15c11-12 speaks of the necessity of discovering "what holiness is," but immediately afterward e1 and e6-7 speaks of the need to "know holiness." Similar collocations without explicit distinction are to be found elsewhere, particularly in the *Meno* itself (75b5 with c5, d6; 79d7-8, c1, 4 with c8-9). But whereas "knowing what holiness is" is naturally associated with the quest for definitions, "knowing holiness" is more readily suggestive of the apprehension of an object. But even in later works, too, Plato tends to leave this distinction without explicit treatment or warning of its existence.[29] This tendency is, of course, inimical to the setting out of the relationship between the two pertinent projects—that of establishing a definition and that of apprehending a Form—and to the explicit treatment of the starting-points and goals of Plato's investigations concerning Forms and definitions. But without the treatment of the starting-points of such investigations, it is difficult to settle the questions how inquiries are to be framed, and what abilities we are granted to recognize their completion.

In the absence of explicit consideration of what the starting point of investigation should be, some philosophers would be inclined to allow us too much rather than too little, but these philosophers are of a different cast of mind from Plato's. That is to say, some philosophers have no tendency to deprive one, at the start, of the necessary wherewithal to frame the inquiries to come. As we have seen, however, Plato's natural inclinations run in the opposite direction, leading him into a more or less sceptical attitude, particularly toward the deliverances of popular opinion (Ch. I, sec. 3). In fact, we have seen what is probably the same tendency at work already in an earlier part of the *Meno*, in the discussion of "τί" and "ποῖον" (sec. 1). For what Plato may have done in the paradox is to retain the idea that we must find a thing and recognize it before we can know facts about it, but to extend the required scepticism to include not only facts of the ποῖον variety, as before, but also those falling under the rubric τί. In this manner we could—though the point is a conjectural one—see the paradox in 80d-e as pressing to its extreme the idea first enunciated in 71b, and as carrying on its sceptical tendency.

Inquiries, then—as opposed to unframed efforts to learn whatever may present itself—must begin with a specification of what they seek, and Plato tends to be insufficiently attentive to this fact, in part because he has not fully formulated the starting points and goals, as he sees them, of investigations concerning Forms and definitions, and in part because he may see such a specification, particularly when he thinks of a definition as playing its role, as something which it would be illegitimate to take for granted at the start. Thus he passes to the general conclusion in 80d that if one can recognize the goal of one's inquiry, then one must have arrived at it already.

I have observed that Plato is correct in thinking that if at the start of an inquiry one is deprived of a specification of its goal, then the possibility of successful inquiry (and, I think, inquiry itself) is destroyed. I have also observed that the specification must be taken as defining the inquiry, so that it is aimed at whatever satisfies the specification. But this observation does not mean, as Plato evidently thought, that the inquirer begins with knowledge that is in any important sense *about* the object that he seeks, and that is somehow inexplicably gained without inspection or investigation of the thing that it concerns. For it is not the *object*, being what it is and independently of specification, that defines the inquiry, and in an important sense it is not the *object* at which the inquiry is directed. Rather, it is the *specification* that defines the inquiry, and it is the specification's being satisfied by *something* discovered, rather than the satisfaction of it by any *particular* thing, that constitutes the completion of the inquiry.[30] To begin with a specification, therefore, is not to begin by taking anything for granted about the object whose discovery will perhaps eventually consummate the inquiry. It is not, as it were, to name the successful candidate; it is only to say what it is that the successful candidate must be successful at; it is about the office, not the holder of it. Or to put the point another way, it is about the directions of our own aims, rather than the things that happen to lie in those directions.[31]

But Plato has a different answer to the paradox, which we must now consider.

5 The Theory of Recollection: Plato's Response to the Paradox

Plato's response to the paradox is simple and straightforward. It is to accept the crucial part of its argument, including the claim that if one inquired after what one did not know, one could not recognize it if one encountered it. Accordingly, in an effort to save, as well as possible, our belief that we do engage in something like successful efforts at inquiry (81d5-e2), he boldly attacks the other part of the argument and maintains that it is after all possible to inquire, in an unusual sense, about what one already knows. For what we usually think of as inquiry, he says, is actually recollection of what we already know but need to recollect.

There are various preliminary difficulties with Plato's response which need to be cleared away. In the first place, he shows some signs of discomfort with the manner of speaking which his solution obliges him to adopt. Thus, although he must say that before the conversation between Socrates and the slave-boy takes place, the latter actually knows the answer to the geometrical problem posed there (85d9-13), he is nonetheless at certain points willing to talk with the vulgar and say that sometimes one fails to know something or other (e.g., at 85c6-7, 86b2-3; at 86b3-4, however, he makes clear that this employment of "know" is a loose one). At other times, he seems to go off on a different track and to maintain that what is—to use his manner of speaking—"in the soul" prior to recollection ought more properly to be called "belief" (δόξα) than "knowledge" (ἐπιστήμη; see 85b8, c4, 6-7, 9-c1, 86a6-8).

The reason is clear: at this point he has focused his attention on the difference between a person with a relatively stable ability to expound the results of an "inquiry," and a person who readily loses this ability after he has seemingly acquired it. That this difference is what is on his mind in talking of "belief" is shown by 98a3-8 and 85c10-d1, where he maintains that true belief has to be changed into knowledge, and that this change takes place by some sort of rehearsal of the process by which recollection originally took place in a person such as the slave-boy.[32] However, this distinction between knowledge and belief is never said to supersede the claim that successful inquiry may only be about what one already knows.

It has often been suggested that the distinction between knowledge and belief toward the end of the *Meno* (96d*sqq.*) already amounts in Plato's mind to the famous distinction made in the *Republic* between knowledge and belief, according to which the objects of knowledge are Forms and the objects of belief are sensible objects (Ch. IV, sec. 1); and it has also been maintained, on the contrary, that since this way of drawing the distinction is nowhere explicit in the *Meno*, it should not be read back from the later work.[33] On the former side of the debate it has been said, first, that the example employed in the conversation with the slave-boy really has to do with "geometrical" rather than "sensible" objects, and that these geometrical objects are among the Forms that are discussed in the *Republic*; and, second, that Plato could not possibly mean to claim that whatever is learned about the most trivial sensible object is actually recollected.[34] Both of these arguments have considerable force. There is no strong reason to deny that even at this early stage Plato would have found it bizarre to suppose that we could recollect sensible objects or facts about them. (Indeed, it is the fact that he shows signs of disliking this supposition that makes it plausible to say that the *Meno* is coming closer to the theory of the *Phaedo*—cf. n. II-42.) While this debate is going on, however, we should not fail to keep our eyes on the point that is really important to the issues on which Plato is working in the *Meno*. It is that the philosophical problem with which Plato is directly concerned, namely the problem that is posed by the paradox, is neutral on the question what manner of object constitutes the subject matter of inquiry and recollection. As far as that problem itself is concerned, they could be anything under the sun or over it. What the paradox seems to Plato to show is that *if* it is possible fruitfully to inquire about a given object, then it must be possible to recollect it. There is no need for him to specify further what sort of things these objects might be, and he has enough on his hands already to make it reasonable for him to avoid this extra issue. And avoid it he does, for the time being.[35]

Another difficult issue in the doctrine of recollection in the *Meno* has to do with the question whether the things that are recollected are supposed to have been known for all past time or were somehow learned before we were born into our current lives. Once again, Plato appears somewhat indecisive.[36] At times he seems to leave open the possibility of prenatal learning (85d13, e9-86a4). On the other hand, 86a8-9 appears to say that one's soul has "*always* been in a state of knowing"[37] and just afterwards he appears to be affirming the antecedent of the conditional in 86b1-2, "If the truth about things is *always* in the soul, . . ." How are we to interpret this vacillation?

An answer to this question suggests itself when we look more closely at the nature of the paradox and his reply to it. The crucial point to notice is that as we have seen (sec. 4), the problem that he confronts in 80d-e, notwithstanding the fact that Plato himself sometimes seems to suggest the contrary, is *not* an argument against all possibility whatever of "coming to know" an object. It does not tend to show, for example, that we could not meet Socrates and perceive all sorts of facts about him. What it does purport to show is that we cannot meet him, *recognize* him as fitting some specification which we had in advance, and describe ourselves as having moved from a condition in which we did not know him *but were trying to come to know him*, into a condition in which we have come to know him. Given this fact, we can see clearly why Plato might have been willing to leave open the possibility that the soul might have learned prenatally, provided it were not claimed that this learning came about as the result of inquiry. (Of course he would also have to admit the possibility that the soul could learn in this life as well, under the same proviso. But this admission would not by any means leave him free to discard recollection altogether, because he thinks it clear that we do, in this life, sometimes learn as the result of what seems to be inquiry, and that only recollection can, in the face of the paradox, account for this sort of learning. Moreover, he must think that we sometimes recollect from before birth, because he thinks it equally clear that sometimes we discover, as a result of inquiry, things that we have not overtly known since that time.) Thus, he is able to avoid committing himself on the question whether prenatal learning occurs, and his failure to issue a definitive pronouncement on this point becomes fully comprehensible, now that we realize what his point is.[38]

These preliminary matters having been disposed of, we are now in a position to examine the nature of Plato's response to the paradox. In a sense it fails, but what is more important than that fact is the fact that it is so constructed, and so viewed by Plato, as to obscure the real nature of the problem which the paradox posed for Plato's nascent epistemological doctrine.

The crucial move made by the paradox of inquiry, as we saw, was the claim that if the object of an inquiry is not in the requisite sense known, then it cannot be recognized by the inquirer (80d7-8). Plato wishes to agree that this is so (that is, that "inquiry" must concern what is already known), but then to insist that what we ordinarily construe as *de novo* inquiry is actually an attempt to recollect. What he is recognizing is the inquiring, and he is maintaining that this effort is in fact the effort that recollection, as we all know, may require. At the same time, however, he must reckon with the fact that the recollection that he is invoking must be a purposive, directed effort to recollect a particular thing or item of information, because it is of course introduced to show how such directed projects as Meno's attempt to gain—or, now, to recollect— knowledge of virtue. So of course it must be claimed to be possible for one to recognize that which one set out to recollect. For if it were not, then recollection would fall victim to a paradox of recollection rather analogous to the paradox of inquiry, whose crucial move would read as a parody of 80d7-8, as follows: ". . . even if you happen to come right upon it, how will you know that it is that which you had not yet recollected?" So it must be claimed possible to recognize the previously known but unrecollected in a way in which it is not possible to recognize the previously unknown. For otherwise the diehard opponent of inquiry will contend that even this stand-in for inquiry will not do, because in order to be able to recognize what one is trying to recollect, *as* the thing that one was trying to recollect, one must already have recollected it.

The diehard's case is not without force, because he can appeal to the idea that, just as one must in some sense have a specification in order to recognize the object of an inquiry, so too one must have a specification of what it is that one is trying to recollect; and he can maintain that if an inquirer's possession of such a specification constitutes already having completed an inquiry, by parallel reasoning a recollector's possession of a specification ought to constitute already having recollected. Certainly this would appear to be the case if we recur to the example of Plato's definitions and Forms from the previous section. For if one is pictured as using a definition as a specification for recognizing a recollected Form, then it would appear that one has already recollected the definition; but it is not clear that Plato ought to wish to allow this possibility. Likewise, if one is pictured as viewing a Form in order to pass judgment on the correctness of a recollected definition, then it would appear that one must already have recalled the Form itself to one's apprehension; but again it is not clear that Plato would wish to allow this possibility.

At the extreme opposite to the position of the diehard opponent of inquiry is the position of the philosopher who wishes to uphold the possibility both of directed efforts at recollection and of directed *de novo* inquiry. His view, of course, is that although one can recognize the successful outcome of such recollection, one can equally frame *de novo* inquiries and recognize their outcomes too, by virtue of the fact that in both cases one may specify the aim of one's project without already having completed it. This person, however, does agree with the diehard in one important respect: he holds that inquiry and recollection are on a par, in that one is possible if and only if the other is. He thinks that they are both possible; the diehard thinks that neither is.

The point that the two make in common is that the possession of a specification of one's goal ought to count as the attainment of it *equally* in both cases; and what they both oppose is the Platonic view that it counts as such in the case of *de novo* inquiry but not in the case of recollection. Their position is enhanced by the consideration that if one is attempting to recollect something, and if one has on hand a specification by the use of which one can recognize it, then it ought perfectly well to be possible to use that same specification to recognize something that one has never observed or apprehended before.[39] For example, suppose that one is trying to recollect a definition, and suppose that a formula is forthcoming from one's memory.[40] By expressing the standards that a correct definition must meet, the specification presumably enables one to decide whether or not the putative definition is correct. But if the specification can do this, then one has difficulty saying why it could not do the same for a putative definition that presented itself not through memory, but for the first time. If, on the other hand, the specification could not be usable on previously unknown candidates, then it is hard to see how it could help one to pass judgment on those dredged up by recall. A usable standard would seem to be a usable standard, whatever the source of the candidates to which it is applied.

But this argument neglects a possibility embodying what customarily appears to us as a special feature of memory, namely the fact that sometimes one simply has the feeling (if "feeling" is the appropriate word) that one is remembering, which one trusts as a warrant for saying that one has correctly recollected what has come to consciousness accompanied by that feeling. For Plato's position can rely on the idea that instead of thinking that a purported definition arises from memory to be tested by an independent standard, what actually happens is this: the *content* of one's recollection is that the recollected formula *is* the correct definition, and one trusts the feeling of recollection as a warrant for confidence in this claim. It is not that you recall the claim that virtue is such-and-such, with the idea that you have heard it somewhere before, and then test it by some standard which you have of what a correct definition should be like. It is rather that you recall—as you feel—that virtue *is* such-and-such, and your reason for accepting this claim is *simply* that feeling of recollecting. How, then, do you recognize that you have in fact recollected what you set out to recollect? What specification did you have to enable you to do so? Simply the idea that you could trust the deliverances of what was felt as recollection.[41] Your ability to recognize the completion of your project is accordingly derived from your confidence that recollection, as you feel it, is veridical. But of course it is implausible to say that if you begin with the idea that the correct answer to the question "What is virtue?" is whatever your felt recollection will present to you as such, then you must already have recollected what virtue is. So it appears that recollection does provide a way in which you can be said to be able to recognize success in recollection without already having attained it.

There are two points to be made about this argument, of which one is the more important for the understanding of Plato's thought. The less important point is that the argument does not succeed. The more important point is that what is crucial about the argument is not that it involves *recollection*, but that if the argument is correct, then recollection has a particular feature which is important to Plato's method, but which is not explicitly recognized by him. First, the less important point. If one can simply trust one's "feelings" of recollection, then of course one can avoid reliance on any independent specification of what one is attempting to recollect. However, there is no more reason to trust one's feelings of recollection all by themselves than to trust the feelings that sometimes come upon one when one is apparently conducting a *de novo* inquiry, and which seem to be to the effect that one has in fact encountered the correct answer to it. The point is that if we sometimes "feel certain" that we have recollected correctly, we also sometimes "feel certain" that we are correct in something that we are discovering for the first time. Moreover, in neither case does one ever rely merely on the feeling; in both sorts of cases one seeks corroborative support. So there is no reason to accept the view that recollection is in fact on a different footing from inquiry. One could equally well begin an inquiry determined to accept whatever struck one with conviction, and one would not plausibly be said already to know what one was aiming at.

The more important point is that what is crucial about recollection, as an answer to the paradox of inquiry, is not that it is recollection, nor that it concerns what one already knows, but that it provides one with a way of beginning one's cognitive efforts short of their goal, while nevertheless being able to specify what that goal is and to recognize it when it is reached. This would be the crucial move in answering the paradox, even if—as I have just denied—the supposition that we recollect were the only possible device for removing the difficulty that the paradox poses. The general problem affects any sort of investigation, whether it be efforts at recollection or *de novo* inquiry. It is a problem of clarifying what the starting point of investigation is to be, how it attains its ends, and how the attainment of its ends is to be recognized. Directed investigation, as I have said, does not begin *in vacuo*; it begins with an understanding of its aims. The appeal to recollection as such tends to obscure this fact, and to turn attention away from what needs attention most.

Plato shows some understanding of this fact. For in spite of the fact that recollection constitutes his official response to the paradox of inquiry, it is not his only suggestion in the *Meno* concerning questions of method.[42] On the conclusion of the conversation between Socrates and the slave-boy, Socrates makes a proposal about how they should proceed with the discussion of virtue. The method that he proposes involves the use of what he calls "hypotheses," and is (in spite of the obscurities surrounding his exposition of it)[43] evidently supposed to be a way in which investigation may begin, if only provisionally. We have noticed earlier, and have been just now noticing here, that one of Plato's chief methodological needs is for a way of explaining how one can begin to gain the sort of knowledge at which he thinks we ought to aim, and the method of hypothesis shows his recognition of that need. For although it is quite separate from the theory of recollection (86c-e makes no attempt substantially to connect the two), it is an attempt to provide us with a way of beginning our investigations and trying to make progress in them.[44] Moreover, the attempt is continued and developed in the *Phaedo*, in which Plato gives a clearer and more complete treatment of it. Accordingly, it will best serve our purposes to examine the method when we treat that dialogue (Ch. III, sec. 7). Let us for now simply note the need, which its introduction in the *Meno* is an initial attempt to fill.

Notes

1. See Jaeger, vol. II, p. 161.

2. For an interpretation linking the *Meno* and the *Euthyphro*, see Allen **4**, pp. 76-79.

3. For some examples, see Quine **5**, Parsons, Bennett, my **2**, Brody.

4. For one such use, see Bluck **4**, p. 392; Dodds, pp. 289-290; as well as 80d6, *Euthyphro* 5c9, d7, 12d (in 5c9 and 12d8 the use of "τί" and "ποῖον" is rather thoroughly scrambled), *Lach*. 194e3 vs. 8.

5. This account of the distinction allows us to get around the difficulty mentioned by Bluck **4**, p. 211, that on Plato's view we ought to be unable in principle ever to *know* about something sensible, such as Meno and his looks. For we can suppose, if we like, that Plato is using the example of Meno simply to illustrate the point, without meaning it to be taken seriously itself as a case of knowledge. Alternatively, we could simply say that Plato has not yet firmly decided that there is no knowledge concerning sensible objects (as is suggested by 96d*sqq*.). Or we can simply say that Plato at this point is not concerned with the question what sort of objects knowledge has to do with (cf. n. II-35). (There is no reason to worry about one of the passages that Bluck mentions: *Symp.* 201d is an example of the looseness with which Plato can use "τί" and "ποῖον"; cf. n. II-4.)

6. Contemporary philosophers have spent time on this notion: see, for example, Hintikka **1**, pp. 131ff., and **3**.

7. I use "*F*-ness" as a stand-in for ways of designating Forms, in spite of the problems which, because of certain features of Plato's views about Forms, attend this manner of speaking; cf. Ch. III, introd., on "self-predication."

8. With an eye to certain contemporary developments in epistemic logic, we can notice the following corollary. It is that by holding this view, Plato has obliterated the distinction, as *some* wish to draw it, between referential and opaque occurrences of singular terms within ascriptions of knowledge (on this distinction, see Quine **8**, pp. 144ff.), or—changing the point slightly—between *de re* and *de dicto* ascriptions of knowledge. Consider the distinction, thus drawn, between sentences such as (1) "Meno knows, concerning Socrates, that he is wise" and (2) "Meno knows that Socrates is wise." It has seemed natural to some philosophers to say that for (1) to be true, though not for (2), it is necessary that Meno be in some sense "acquainted" with Socrates. What Plato has done, in effect, is to say that (2) can be true if and only if (1) is, thus wiping out the distinction, thus construed. Beside this dislike of knowledge-ascriptions based on hearsay, there is another reason why Plato would have been led in this direction. It is the well-known fact that Greek has a grammatical construction

of which a literally translated instance would be "Meno knows Socrates, that he is wise," of which the first three words can form an independent sentence translatable by "Meno knows Socrates" in the sense roughly of "Meno is acquainted with Socrates." This fact would evidently make the contrast in question less obvious to Plato. On the other hand, Plato does sometimes show a glimmering of the distinction, and even in the *Meno* itself. The relevant passage is 77b-e, which is designed to show that no one ever desires what is bad (κακόν) for him. First, at 77c6, d5, Plato uses the construction "γιγνώσκειν τὰ κακὰ ὅτι κακά ἐστιν", which can and should be translated here "know, concerning bad things, that they are bad." Even more important is 77d7-e2, which runs:

> So it is clear that these people, those who do not know the bad things, do not desire the bad things but rather those things which they think are good but which are in fact bad; so that those who do not know them and think they are good clearly desire the good things.

What emerges from this passage is that Plato can make a distinction between "desiring bad things" and "desiring things which one thinks are good but which are in fact bad," which is pretty close to the distinction at issue here. But it is one thing to see the contrast in a relatively restricted type of case, and quite another to transfer this recognition to other, less obvious, cases. (Sharvy, pp. 119-120, sees a related distinction at *Euthyphro* 8b, but he highlights it strongly, whereas Plato's way of putting it makes it at best hardly recognizable.)

9. We see signs of similar distinctions in the *Phdo.*, the *Crat.*, and in *Ep.* VII; see nn. VI-20, VI-21, and VIII-26. Once again, though, it would be a mistake to think that Plato kept precisely the same distinction in view throughout his career.

10. See Robinson **1**, pp. 54ff; Allen **4**, pp. 118-120. The common view (expressed, e.g., by Allen, p. 119) that *Lysis* 219-220 shows a notion of "eponymy," is dubious: see Owen **3**, pp. 163-190 (esp. 182-183, with references). (Allen also fails here to provide any arguments for his claim that "there is no incompatibility between the theory of Forms and the eponymous use of terms" (p. 119); but some kind of argument would be desirable, in view of Aristotle's attack on this claim (cf. Owen, pp. 185-189), and Allen might refer to what he says in his **2**.).

11. See *Euthyd.* 277esqq. For the *Phdr.* and the *Crat.*, see Ch. V, secs. 1-2, and Ch. VI, sec. 2; and see also Ch. VIII, sec. 3, on similar matters in *Ep.* VII.

12. See *Phdo.* 102-103, with Ch. III, sec. 5, and perhaps also 99d-100a, along with (perhaps) *Rep.* 435a-b and Ch. IV, sec. 1.

13. On this point, see Robinson **1**, pp. 54-58, and Bluck **4**, pp. 230-231.

14. Robinson rightly diagnoses the problem in Plato's argument (pp. 54-57) but he underestimates the importance of the fact that Plato gives it (p. 57), and so (I think) does Allen **4**, p. 120.

15. Robinson and Allen do not make anything of this fact (*locc. citt.*), though of course Robinson is treating primarily Plato's earlier dialogues. Allen claims that the slogan "*unum nomen unum nominatum*" is in this context "best taken as an

ideal for the improvement of language . . ." (p. 119). This is correct, as applied to the *Crat.* (Ch. VI, sec. 2), but is beyond anything that Plato says in early works.

16. The material of this section and the next two is also covered, with additions, in my **3**. (On points of difference, this treatment supersedes that one.)

17. *"The* paradox": some have suggested (e.g., Moravcsik **2**, p. 57) that there is meant to be a difference between the formulations of the puzzle by Meno and Socrates. There is indeed a difference in wording on which we might want to dwell in *our own* philosophical reflections, but to suppose that Plato intended to be propounding two different problems leaves quite unexplained why he never mentions the fact, and thenceforth acts as though he has only one puzzle to face. (Moravcsik's account also requires us to suppose that after setting two puzzles, Plato for some reason entirely neglects one of them.) What Socrates does is simply to make clear that Meno's puzzle can be cast in the form of a dilemma (e5 must be simply a terse reformulation of d6-8, or else Plato would surely have remarked on the difference).

18. For an awareness of this fact, see Cherniss **3**, pp. 71ff.; Wieland, p. 77; and Moravcsik **2**, pp. 56, 63. (There seems to me to be no foundation for Wieland's claim, *ibid.*, that *Soph.* 229b*sqq.* is also directed against the paradox.) Most likely, Aristotle too was alive to this fact; cf. n. II-25. No one, to my knowledge, has ever denied that the theory of recollection was supposed to disarm the paradox, but some have minimized or ignored the fact. Of course, the ideas of transmigration and recollection have a pre-Platonic history, but Plato is making his own use of them; see Gulley **2**, pp. 4ff. (esp. pp. 10-11), and Bluck **4**, pp. 61-75.

19. According to Gulley (p. 13), "Plato makes quite clear that the theory of recollection is introduced as a foundation for the Socratic dialectic," but he does not see the connection with the paradox. Thus he says, "For if knowledge is recollected knowledge then a criterion of truth above mere consistency and individual agreement is available to guide inquiry . . . ," but he fails to give any explanation of why this is so. He is right, however, to emphasize Plato's desire to have more to rely on than mere agreement: see Ch. I, introd. and sec. 3.

20. This is not to say that the paradox had this purpose in other hands. For other appearances of it (including *Euthyd.* 275ff.), see Bluck **4**, p. 272.

21. Grube, p. 12, speaks of the paradox as a "tiresome sophism," without venturing to suggest how it might be solved. He does see that the theory of recollection is designed to meet the paradox, but he says (as does Burnet **2**, p. 157) that it is introduced "in a mythical vein." Evidently he means that neither the paradox nor the theory is to be taken seriously. It is true that the first introduction of the theory of recollection is mythological (81a-d), and that some reservations about the theory are expressed later (86b). The former fact is explained by noting that Plato is appropriating an idea which had been expressed in a mythological way—though by whom we do not know (see Bluck **4**, pp. 61-75, 274-276). The latter is explained by the fact that the theory really is, as Plato could see, quite a lot to swallow. Neither fact, however, tells against

philosophical seriousness on Plato's part, in connection either with the paradox or with the theory.

22. Cf. *Lys.* 211b8, and *Soph.* 225c9 with a2, and Gulley **3**, p. 206. Henricus Aristippus got it right: *litigiosum*.

23. "To search for or inquire after": we shall see that Plato does in part have in mind the idea of in some sense literally searching (cf. my **2**, pp. 296-297). This is guaranteed by 80d7-8, where the question arises of *recognizing* the thing for which you are searching. (For similar uses of "ζητεῖν" and cognates, see for instance *Rep.* 368c7, d2, e1, and *Crat.* 436a5, 7. For coordinate uses of "εὑρίσκειν", see *Crat.* 436a4, 5, 7, 438a8, 439b4, 7, and *Tht.* 148d2. On this last, see McDowell **2**, *ad* 147b4-5 and 148c6-7.) The paradox should thus not be confused with others which are superficially similar to it, but which do not involve just this notion of searching (cf. n. II-17). Notice in particular that most versions of the so-called Paradox of Analysis, although similar to the paradox in the *Meno* (see Hare **3**, Moravcsik **2**, pp. 63-64, and Nakhnikian, pp. 129-130), are distinct from it. (For the original modern version of the Paradox of Analysis, see Langford, p. 323.) On this matter, see my **3**, pt. IV.

24. The verb "ζητήσει" in e5 is a Deliberative Future (see Smyth, secs. 2549-2550), so we could translate "he does not know what to inquire after;" but it does not matter to the point of the clause.

25. Something else that is not Plato's problem here is what Aristotle seems to read into the passage (*An. Post.* 71a29-31; cf. Cherniss **3**, p. 71). But a comparison of *An. Post.* 71a29-31 with 67a16-26 (cf. also 86a10-13, 22-30) indicates that Aristotle realized that the theory of recollection was used in the *Meno* as an answer to the paradox. (This contention is not weakened by the fact that no trace of the paradox appears in the *De Mem. et Reminisc.*, since there Aristotle has no concerns that would make the paradox pertinent.)

26. See further my **3**, pp. 299-300. But notice that the points in this and the following sections will stand, though with less generality, if not all inquiries are framed by specifications (but instead require merely the ability, somehow conceived of as not involving any ability to produce a specification, to recognize the successful outcome of the inquiry). For certainly many are, and they can be the ones which are seen as raising the problem that the paradox of inquiry poses.

27. See *ibid.*, p. 300, n. 17.

28. Not wishing to encumber the present discussion with issues concerning the notion of reference and the like, I leave aside the question whether *there is* in such circumstances an inquiry or an object thereof at all. See infra, n. II-31.

29. See Robinson **1**, p. 103, on the disagreement that has arisen partly because of this lack of treatment. For the lack of treatment (and even evidence for a certain degree of outright confusion) see e.g. Hare **2**, esp. pp. 22-24, and Vlastos **9**, p. 165. One may see much the same phenomenon within the conversation between Socrates and the slave-boy. In a good deal of it, the aim would seem to be to answer the question, "How long is the side of a square of (e.g.) an area of eight square feet?" Elsewhere, however, Plato writes as though there

were an object that was the object of inquiry, namely here, *the side* of the square whose area is eight square feet; see 84a4-6, 84c5.

It is common in this connection to invoke Russell's distinction between knowledge by acquaintance and knowledge by description (and likewise the distinction between *kennen* and *wissen*, and between *savoir* and *connaître*, and to say that Plato did not clearly draw it. I myself avoid this invocation (esp. in Ch. VII, secs. 2-3, 5, Ch. VIII, secs. 3-4, and Ch. IX, sec. 2 with n. IX-14). The reason is that there seems to me to be great unclarity in this distinction, as it is normally expounded by Russell and others (see esp. his **5**). In particular, it is quite unclear to me whether Russell thinks that a person who is acquainted with an object *a*) can, or *b*) must be said to recognize, or to be able to recognize, that object. For my purposes here the crucial distinction (which of course requires much more treatment than there is space to give it here) is between somehow "*apprehending*" something and *recognizing* it, in the sense of recognizing that it fits some specification (usually what is in question is a singular specification, but cf. my **3**, sec. II). I do not think that this is the distinction that Russell intended, though it is obviously connected with it.

30. See further my **3**, sec. III, in which this view is also shown to have its difficulties; in my opinion, however, they are not as great as the paradox of inquiry.

31. For related matters, see Quine **8**, pp. 134, 151-156, but notice that the question at issue here is not precisely the same as the question how we should parse sentences involving "to search for" and the like. It is because the situation is complicated in this way that one cannot be content with the response to the paradox that simply says that searches are directed at what we in one sense know but in another do not (see, e.g., Bluck **4**, p. 272). Note too that it is an oversimplification to see the paradox as arising simply from a confusion between, as it were, *quid* and *quod*, that is, between "knowing what" in the indirect-interrogative sense of "what" and "knowing that which" (see Austin **3**). Although this confusion might have played a superficial role in the formulation of the paradox, the root of the matter goes much deeper.

32. For this point see Vlastos **9**, pp. 152-153.

33. On this issue see respectively, e.g., Allen **1**, esp. 172-174, *vs.* Bluck **4**, pp. 30ff., and Cherniss **2**, and **6**, esp. p. 421.

34. See Moravcsik **2**, p. 60. Another way of linking the *Meno* with later discussions of the Forms has been to see a connection between the claim in 81c9-d1 that "all nature is akin" and the "associationist" conception of recollection in the *Phaedo* (73c*sqq.*). For criticism of this idea see Tigner, pp. 1-4, who also points out flaws in other accounts of the "kinship." His own interpretation, although not to my mind quite satisfactory, is on the right track, particularly in claiming that because the idea of the kinship is introduced so casually, Plato cannot have hoped to require his readers to extract anything very elaborate from it, or very elaborately connected with his line of thought. (Of course even if Plato's use of the kinship was not elaborate, its use by its originators could have been as complicated as you like.) Tigner thinks that Plato holds all nature

to be akin in the sense of belonging to "the same ontological family." What one might quarrel with here is merely the way of putting the matter, which suggests that Plato had a notion of "ontological family" which he could briskly deploy in this way. But the truth seems to me very close to what Tigner says. The point to emphasize is that Plato is not attempting here to show, or even to allude to in the vaguest way, a *method* by which all things may be recollected once one thing has been. He is merely anxious to point out that there is nothing *preventing* one's recollecting all things once one has recollected one. And this means *merely* that there is nothing in the nature of things that would prevent it from being the case that if you can recollect one thing, then you can recollect everything. The passage does not say that there is any closer kinship among things than that.

35. See also n. II-7. Plato's use of the word "μαθημάτων" at 85e2 does not require that mathemetics be the sole subject matter of recollection, because the word is much broader, and covers whatever one can μανθάνειν, as one can see from 81c6-7, and *Rep.* 475c6-7, d3, e1, 485b1, d3-4, 521c7, 522b6, 529b-c. Most commentators, down to and including Gulley (**3**, pp. 16ff), Vlastos, and Moravcsik, believe that recollection has to do exclusively with *a priori* knowledge in something like the modern sense. Thus, for example, Vlastos **9**, claims that "what Plato means by 'recollection' in the *Meno* is any enlargement of our knowledge which results from the perception of logical relationships" (pp. 156-157). Now it is probably true that this sort of knowledge is what Plato has chiefly on his mind. But he does not say so in the *Meno*. Why not? Because he is primarily using recollection to solve the paradox and can thus say neutrally that we can recollect *whatever* we can be said to come to know by inquiry. If he thinks that we can know only what we can know *a priori* (as he certainly believed later, though under a somewhat loose sense of "*a priori*," by some modern standards) then of course he must think that we can recollect only what we can know *a priori*. But in the *Meno* he is simply not tackling this particular issue of the logical and epistemological status of the recollectable. In particular, he does not broach the matter in his use of the phrase "αἰτίας λογισμῷ," as Vlastos claims (pp. 152-156). Although "λογισμός" can indeed carry the sense of "arithmetical reckoning," its ability to do so is not enough to show what Vlastos wishes, that what is involved *here* is *logical* necessity (Vlastos' use of "δήσῃ" in 98a3 to bring in the notion of "ἀνάγκη," and his appeal to Parmenides to show that we must be dealing with logical necessity, are insufficient.) Plato here says nothing explicitly to tell us what kinds of things can be "bound by the calculation of *aitiai*," because—to repeat—it is not necessary for him to do so. (Of course, it follows that neither is he concerned to claim that what we recollect must be things from previous incarnations, as is claimed by Buchmann, pp. 66-73.)

36. See *contra* Cherniss, *locc. citt.*

37. The use of "ἀεί" here shows that "μεμαθηκυῖα" cannot literally mean "have learned," so Plato is not here necessarily alluding to some point at which the knowledge was acquired. The same point can be claimed about 86a1, where he carefully uses the pluperfect, "ἐμεμαθήκει:" "If he did not acquire

(these *doxai*) in his present life, then is not this clear, that he had them (εἶχε) and *had learned* them in some other period." Surely if Plato meant to indicate unambiguously that the *doxai* were acquired, he would have said simply "that he learned them (ἔμαθεν) in some other period." On the other hand, it cannot be claimed that he clearly indicates that they are *not* acquired. It is sometimes contended that they could not be, on the ground that to suppose that they were would be to reinstate paradox (e.g., Gulley **3**, p. 17); but the point being made here is that this is not so, because mere learning, without recognition of what one has learned as something after which one was inquiring, is not affected by the paradox.

38. There are two sorts of thing for which the term "recollection" can be used: 1) apprehending something and recognizing it as some particular thing previously apprehended, or 2) calling to mind some "image" of a thing and recognizing it as the image of some particular thing previously apprehended (see my **3**, pt. V). Plato does not mark the distinction, but the same problems of recognition arise in either case; cf. n. V-7. (Some ideas related to this matter are discussed by Prauss, pp. 110ff., and esp. pp. 113-114; but it seems to me that his account is unsatisfactory, because his use of the notion of "*identifizieren*" leaves it up in the air just how this *Identifizieren* is to be performed or verified, and even just exactly what it consists in.) Notice that it will not solve the paradox to say, as many do, that recollection involves an appeal to "latent" or "potential" or "virtual" knowledge, since the problem of recognizing the particular thing that you wanted to know "overtly" or "actually" is just as acute as ever (cf. my **3**, pt. V). (For the idea of latency, see Cherniss **3**, p. 76, and Vlastos **9**, p. 164—though cf. p. 153, n. 14.) Nevertheless, these terms may well represent accurately what Plato intends (though they are a little clearer than what he actually says).

39. Note that there is the further complication concerning specifications for inquiry (cf. my **3**, pp. 291-292, 294ff.) that one's initial specification need not be one by which, itself, one can recognize one's quarry; but if it is not, then one needs to be able to find an equivalent one which is.

40. As I have indicated, the issues are basically the same whether the inquiry is aimed at finding an object in a narrow sense or at finding the answer to a question (cf. my **3**, pp. 296-297, where, however, I tended to talk too much as though in Plato's view inquiries *must* primarily be of the former sort).

41. See my **3**, pp. 291-292, 294ff. Strictly, what happens is that one's initial specification is something like "the definition of virtue"; but on the strength of one's willingness to trust one's feelings of recollection, one concludes that this is equivalent to something like "the formula that may come to my mind accompanied by the feeling of recollection," and one uses this latter specification to recognize (what one takes to be) the definition. (Thus, the defense of Plato made in this paragraph fits the general scheme of my **3**, though I did not there give it its due.)

Note, too, that the supposition that Plato is thinking along the lines represented in this paragraph disarms what is probably the most common objection to his argument, that during the conversation between them, Socrates, by his hints, in effect *tells* the slave-boy the answer to the geometrical problem. The rejoinder is that what recollection is supposed to enable the latter to do is not to dredge up the solution, but by his sense or feeling of recollection to recognize it as the correct answer to the problem. Still, it might (or might not) be going too far to attribute to Plato any very vivid account of the matter.

42. It is interesting to observe that although the *Phdo.* makes crucial use of the doctrine of recollection (72ff.), and even alludes to the account of that doctrine in the *Meno* (*Phdo.* 72e-73b), the *Phdo.* does not present that doctrine as an answer to the paradox, but makes a quite different use of it. But this fact does not mean that Plato no longer thinks that the doctrine can be used against the paradox, but only that he has other work for the doctrine to do as well. The same is true in the *Phdr.*, where the doctrine appears but the paradox does not (cf. n. III-14 and Ch. V, introd.).

43. See esp. Robinson 1, Ch. VIII, with his discussion of the ideas of Cherniss and Friedländer, and esp. pp. 117ff.

44. As Robinson's account shows, Plato's method of hypothesis develops out of the (probably Socratic) procedure of *elenchus*; and Irwin correctly points out (p. 754, n. 4) that the questioning of the slave-boy by Socrates follows the pattern of *elenchus* as it is presented in Plato.

CHAPTER III

The Phaedo:
The Growth of the Theory

The *Phaedo* is the first dialogue in which Plato seriously attempts to elaborate his views about the objects that we have been calling "Forms" (εἴδη ἰδέαι—cf. n. I-21), to say something about what these objects are like, and about various relations between them and the more hum-drum objects that figure in our day-to-day life. It is the earliest work that contains, in any explicit way, what could reasonably be called a *theory* of Forms.[1] The results of this elaboration of his views run broad and deep, and have a profound effect on the course of his future epistemological reflections.

It is in the *Phaedo* that Plato begins to expound his famous view, already adumbrated before, that Forms are in some way models or paradigms of which sensible objects, as he thinks of them, are imita-tions or copies,[2] and begins to develop the semi-technical terminology that is built around this view.[3] The form of *F* (also spoken of as the *F* Itself, or the *F*) is thus seen as in some way the perfect sample of a thing of which the predicate represented by "*F*" is true, whereas sensible objects are only, in a way to be discussed, defectively *F*.[4] This way of thinking of the Forms, according to which, e.g., the Form of Large is itself an object that is large (though in a special way), has often been expressed in recent times by saying that the Forms are "self-predicative," or that "self-predication" holds for them.[5] This manner of speaking has its drawbacks, but it will be convenient for us to use it from time to time. It is thus clear that the manner of speaking that I have adopted heretofore (in order to avoid a too direct allusion to views that are not yet in play in the early dialogues), according to which the

Form of *F* is called "*F*-ness," has to be taken with a grain of salt. For it can seem quite mistaken to think that, in general, *F*-ness is an object which is ("predicatively") *F*, e.g., that Largeness is large, and there is good reason to say that this notion makes trouble for Plato later on.[6] Nevertheless, Plato himself uses expressions of the type of "*F*-ness" along with expressions of the type of "the *F* Itself" (largely, as many though not all would agree, because he is sometimes inattentive to the difference between saying, e.g., that an object is Largeness and saying that it is large),[7] and I, for convenience, shall sometimes do so too. It is to be borne in mind that although the assimilation of these two manners of speaking, with its associated notion of "self-predication," will not often be explicitly under consideration, it is always in the background.

Though they are thus newly decked out, the Forms are still expected by Plato to perform the same philosophical functions which he had begun to assign to them before. Earlier on (Ch. I, sec. 1), I drew a rough and ready distinction among three tasks to which the Forms were put, labeled "metaphysical," "semantic," and "epistemological." The *Phaedo* has a good deal to say explicitly on the first front, with its claim that Forms are in some sense "causes" (αἰτίαι).[8] For instance, things other than the Beautiful Itself are said to be beautiful "because of" the Beautiful Itself; it is the Beautiful Itself that "makes" these other things beautiful (100c-d). On the epistemological and semantic issues, however, matters become more involved, and we must take some time to untangle them.

1 Sensing and Thinking

The most important epistemological departures in the *Phaedo* are the steps that it takes toward maintaining that Forms are—to put it very roughly at first—more epistemically tractable than sensible objects. These steps are a move along the path that arrives, in the *Republic*, at the claim that it is the Forms that are "knowable" (γνωστά), whereas sensible objects are merely "opinable" (δοξαστά), or are the objects of "opinion" or "belief" (δόξα).[9] The *Meno* had not gone so far as to make these claims (cf. Ch. II, sec. 5), but the *Phaedo* starts almost from the beginning to downgrade the epistemic status, so to speak, of sensible objects and our sensory apparatus, as compared with the Forms and the powers of the soul or mind (ψυχή).

The move begins when Plato starts to speak disparagingly of the body in contrast to the soul and suggests that the philosopher ought to pay more attention to what he thinks of as the desires of the soul than to what he regards as the desires of the body (64c-65a). "And what," he suddenly asks (65a9), "about the acquisition of knowledge (φρόνησις)?" He asks rhetorically whether sight or hearing "has any truth" (ἔχει ἀλήθειάν τινα), and quotes "the poets" as saying that we neither see nor hear anything "accurate" or "clear" (ἀκριβεῖς, σαφεῖς, in b5). He goes on to maintain, again without argument, that the soul is hindered by the body in apprehending the truth, and that the soul in particular "calculates" (λογίζεσθαι) best when various bodily faculties do not interfere. What he rather clearly has in mind, for example, is that we are best able to think through a problem of arithmetic when we are not paying attention to what we are seeing or hearing, or to pains or pleasures which we might be experiencing (c2-9).

Another idea that he may have in view can be seen when we consider his firm distrust of hearsay, and belief that one ought whenever possible to get one's information firsthand (Ch. I, introd. and sec. 4), and links from his attitude on these matters to his view of the relation between body and soul. Plato holds a view that could be expressed, with a little strain, by saying that a person *is* his soul, and that the soul is an entity quite distinct from the body (115c-d). Given this view, however, he evidently believes that gaining information from the use of one's senses (which are part of one's body, 64d*sqq.*) is, in effect, a case of gaining information at secondhand. For in 82d-83b, he contrasts the soul's gaining of information "by itself" (σκοπεῖσθαι τὰ ὄντα ... αὐτὴ δι αὑτῆς, 82e3-4), with its doing so "through" (διά) the body or the senses,[10] in which case there is a possibility of "deception" (ἀπάτης, 83a4), and he concludes that the soul should "trust nothing but itself" (a8-b1).

Having distinguished sensing and thinking, and having disparaged the former in contrast to the latter, he makes his crucial move. He suddenly induces his interlocutor, Simmias, to agree without argument that there are such things as the Just Itself, the Beautiful Itself, and the Good Itself, and that these are not visible, but are apprehended by thought (διάνοια), acting without the hindrance of the body. He is now claiming that it is in apprehending these entities, by means of one's soul, that one "gains truth and knowledge" (66a6).

Notice what has happened. We have gone from saying that the mind is most apt to discover the truth when it is acting without the interference of the senses to saying that it is concerned with a special class of objects, which are not sensible, about which it is possible to apprehend the truth. Leaving out of consideration several points on which these claims might be pressed, we can see that one possibility that is notably neglected is that there might be truths to be apprehended by the soul about sensible objects themselves. There are philosophers who would want to argue against this possibility, and Plato would no doubt be among them,[11] but the fact to notice is that he here simply ignores the possibility rather than arguing against it.

We have thus slipped quickly from saying that there are two different sorts of things that we do, sensing and thinking, to saying that there are respectively two different sorts of entities concerning which we do these two different things. By contrast it is possible, while admitting a philosophically important difference between sensing and thinking, nevertheless to deny that there are objects that are exclusively the subject matter of either activity to the exclusion of the other, or that there are any objects that are, themselves, exclusively apprehended "by sensation" or "by thought."[12] For example, the number five seems to be a good candidate to be an intelligible and non-sensible object. But one might well claim that I must apprehend at least partly by sight that the number five is the number of the fingers on my right hand, and that that is something "about" the number five.[13] On the other side, my right hand might seem to be an indisputably sensible object, but again one might contend that I must apprehend at least partly by "thinking" and not solely by sensation that it has fingers to the number of the cube root of 125. So Plato is here taking a disputable step.

2 Sensible Fs and the Form of F

But Plato says more here than that certain objects are sensed whereas others are apprehended by thought. He also says that thought apprehends "truth" whereas sensation does not, and in effect that judgments made by thought are "accurate" and "true" (ἀκριβής and ἀληθής) whereas those that are made by sensation are not (65a-b). We must try to discover what he means by this, and what his grounds for it are. For in connection with this claim there arise some of his most important contentions about the nature of Forms.

The argument for this claim does not begin to emerge until the extended passage in 72e-77a, which is an attempt to show, ultimately, that one's soul can recollect, that therefore it must have existed prior to one's birth, and thus (though Plato quickly admits, in 77a*sqq.*, that this inference is fallacious) that it is immortal. The important part of this passage for us at the moment is the brief argument which appears in 74a9-c5.[14] The claim which he makes here, which has been much discussed in recent years, is to roughly the following effect.[15] If we consider a predicate such as "equal," we shall notice that no sensible object (and I shall henceforth connive with Plato, as I have done already, in employing this notion) can be said to be simply and flatly equal without any qualification. Every sensible object that is equal is also unequal, because every sensible object that is equal to one thing is also unequal to some other thing. However, Plato claims, there is also an object, different from any of the sensible objects, which is equal but not qualifiedly so, and this is the Equal Itself or the Form of Equal. This object is not equal to one thing and unequal to another, but, paradoxically (in a way that was observed by Aristotle and perhaps, later in his life, by Plato himself) simply equal.[16] Some have thought that Plato's point here is, instead of what I have claimed it to be, that whereas sensible equal objects can appear to be both equal (to one person) and also unequal (to another person), the Form of Equal can never *appear* to be unequal.[17] Now we shall see that Plato may sometimes believe that in certain circumstances the Form of Equal cannot appear to be unequal (see 74c1-2 and Ch. IV, sec 1) though there are also obstacles to this interpretation. But the passage also makes clear that he thinks that one trouble, at least, with sensible equals is that they *are not* perfectly and unqualifiedly equal (see esp. "εἶναι" in 74d7, e1, 75a2, d7, and "ἐστιν" in 74e2, 75b2, 8); and thus the Form must be something which *is* unqualifiedly equal (regardless of what we say about how it appears.)[18]

Plato's use of this example raises a problem, by the way, which we must briefly examine. I have said that this argument concerns predicates "such as 'equal.' " But which are these predicates? One suggestion is that at this point Plato has in mind a more or less loosely marked-off set of predicates which he thinks of as "incomplete," and as requiring qualification whenever they are applied to sensible objects, but also thinks that there are other predicates for which the sensible world supplies unproblematical and unqualified instances. It can then be claimed that he later came to believe that since any predicate that is true at a given time of a given object will at some later time be, or at some earlier time was, false of that object, no sensible object serves as an instance for a predicate without some *temporal* qualification. (The Form, on the other hand, would be the only thing of which the predicate is true without temporal qualification.)[19] On the other hand, there are also reasons for thinking that Plato might have meant the argument to apply to all predicates (or at least those that he thought to be at all relevant) from the start.[20] Fortunately, we can afford, for our purposes, to allow this issue to remain unsettled. I shall in the following pages sometimes speak unguardedly, as though Plato thought that all

predicates were covered by his thesis, but the reader may, when necessary, read in the appropriate qualification.

It has been repeatedly pointed out that Plato's line of thought here
goes astray, because of a failure on his part to take account of the
workings of, in particular, relational predicates.[21] Wanting an unqualified sample of "large," *tout court*, but finding the sensible world full
only of samples of "large compared to," or like predicates, he looks
elsewhere for the unqualified instance which he wants. What he did not
consider was the possibility that he *should* have been looking only for
samples of the latter predicate, and that there was something wrong
with the former which made it misguided to think that it might be
instantiated at all, or even that it made sense. If he had considered this
course, then he would have realized that there *are* unproblematical
samples of "large compared to" in the sensible world, or—adding on
temporal qualification—"large compared to X at time T."[22] (But this is
not to say that Plato pays no heed at all to relations; see n. III-16.)

From considerations such as these, Plato arrives at his well-known
doctrine that sensible objects are in some sense copies, or poor imita-
tions or replicas, of Forms. This move presumably came about in
something like the following way. First, given the reflection that the
Form of F is in this way "unqualifiedly" F whereas sensible Fs are only
"qualifiedly" F, it was easy enough to think that in contrast to the
Form, which is fully F, the sensible Fs are defectively F. Second, the
relation between a defectively F object and the fully F object comes to
be regarded as similar to the relation between an object and a picture
or copy of that object. Both of these steps are, of course, dubious,[23]
but it is not too difficult to see why someone would be tempted to take
them. Plato's temptation to take the latter step becomes especially
understandable, moreover, when we reflect that he was already willing to think of the term "Simmias" as correctly applicable both to the
man Simmias and to a portrait of him (the latter application being
somehow less proper and privileged than the former), and similarly
of the general term "horse" as truly applicable (though with the same
difference) both to horses and to pictures thereof.[24]

It is about the Forms, construed in this way, that Plato had said that
we can make judgments which are "accurate" and "true" (65a-b). What
supports this claim? Simply that it is to these objects that we can apply
predicates without qualifications.[25] A judgment of the Form "X is
equal," *tout court*, can be made only about the Form of the Equal; when
it is made about a sensible object it has to be qualified. This is not to say
that we have to make formally contradictory statements about sensible

objects; Plato does not believe that a sensible object can be both equal and unequal to another sensible object("at the same time, in the same respect, etc.").[26] He has, however, adopted the view that there is something wrong with a sensible object, because he has slipped into supposing that it is legitimate to suppress the necessary qualifications, and to say that the object is both equal and unequal. But this difficulty—as he takes it to be—is something to which the Form is immune. It can be said, without such qualification, to be equal. It has been realized since Aristotle that Plato was mistaken on this issue, as I have remarked, but the way in which the mistake works on him must be clearly seen. It is that he recognizes the need for adding what I have been calling a "qualification" onto a predicate such as "equal" clearly enough to observe the importance of remarking that a sensible object may not be both equal and unequal to the same thing ("at the same time," etc.). But he does not see it clearly enough to realize that it makes dubious sense to say that *any* object is equal unqualifiedly (i.e., without being equal to anything).[27] Therefore, he can think that the Form is unqualifiedly equal and thus regard it as a defect in sensible objects that they are not so. And now that he is preoccupied with judgments of this unqualified type, and downgrades judgments of the type of "X is equal to Y," he can easily believe that judgments about Forms (i.e., unqualified judgments) are in a sense more accurate than judgments about sensible objects ever could be.

Once Plato has arrived at this point, it is easy for him to connect this view with his earlier claim that thinking is a better guide to the truth than sensing. That claim at first seemed to get its plausibility solely from the citation of cases in which we are distracted by vivid visual spectacles from our arithmetical computations (and a neglect of cases in which we are distracted from visual spectacles by vivid arithmetical computations). Now, however, Plato thinks he has shown that the judgments that we make about visual spectacles, and other matters on which we bring our senses to bear, are themselves inevitably flawed. Given his view that the senses can yield to us judgments only about such matters, and never about Forms (which view was treated in the previous section), he thinks that he is in a position to disparage the usefulness of our sensory apparatus itself. What this means, of course, is that he is *not* saying that our senses do a bad job, given the subject matter with which they have to work. Rather, their defect is that they are incapable, he thinks, of providing us with judgments about more tractable objects.

3   A Metaphysical Corollary of the
New View of Forms and Sensible Objects

Some will be inclined to think that the view just now described is too clearly mistaken, and even bizarre, to be rightly ascribed to Plato. Such an impression, I think, is the result of an overexposure to contemporary philosophical discussions, in which such logical and quasi-logical matters as relational predication are so thoroughly and unremittingly scrutinized. Even Aristotle, who criticized this aspect of Plato's doctrine, himself had no very clear understanding of relations (as a glance at *Categories* 7 and *Metaphysics* V.15 will show), and perhaps nobody did until late in the last century.

A feeling for Plato's position, and for the plausibility to him of the views that I have just explained, can perhaps be gained from seeing a bit of the general metaphysical picture within which it finds its place. I shall accordingly say something further here about his division of the universe into the sensible and the intelligible, drawing on some material that is somewhat out of our line of march.

There is a view with which Plato flirts, which—although Plato would not put it in this way—can be expressed by saying that for him sensible objects are "relational objects," whereas Forms are not. What is a relational object?[28] Roughly characterized, a relational object can be thought of as an object that cannot be described except by reference to something else; in other words, as an object of which no atomic monadic predicates are true,[29] but of which polyadic atomic predicates are true. By contrast, a nonrelational object is an object of which some atomic monadic predicates are true. Now there are many possible objections to these notions of relational and nonrelational objects,[30] but what is important about them for our purposes is simply that they provide a tolerably clear way of understanding one of the contrasts that Plato wants to draw between sensible objects and Forms, and of understanding it in a way that fits well with the general run of interpretation of his doctrine. The idea that it helps us to understand is that the Forms are in some way independent entities, whereas sensibles are somehow dependent entities.[31] For we can roughly think of dependence as an inability, and independence as an ability, to be described without further mention of some object or other.

There are two ways of regarding sensible objects as, on Plato's view, relational. One is based on the idea that we have already seen, that whatever can be said about sensible objects has to be "qualified" in the manner that we have discussed, and that the qualifications make reference to various objects.³² It is just possible—though Plato does not pronounce on the matter—that he thinks that the qualification must contain a reference to a sensible object. But we might also push this interpretation further, by saying that in all cases the qualification must contain a reference to some object *other than* the thing that counts as the subject of the predication.³³ (This allows us to say that *a* is, e.g., equal to itself, so long as the rest of the qualifying phrase—"at time *t*, etc."—mentions some object other than *a*.) If we push it in this way, in fact, we get a far more full-blooded version of the metaphysical idea of dependence, since we now picture an object as in this way "dependent" exclusively upon objects different from itself.

The other way of picturing sensible objects as relational sits even more comfortably in the Platonic texts. This time the idea is that the only way in which a sensible object can be described is by reference to a Form, and it is often accepted that Plato did believe something like this.³⁴ Thus, any predication about a sensible object—"a is *F*"—contains a term—"*F*"—which refers to a Form, and similarly any phrase referring to a sensible object—such as "the thing which is *F*"—contains a reference—"*F*"—to a Form.³⁵ There might also have to be references to other things as well, in the qualifying rider, but at least the reference to a Form would be obligatory.

The Form of *F*, by contrast, is immune on both of these accounts. Forms can receive predicates without qualification, and thus at least some things can be said about them without reference either to other Forms or to sensible objects.³⁶

4 The Repercussions of the New View of Forms on the Quest for Definitions

There are crucial consequences for Plato in the view that sensible objects are somehow constituted as not to admit of unqualified predications. From all indications, one of his tasks in the earlier dialogues, in trying to provide a definition for a term such as "holy," was to give us a way of telling which things are holy and which things are unholy. It is not hard to see that this task, so construed, has been subverted by the developments examined in section 1. For although there is doubt, as we saw, about which predicates Plato initially regards as applying to sensible objects only with qualification, it is clear that the list of them includes the predicates, such as "holy," for which definitions had been sought in order to determine their extensions.³⁷ But determining which things are holy and which are unholy now seems less significant a project than it did before. For it now appears that everything in the sensible world that is holy is also unholy, and *vice versa*. (This fact, of course, need not mean that everything sensible is both holy and unholy, though Plato does not tell us whether he thinks that there are things that are neither.)[38] How, then, can we provide a definition that will apply only to the one group of things and not to the other? And why are we bothering to try to separate the two groups in the first place, since they turn out to coincide?

It has often been thought, for reasons such as this, that Plato believes the sensible world to be, as it were, so totally chaotic that there is no real point in saying anything at all about it, and that one must restrict one's intellectual activities to matters entirely concerning the Forms.[39] But this view goes too far. Plato does, to be sure, believe that one is far better off if one confines one's judgments to the world of the Forms.[40] He does not, however, think that the only judgments to be made about the sensible world are, at the best, judgments of the form "X is both F and non-F." He is, in fact, committed to supposing that there is a good deal more about the sensible world that we can reasonably judge. It is not simply that he himself, in the course of his dialogues, incidentally makes statements about the sensible world. Rather, it is that certain central views of his seem to rest on the assumption that there is some point in making certain judgments rather than others about sensible objects. One notable case in point is an important theme of the *Republic*, that the rulers of a city ought to work to make their city resemble as closely as possible the pattern of justice which is there to be imitated.[41] This conception would be a pointless absurdity if the most that one could conceivably say about a city in the sensible world is that it is both just and unjust, or in general that it is both F and non-F. But this is not all that Plato allows us to say. Instead, he provides us with the notion that a sensible object may be a more or less close approximation or imitation of a Form—the rulers' job in the *Republic* being to make their city imitate a model as closely as possible. Certain sensible things, then, while both just and unjust, nevertheless partake in or resemble the Form of Justice more than others do.[42]

Another indication that Plato believes that there are some judgments to be made about sensible objects is the fact, already noted (sec. 2), that he takes some pains to emphasize that no object whatever may have contrary attributes at the same time in *every* respect, thereby making it clear that he does not claim that formal contradictions hold for sensible objects. This claim would be false if one could truthfully deny everything that one could truthfully assert about a sensible object; and it would be pointless if Plato took no account whatever of any statements except the unqualified predications that can be made about Forms. As he sees them, sensible objects can be talked and judged about—only not in the unqualified manner that he thinks important.

Because of Plato's shift in view regarding what judgments about the sensible world have to be like, we thus arrive at the notion that the purpose of knowing a Form, or using it as a paradigm, can no longer be to separate the just from the unjust, e.g., but instead to determine something like the degree of justice and injustice in sensible things.[43] But the shift also confirms a view that had already appeared in earlier works, namely the view that definition must in an important sense be about Forms (Ch. I, sec. 4). For only if the definition is about the Form, Plato thought, could it avoid being as much about things that are unjust,[44] and thus make any claim to explain the notion of *justice, tout court* and free of qualifications, in the way in which Plato expects it to do.[45] When we say in general, therefore, that the *F* is such-and-such, and mean thereby to be giving a definition, we must now regard ourselves as talking about a Form. Plato had already of course, been inclined to believe this, for reasons that we have seen. Now his view is even more settled.

Another view of his has also been strengthened. I have dwelt on what I called Plato's refusal to trust hearsay when searching for a definition (see esp. Ch. I, sec. 3). Roughly, the idea was that Plato would not grant that the observation of the way in which a term was customarily used, or the expressed views of ordinary speakers on its meaning, could be taken as evidence carrying any particular value. His new view of sensible objects plainly strengthens this tendency. If all just actions and other things in the sensible world are also unjust, and *vice versa*, then this fact will discredit the claims of any ordinary usage which says, or supports the view, that a particular action is unqualifiedly just, or is a paradigm of justice, and it will also discredit any ordinary or common-sense attempt to divide actions into the flatly just and the flatly unjust.[46] In the same way, too, definitions by examples will plainly be ruled out if they are meant to provide cases of things to which a predicate applies without qualification. What a particular case may do, of course, is to remind you of a Form (74d-75a, 76a). But this fact does not license defining by citing cases, especially as Plato thinks that what reminds you of a Form may be to any degree either similar or dissimilar to it (*Phaedo* 74a).[47] Accordingly, Plato can now feel that he has firm grounds for rejecting any appeal to usage or ordinary opinion about the application of terms in his quest for definitions, as he thinks that usage and opinions about it are based on the mistaken view that predicates apply to sensible objects unproblematically.[48]

Later on in the *Phaedo*, in 89-91, Plato makes it clear that the claim that terms can be applied to Forms unproblematically performs an important philosophical function of counteracting what he calls "μιοολογία," or "hatred of words."[49] He observes that someone who notices that words can be used both truly and falsely is likely to come to the conclusion that there is something wrong with words. What he should do instead, Plato thinks, is to reproach his own lack of skill with words (90c8-d7). There is nothing wrong with words *per se*, he is claiming (d9ff.); it is rather that one must take pains to find uses of language that are "true and stable" (ἀληθοῦς καὶ βεβαίου λόγου, c8). What he must have in mind here is the use of language in talking about the Forms.[50] It is important to notice that this is a far cry from certain disparaging views about language in general which he shows signs of holding in later works. We shall investigate that matter later, in the light of the fact that he is here endeavoring strenuously to rescue language from any blanket indictment.[51]

5   Forms and Terms

According to a view held by Plato, when we want to know whether— or rather now, instead, to what degree (sec. 2)—a certain sensible thing is just, we are supposed to compare it in some way with the Form of the Just, to see how closely it resembles that Form.[52] For Plato thus far, there has appeared to be no problem about the supposition which this view embodies, that there is a certain Form which is correctly called "the Form of the Just" (or better, αὐτὸ τὸ δίκαιον, or the like), and he has raised no questions about the matter. Indeed, the tendency of his attack upon "misology" (sec. 4) is to place such questions in the background, in so far as it suggests that there are no pressing difficulties of principle about the way in which words are properly applied, so long as we see that they are properly applied, strictly, to Forms.

It is in *Phaedo* 102-103 that Plato shows this attitude most clearly. There he suggests that if a given sensible object partakes in a certain Form, it "has" (ἔχει) the "name" or "appellation" (ἐπωνυμία) of that Form (102b2, c10, 103b7-c1).[53] Thus, if Simmias partakes in the Form of the Large (to some degree or with qualification—though I shall generally leave such riders out for the sake of brevity), then he can, as it were, be "called" by the name of that Form, i.e., by the word "large." (We can see here clear traces of the view that Forms are "self-predicative" — cf. Ch. III, introd.)[54]

What is it to say that "large" is the name of the Form of the Large? The problem is not the one that earlier dialogues might seem more directly to have raised, namely the problem of how one might tell, in apprehending a certain Form, that it is the Form of the Large. Rather, it is the closely related problem concerning what it is, so to speak, that makes a particular Form *correctly* called "the Form of the Large."[55] Using another manner of speaking than Plato's, we might observe that in his view, when we want to become clearer about the extension of a particular term in the sensible world, we look to the Form "corresponding" to that term, to see in what degree various sensible objects resemble it. But wherein does this "correspondence" consist? How is it set up? What is it that could bring about a right and a wrong, a fact of the matter, about which Form is pertinent to which predicates?

A tempting response to these questions, of course, is to say that it is human usage and conventions that establish such correspondences between terms and extralinguistic reality. This response is one to which Plato will give attention in the *Cratylus*, when he pits it against a rival theory, to the effect that the correspondence is somehow fixed by nature, in contrast to human practices. Neither the *Phaedo* nor any other early work takes a position on this issue. All that is notable is that no mention is made of any role for arbitrary human activity in the forging of the links between Forms and their "names," and the links are left unscritinized.

But the links exist because, as we saw, the Forms are not regarded by Plato simply as unreal shadows lurking behind linguistic reality (see esp. Ch. I, sec. 4). There are facts of the matter about Forms, and we must find out what they are.

6 The Semantic Consideration in the *Phaedo*

What was earlier called the semantic consideration for the existence of Forms (Ch. I, sec. 1) is closely linked with the point just discussed. It also plays an important role in one argument of the *Phaedo* which bears on the theory of Forms.

The semantic consideration had to do with the view that the Forms could be used to explain how it is that terms are meaningful or significant. In the earlier dialogues this view was in evidence, but it was not very much elaborated. In the *Phaedo*, however, it receives further development, in a manner which has in fact already been adumbrated earlier in this chapter (sec. 2). Let us reconsider 74a-77a. In that passage, Plato is emphasizing not so much the notion that we can and ought to compare sensible objects to Forms, but rather the idea that we *do* make such comparisons, and that such comparisons are involved in our judgments about the sensible world immediately from birth (75b10-11). The contention appears to be that because we use our senses as soon as we are born, we must already have some knowledge of the Forms (c1-5); it is this that provides Plato with a crucial step in his argument for the claim that we recollect. He seems to believe that even in our first use of our sensory apparatus, we make some use of knowledge of the Forms, which knowledge we must therefore have acquired prenatally (c8-10). Some would raise an objection to this claim, by saying that our earliest feats of sensing involve no "conceptualization" of the sort that would require one to posit any prior "acquisition of concepts" or knowledge of Forms or the like.[56] We need not, however, delve here into this debate. What is important is that Plato thinks that our very earliest judgments, and indeed our very earliest use of our senses, involve comparing sensible objects with Forms (75b5-6) and being reminded of Forms by sensible objects. Anyone who makes a judgment, whether he is able to express it overtly in words or not, is in some sense thinking of a Form or Forms, and it is this thinking, whatever precisely it amounts to, that makes it possible for him to make judgments at all.

Though many questions could be asked about this claim (and Plato does not go into it deeply here), and objections could be raised to it, it can clearly be taken as an elaboration of the "semantic" consideration for the existence of Forms.[57] For Plato is indirectly contending that the Forms, and our apprehensions of them, are to be brought in to explain how it is that we can understand words.

Questions press in on this contention which have already appeared before. Plato is plainly treating as unproblematical our ability, when we acquire the use of language, to link with Forms the words that we use to correspond to them. No worries are given over to the question how the correspondence is mastered by a given person nor how it had been established before that person appeared on the scene. For present purposes, it is treated as fixed, there for us somehow to learn. It is true that although Plato does think that we apprehend Forms in some degree from the time of birth (75c1-5), he also wishes to deny that our knowledge of them at the start is, in some sense, as complete as it might be. For this reason he wants to claim that we must still recollect them (76c1-4). Part of his reason for saying that we do not "know" them in a sense is that we are often unable to give a *logos* (λόγος) for the terms that we use, and that one must be able to give such a *logos* of it if one genuinely knows it (76b4-9). By *"logos"* he here means "definition," [58] and so he is harking back to a claim that we have seen before, that being able to give a definition is required for sure application of predicates to particular sensible objects. What now needs to be explained, then, is the nature of the difference between the state in which one can, even as an infant, make sensory discriminations by virtue of the fact that one has some sort of knowledge of Forms, and the state in which one is able to give a definition and is to be regarded as genuinely knowing the Form. Once again, that is, the link between definitions and knowledge of Forms demands explanation.

7   The Method of Hypothesis

The method of hypothesis is Plato's great attempt to show how investigations of the sort that he favors may be begun and carried on. The method, which is first unveiled briefly in the *Meno* (Ch. II, sec. 5) is unfortunately expounded in such a way as to be difficult to follow, and it is not at all clear that the descriptions of it are fully consistent with each other, or even within themselves.[59] The idea behind the method, however, is for our purposes clear enough.

As it appears in the *Meno* and the *Phaedo* (see esp. *Meno* 86c-87d, 89a-d; *Phaedo* 99-101), the method is not designed to establish conclusions which are to be regarded as fixed and unshakable, but rather as a way of reaching provisional conclusions based on provisionally accepted premises or assumptions.[60] In this respect, it is in a certain sense exactly what Plato seems to need. He does not wish to accept the deliverances of common opinion as certain (Ch. I, sec. 3), but he does need a way in which investigation, and also debate, may be conceived of as beginning, so as to have some hope of making progress. In the version offered in the *Phaedo* (the account in the *Meno* may perhaps be different in problematical ways),[61] the idea appears to be that a hypothesis is laid down, and tested by seeing whether it has any absurd or unacceptable consequences. If it passes this test but disagreement nevertheless persists among those in the discussion, then a search is made by the proponent of the hypothesis for a "higher hypothesis" which entails the original one, and this new hypothesis is tested in the same way. The process continues in this way until, one hopes, agreement is reached, but it is not said that the method can thus attain more than such agreement among those who are present.[62]

It is important to notice that the method is not pictured as starting from common or ordinarily accepted opinions (cf. Ch. I, sec. 3). Rather, whoever wishes to begin a discussion on some topic may do so by "hypothesizing" what seems to him "strongest" (101a3-4). He is of course subject to questioning and must argue his position to those who request him to do so, provided they observe certain formalities (101d3-7). But no special prominence or respect is accorded to any particular source of hypotheses or objections to them.

Simple as it is, Plato's account of this method presents something which is, details aside, highly important to his conception of his procedures, and vital to their success. It presents the sketch of a starting point. What needs to be done now—and what the *Phaedo* declines to attempt to do—is to show how the starting point is to be linked to the destination, that is, how one can pass from mere agreement of present company to something that has a somehow more robust guarantee of truth. As part of this effort, he must show how the method of hypothesis is to be joined with the project of apprehending Forms and to show clearly how the establishment of definitions figures in both. These tasks are taken up in the *Republic*.

Notes

1. Thus Ross **2**, p. 22.

2. I leave out of consideration here the—for our purposes irrelevant—question whether in addition to Forms and sensible objects, Plato also believed in what Bluck calls "Form-copies" (see his **1**, pp. 17-18, and Brentlinger). If these played any essential role in Plato's epistemology—and I do not believe that they do—they would merely complicate our story without changing it in any crucial respect.

3. "*Semi*-technical": see n. I-21.

4. On this theme see esp. Owen **2**, pp. 302-309; and Vlastos **8**, pp. 10-17.

5. The phrase has been used since Vlastos **2**.

6. In particular it brings on the notorious Third Man Argument. See Vlastos **3**.

7. See Vlastos, p. 250. Shorey maintains that Plato grasps the distinction, e.g., at *Rep.* 509a3; see **3**, pp. 343-345, but that is compatible with his sometimes not sufficiently attending to it.

8. We must be careful, though, over the translation of "αἰτία" by "cause": see n. I-35.

9. On this contrast in the *Rep.*, see esp. 476-480, 506c, 509d-511e.

10. I do not say that this is his only reason for disparaging senses and sensibles; cf. sec. 2 and Ch. IV, sec. 1. In the later *Tht.* (184c-d) this same

proposition is used, but the contrast between what is firsthand and what is secondhand is not; cf. n. VII-44.

11. But there is reason to think that later he may have changed his view; see Cooper. Compare Russell's view that "all *a priori* knowledge deals exclusively with the relations of universals," (**1**, Ch. X).

12. I do not know of anyone on whom this view can be directly fixed. Note that I have put it somewhat vaguely, particularly in that I have left quite unexplained what is meant by "apprehended by sensation" and "apprehended by thought." It is important to notice, however, that it is possible to hold this view while still believing that certain propositions are *a priori* and others are *a posteriori*, if you do not say that certain objects have only *a priori*, or *a posteriori*, propositions true of them. For to say that all *a priori* knowledge deals exclusively with the relations of universals (cf. previous note) is not to say that *a priori* knowledge deals exhaustively with the facts about universals.

13. On some problems connected with these issues, see Steiner and Benacerraf.

14. Notice that the theory of recollection is here not called on to do the same job that it does in the *Meno*, that of answering the paradox of inquiry (cf. Ch. II, sec. 5). Instead, Plato alludes simply to the conversation with the slave-boy (72e-73b). There is no reason to believe that he now doubts that the theory does answer the paradox. On the contrary, he must think that the paradox has been disposed of (otherwise we should expect to hear something about it), and he now has other matters to attend to, and another use for the theory of recollection itself. Cf. n. II-42.

15. On this matter see esp. Owen **2**, and also Vlastos **8**.

16. The paradoxicality of the idea is observed by Aristotle in, e.g., *S.E.* 181b25ff. (cf. *Cat.* 6b28-33) and *Met.* 990b16-17, along with Owen **2**, pp. 302ff.

There are, to be sure, passages in which Plato shows an awareness of relations which cannot be denied. Some of them are: *Charm.* 168b, d; *Lysis* 212a, 218d; *Phaedo* 102b-c; *Rep.* 438b, 475b4-6, 575c2; *Symp.* 199d-200a; *Tht.* 204e11-12, 160a8-b3, perhaps 157a3-6; *Parm.* 132b8-9; *Phileb.* 35b1. But these passages themselves do not show the right sort of awareness to extricate Plato from all confusion or to make him realize the full paradoxicality of his view of Forms like the Equal. For it is one thing to notice (to use a non-Platonic example) that each brother in the sensible world is a brother of something, and another to see why it makes no sense to say that there might be a (non-sensible) brother which is a brother of nothing. (It is the failure to notice Plato's view about Forms that damages the sophisticated attempt by Castañeda to show that Plato had a good grasp of relations.) Cf. n. III-36.

There are, however, signs that Plato may have become clearer on this point later in his career. *Not*, I think, in *Soph.* 255c12-13, even if Owen and Frede are wrong in denying that it treats of a distinction between relational and nonrelational notions (I believe, however, that they are right; see Frede, pp. 12ff., and Owen **11**, pp. 252, 256-258). Rather, the signs are in *Parm.* 133b-134e, where

Plato seems to admit the possibility that Forms might be—as it were (cf. sec. 3)—relative to other Forms, so that the Slave Itself would be slave of the Master Itself (see esp. 133c8-9).

17. This interpretation is in fact the majority view, embodied in most translations. See, e.g., Ross **2**, p. 23; Burnet **1**, *ad* 74b8; and the vast majority of translations. (For "τῷ μέν ... τῷ δ' οὔ in b8-9 there is also the manuscript variant "τότε μέν ... τότε δ' οὔ," but it is easily explicable as a gloss, induced by the Platonic doctrine of the mutability of the sensible world.)

18. On this reading, Plato's argument escapes the obvious objection forced on it by the traditional interpretation of 74a9-c5 (see previous note), that the fact that X and Y seem unequal to someone does not mean that they are unequal (see, e.g., Gulley **2**, p. 29). (Thus, the argument moves [to omit most of the steps] from the claim that sensible equals *are* also unequals to the claim that there must therefore be something perfectly and unqualifiedly equal. If we take the traditional reading of 74b8-9, then the argument must involve a begging of the question. It is admitted that there are things that are sensible, and which appear both equal and unequal. From this premise, we wish to conclude that there is something, distinct from all of the sensibles, which never appears unequal but always appears equal. But the premise used to help us reach this conclusion (74c1-2) cannot legitimately do so. Taken opaquely, it says "It never appears that equality is unequal," in which sense it cannot be used to conclude that *there is* such a thing as Equality, which never appears unequal. (It cannot be so used, any more than we can infer "There are pink ghosts" from "It never appears that pink ghosts are green;" for the notion of opacity, see n. II-8. But taken transparently, it would not properly be accepted by anyone disputing the conclusion to be drawn. It must be admitted, however, that the fact that the argument is thus flawed is no insuperable obstacle to attributing it here to Plato, as we have seen that he is capable of overlooking this matter of opacity and transparency; cf. n. II-8.

19. For this line of interpretation see Owen **2**, pp. 305-308.

20. One such reason is that *Phaedo* 65d11-e1 seems to hint at no such restriction on the class of Forms as this interpretation would require. Another is that it is not clear that Plato was any less preoccupied with the mutability of sensible objects at this stage of his career than he was later. If he was not, then it is difficult to maintain with Owen **2**, p. 307, that he only later came to the view that considerations involving temporal qualifications required Forms for a much broader range of predicates.

21. Plato is to some extent defended in this regard by Scheibe, but the question is whether the notion of *"Relativa"* which he uses to do so does not encapsulate just the confusion of which Plato is accused (cf. sec. 3). Cf. n. III-16.

22. It is arguable that this move will not work for all of the predicates that Plato uses in this way, on the ground that many of them are not relational (see Owen **2**, p. 306), but instead involve "syncategorematic" terms, or adverbial expressions not subject to a relational interpretation. (This use of the term "syncategorematic" is borrowed from Quine **8**, p. 103.) I do not enter into this

matter here, except to remark that many still remain puzzled over these sorts of predicates. For some worries over adverbs, see, e.g., Wallace (he objects mildly, pp. 696-697, to construing adverbial constructions by means of relational expressions, on the complaint that it is "unnatural and counterintuitive," but offers no argument).

23. For a criticism of the former, see Aristotle, *E.N.* 1096b3-5. The latter, so far as I know, was not attacked by Aristotle, and he classes both relations as giving rise to homonymy: see *S.E.* 181b33-34 with Owen **3**, pp. 187-189. Owen there discusses the notion of "focal meaning," which must have been suggested in the Academy as a way of linking the senses in which a term was applied both to a Form and to its instances (p. 187). Now if this is so, then the suggestion must have been made after the two steps that I describe had already been taken. For the suggestion is a development of their conclusion.

24. See *Phaedo* 73e, 102b2, c10 with 74e-75a; *Rep.* 596e10, 597b5, 11. (I owe to Owen the realization of the importance of the particular way in which Plato expresses himself in *Phaedo* 73e.)

25. This is substantially Vlastos' point in his **8**, but there is one relevant part of his discussion that raises difficulties. It is his claim that the Forms are thought by Plato to be "real" *in the sense of being* "cognitively reliable" (*passim*, and esp. p. 17). Rather, Plato thinks that Forms are perfectly "real" in the sense, explained by Vlastos, that they are the subjects of unqualified predication. It is then *because* they are "real" in this sense that Plato feels justified in regarding them as "cognitively reliable." They are not called "real" *in the sense that* they are "cognitively reliable"; but they are rather called "cognitively reliable" on the *ground* that they are "real," in the *sense* that they are the subjects of unqualified predication.

26. *Rep.* 436b, e-437a, with Vlastos **8**, pp. 14-15.

27. Cf. n. III-16.

28. It is difficult to be sure, but I think that one could fasten on Bradley the view that all ordinary objects are, in the sense to be specified, relational objects (see his pp. 16-25). It should be noticed that this view is distinct from the view, attributed to Bradley by Moore and discussed in detail by the latter, that all relations are "internal" (see Moore **3**, pp. 276-309). For it is one thing to say that all relational predicates that apply to a thing do so essentially, and quite another to say that all of the predicates that apply to a thing are relational.

29. That is, no atomic predicate of the form "Fx." It is a simple matter, given that an object stands in some expressed relation or other, to construct a monadic predicate to be true of it, such as those of the form "$(Ex)Rxy$," and it would seen extraordinarily artificial to try to block these. Note that we could formulate a somewhat different view of the relationality of an object by basing it on the claim that such objects have no atomic monadic predicates *essentially* true of them (in one sense or another of "essentially").

30. For one thing, as I have described it, it is subject to the objection that it is easy to introduce a one-place predicate which is simply stipulated to be true of whatever object you like, so that an object could, ironically, be relational only

relative to those languages in which no one-place predicates happened to be true of it. I take it, however, that someone defending the notion of a relational object would have to say that there is something wrong or illegitimate about those languages in which there purport to be one-place predicates which are true of such objects. I do not know how this assertion might be defended. Aside from this matter, observe that this account of what it is to be a relational object does not require that the relational predicates true of the object be true of the object together with objects *not identical with it*. This point could be remedied in various ways (subject to the problem mentioned in the previous paragraph). One brisk and informal way is used in the text, *infra*.

31. Thus, Forms are described by the phrase "αὐτὸ καθ᾽ αὐτό" and the like, by contrast to sensible objects: see, e.g., *Symp.* 211b1; *Phaedo* 75d5-6, with Zeller **2**, pp. 662-663, 706. Consider also the way in which sensibles are said to depend upon Forms in *Timaeus* 48ff., esp. 51a7ff. along with Lee and Mills. Although I think that there are *some* elements in their accounts that make them closer to the text than mine is, I prefer my account of philosophical grounds as a clearer explanation of a view that Plato is getting at. (For points of contact see esp. Lee, p. 365, and Mills, pp. 161-162.)

32. We might want to be a little wary about the use of the word "object" here, because it is not clear that all of the things that are mentioned in qualifications would be counted by him as on the same footing (see the examples in Owen **2**, pp. 304-305, along with the noncommittal wording of *Rep.* 436b8-10, e8-437a2, and *Symp.* 211a2-5).

33. This issue would require a fairly extensive study on its own account (see esp. *Charm.* 165ff.), but Scheibe has suggested along these lines that "das Einzelding nicht unabhängig von der äusseren Situation, in der es notwendig auftritt, gekennzeichnet werden kann"; see his p. 45. In addition, there is the fact that in the early dialogues at least, Plato seems to have had some doubts about whether—as we might put it—there are any reflexive relations (see Scheibe, pp. 35-38).

34. See, e.g., Burnet **2**, p. 165 Taylor **2**, p. 76; Hackforth **3**, p. 154; Lee, *op. cit.* This is not to say that their ways of putting the matter are the same as mine or as each other's. (In connection with this idea one should also consider the view, which has been proposed from time to time, that Plato regards sensible objects as somehow bundles or collections of qualities or the like; see variously Taylor, *ibid.*, T. M. Robinson, p. 93, and McDowell **2**, pp. 143-145.)

35. The term "reference" must be taken in an accommodating way both here and elsewhere, in view of Plato's lack of precision on such matters (cf. n. I-42). Logically, proper names and demonstratives must also be disallowed as ways of referring to sensibles; indeed *Tim.* 49c*sqq.* seems to be making just this point about demonstratives.

36. That is, the Form of *F* will at least be *F* without any qualification (*Symp.* 210e6-211a5, e.g.), and perhaps this is all that Plato is committed to. It must be admitted, however—though this is not the place to explore the matter in

full—that there are signs at least that at this stage Plato wants to say something more than this, that *no* true predication about a Form need carry a qualification. It is tempting to put this interpretation on the phrase "αὐτὸ καθ' αὐτό" in such passages as *Phaedo* 78d5-6 and *Symp.* 211b1. Indeed, it is also tempting to attribute to him at this stage, particularly on the basis of *Symp.* 211a5-b5, the view that *nothing whatever* may be properly said about the Form of *F* except that it is *F*. If this were correct, then the Forms would in yet a more extreme way fail to be relational.

It does not seem, however, that we can say that Plato accepted such an extreme view as this in any wholesale way, and plainly in his later works he saw that it could not possibly be right. On the first point, the view seems pretty clearly incompatible with any likely interpretation of his ideas about Forms and dialectic (cf. Ch. IV, secs. 3-4), which involve saying a good deal more about the Form of *F* than simply that it is *F*. For another thing, such texts as *Symp.* 211a-b are adequately accounted for by the interpretation that I have given above, which simply insists that the Form of *F* be *F* unqualifiedly. On the second point, such passages as *Parm.* 133c8-9ff. and *Soph.* 259e5-6 (along with the surrounding text) show Plato emphasizing the necessity of saying quite a lot about each Form, and particularly about its relations to other Forms. Thus, if Plato ever did hold the extreme view described, he changed it later on. (That he is thus changing his mind in the *Sophist* would be confirmed if we could be sure that *Soph.* 251a*sqq.*, concerning the "late-learners," is a criticism of an earlier view of Plato's own, as some have thought.) Of course, he might never have held it, but he still may have wanted to combat it later, thinking that it might appear, though wrongly, to be an implication of some earlier thing that he had said. And indeed it is not, given the above, too hard to see why he would have been *tempted* at some times and for some reasons, to hold it.

There is another point to be remarked on concerning this suggestion. It is that there is little doubt that when Plato considered matters having to do with relations, he thought primarily not of *predicates*, in the linguistic sense, which are relational in the sense of being many-place, but rather of "relational *things*," such as—to put it more or less in his way—things which are larger (compared to other things), things which are equal (compared to other things), and so on. (For a closely related point see Scheibe, pp. 30-31.) Now because he thought of the matter in this way, it was much easier for him to suppose that there could be an object such as the Form of Equal that was equal but not equal to anything (cf. sec. 3) than it would have been if he had thought of the predicate "equal" as itself two-place. For in the latter case he would have seen that something peculiar happens when you try to apply *that* predicate to that single object (on its being a single object, see Owen **10**, Owen **9**, pp. 114-115). But when you start out observing—in this manner of speaking—that all of the equal *things* one comes across seem to be equal *to* something, then it is easier to entertain the idea of a different sort of equal thing, not equal to anything else.

37. See Owen **2**, p. 307, and compare n. I-59 on the question whether there is a fact/value distinction in *Euthyphro* 7b-d. The point that

qualified instances are useless for definition is made at *Rep.* 524a-c and 538d6-e3 (see also Allen **4**, pp. 154-155, and Prauss, pp. 22ff.), and *Parm.* 135e1-4 is presumably registering the same idea (depending on whether or not "λόγος" there means "definition"). Cf. also Aristotle *Met.* 987b6-7.

38. Which are neither, that is, in the sense that—as some put it—neither word properly "applies" to them, not in the sense in which an "intermediate" like gray is neither black nor white. (For obviously Plato thinks that there are things that are intermediate between being completely holy and completely unholy.) There is little sign that Plato thought of this sort of case, unless 491d4-5 is one (cf. Shorey **5**, *ad loc.*, and **4**, pp. 563, 595; *Symp.* 202a-b has to do with the other sort of case, whereas *Soph.* 257b is unclear).

39. For one application of this view, and a reply to it, see Gould, Part II, and Vlastos **4**, (see esp. pp. 232ff). On the right side of the issue, see also Shorey **5**, vol. II, p. 180, n. *a*; p. 187, n. *c*; p. 190, n. *d*; p. 228, n. *d*; and **2**, p. 45.

40. Thus for example see *Rep.* 478e-480a, 506c, 509d-511e, and bk. VII, *passim*.

41. See *Rep.* 471c-473b, 520c, 521b, 592a-b.

42. Another view of Plato's that would be nonsense if we did not allow degrees of resemblance between sensibles and Forms is the doctrine concerning the arts which he expresses in *Rep.* X, and particularly the idea that a painting of a bed, say, is a poorer imitation of the Form of Bed than an ordinary bed is (596e-597b, 598b-c, 602b, 603a-b). In addition, 520c3-6 makes it clear that Plato believes that certain sensibles are images of certain Forms rather than others. A contrary impression might be given by 479b3-10, particularly the words "ἧττον" and "μᾶλλον" in 3, 7, 9. Thus, Shorey translates, ". . . and again, do the many double things appear any less halves than doubles? . . . And likewise of the great and the small things, the light and the heavy things—will they admit these predicates any more than their opposites? . . ." But Plato is not saying that anything which is *F* is *to an equal degree* non-*F*. Rather, the idea is that given something that is double, it will *equally be the case that* it is half, and so on. This is shown by the replies that Socrates receives when he asks these questions, both in b8 and in b11-c5. For example, in response to the second question in the passage just quoted, namely "And likewise of the great and the small things, the light and the heavy things—will they admit these predicates any more than their opposites?" We have "No, each of them will always . . . partake of both," which would be nonsense if the question had been meant to suggest that the degree of partaking was always equal. In b9, Shorey correctly renders "μᾶλλον" by "rather." (In c8-d9, on the other hand, "μᾶλλον" *does* mean "more": the idea is that nothing can more "not be" than what "purely is not," and that nothing can more "be" than what "purely is" [cf. d5].)

43. It is of course neither surprising nor coincidental that Plato should have arrived at this notion in the same work in which he began to extol the condition of the disembodied, by contrast with the embodied, soul. See (with qualifications) Gulley **2**, pp. 23ff.

44. For a slightly different point see Shorey **5**, p. 530 n.*a*. This is the

other side of the coin which we see in the argument concerning "Forms of relatives" in Alex. Aphr. in *Met.* 82.11ff. (Hayduck; see also Ross **3**, pp. 124-125), esp. 83.7-8. Cf. Owen **2**; the part of the argument is that part labelled "II" by him.

45. This is an obvious corollary of the point which Plato makes at *Rep.* 523e-524a.

46. See esp. *Rep.* 478e7-479a8, d3-5, along with Owen **2**, pp. 302-309, and Vlastos **8**, pp. 10-17.

47. The point is that we cannot give a definition to someone by telling him that the Form of *F* is the Form of which such-and-such a sensible object, or set of sensible objects, will remind him. Likewise, of course, we cannot give him a definition by telling him that the Form of *F* is the Form to which such-and-such a sensible object (or set of sensible objects) is similar, because after all, if each sensible object that is *F* is also the contrary of *F*, the sensible object pointed to (or, each member of the set) will be both similar and dissimilar to the Form of *F* and also similar to the Form of non-*F* (i.e., the Form contrary to the Form of *F*—whether there is such a Form is a subject of debate; but see Vlastos **8**, p. 8, n. 1). Some have wanted to claim that Plato must allow to sensible objects an epistemically more privileged position than this account would suggest. Thus, Gulley **2**, apparently maintains that the argument in 72ff. relies in a certain way on the correctness of our sensory observations (pp. 34ff.). This is a philosophically defensible view, but it requires considerable argument, and it is of course certainly not Plato's view.

48. Most people, he thinks, do not clearly recognize that they do not thus apply (e.g., *Rep.*, 476b-e, 478e-480a), though he thinks it relatively easy to induce them to recognize this (if 479a-d is any indication), and also thinks at least some of the time that such people's judgments about their perceptions involve some sort of comparison of sensible objects with Forms, whether they realize it or not (cf. *infra*, sec. 7 with n. III-57).

49. On the question whom Plato is accusing of falling into this error, and to whom he means to allude with the phrase "ἀντιλογικοὺς λόγους" in 90c1, see the remarks of Burnet **1**, *ad* 90b9, c5, 91a2, and Hackforth **3**, p. 108, n. 1, pp. 110-111. It is plain from 90c1-6 that Plato has in mind people who are driven to a total distrust of language by frequently seeing a single statement apparently both proved and disproved, and that in this connection he means to remind the reader both of Heraclitean ideas (see Burnet *ad* c5, along with *Crat.* 440c6ff.) and of argumentative techniques of the sort associated with the Sophists, and particularly with Protagoras (see esp. Diels, vol. II, 80 A1, 19, 21). Now whatever Plato's reasons for making the association, it is clear that he regards the sort of confusion and scepticism engendered by it as his main adversary at this point. (I suppose that this passage forms part of the support for Aristotle's statement (*Met.* 987a32ff., 1078b12ff.) that Plato was stimulated to develop his theory of Forms by a combination of Socratic and Heraclitean influences.)

50. Compare 76b, where he says that anyone who knows must be able to give a *logos* of that about which he knows, and where Plato is clearly talking about

Forms (cf. 75c7, e1-7, 76a1-7). Plainly this use of "*logos*" is the one that Plato wants to vindicate. See also Shorey **5**, vol. II, p. 224, n.c.

51. On these matters, which have to do particularly with the *Phaedrus* and *Epistle* VII, see Ch. V, sec. 2, and Ch. VIII, sec. 3.

52. Cf. Ch. I, sec. 2, along with *Phaedo* 75b, 76d-e; *Rep.* 500e-501c, 540a-b, 596a-b; *Crat.* 389a-b. Notice that some of these passages involve looking to Forms not merely for the sake of making judgments about sensible things, but also for the sake of fashioning sensible things after the Forms. It goes without saying, however, that when one fashions a thing after a Form, a reason why one must look to the Form is to tell how and to what degree the thing on which one is working thus far resembles the Form.

53. See also 78e2, "ὁμωνύμων," and note that at *Parm.* 130e5-131a2, where Plato is presumably sketching what he at that later date viewed as an original motivation of the theory of Forms, introduces the very same idea. It is perhaps also present at *Rep.* 515b5, if "ὀνομάζειν" is read (for a defense of the reading, see Shorey *ad loc.*).

54. The traces are in the idea of his being "called by the name of" the Form. This shows that Plato is not here distinguishing between "large" used as a predicate to describe things, and the same word used to denote the Form. From the fact that it can be used to denote the Form, he slides to the idea that it must *ipso facto* be descriptive of the Form. Cf. n. III-7. If he had not been making this confusion, it is difficult indeed to see how he could so blithely have spoken here of a sensible object's being "called by *the* name of the Form."

55. One should perhaps regard Gulley **2**, pp. 34ff., as in part pressing both of these questions (though especially the former; p. 35).

56. Thus Cornford **2**, p. 51. On a related problem that crops up in the *Tht.*, see Cooper, with my n. VII-11, and also Urmson.

57. Roughly, the assumption motivating Plato is that for it to be possible for me to say, intelligibly, that a certain thing fails to be unqualifiedly large, and in particular, for the phrase "unqualifiedly large" to make sense, there must be some object of which that phrase is true. It can be seen working, for example, in *Phaedo* 74d9-75a4 (that it is being assumed here, rather than proved, is important; cf. n. III-54), though Plato is there giving a principle of more general application. It is equally working in the first premise of the argument from πρός τι given by Alexander, *in Met.*, 82.11ff. (i.e., in 82.11-83.6, the part labeled "I" by Owen **2**, p. 294). The assumption packed into this premise, that the three alternatives given in it exhaust the field, is tantamount to the assumption in question, because it leaves no room for the claim that there might be many things capable of being labeled "almost (or, qualifiedly) thus-and-so" without there being anything capable of being labeled "(utterly, or unqualifiedly) thus-and-so." So far as I can see, the idea behind this assumption is most likely to be that the predicate represented by "(unqualifiedly) thus-and-so" could not make sense if there were nothing of which it were true. It is obvious that this is an application of what I have called the "semantic" consid-

eration, but it is more than that, too, since the semantic consideration *by itself* does not require that there be something in the extension of every general term. What we have in addition, it seems to me, is the same sort of slide that leads elsewhere to the "self-predicative" view of the Forms. From the idea that there must be an entity that corresponds to a general term and somehow explains the fact that that term is meaningful (which is one version of the semantic consideration; cf. Ch. I, sec. 1), Plato is unable at this stage to resist sliding to the claim that there must be an entity of which that term is true. Cf. n. III-54. This is not to say, however, that Plato always succumbs to this tendency, or that he did not start to extricate himself from it later (cf. n. I-44 and Owen **1**, pp. 318-322).

58. Cf. 78d1 with Burnet **1** *ad loc.* and *Rep*. 507b5-7, 534b3-6 (with n. IV-23), and 531e4-5 with 532a7. "*Logos*" can, of course, be used in a more general way (thus often being translated "account"; cf. Shorey **5**, vol. II, p. 195, n. *f*, and Thompson, p. 90). There is little to be said for Archer-Hind's rendering of 78d1-2 (where "ἧς λόγον δίδομεν τοῦ εἶναι" comes out "as whose principle we assign being"), and Bluck and Hackforth both go too far in translating "τοῦ εἶναι" respectively by "essence" and "existence." Burnet has the point just right; cf. Shorey **5**, vol. II, p. 97, n. *d*.

59. See Robinson **1**, Chs. VII-IX, esp. pp. 121-122, 117.

60. Robinson, pp. 136-141.

61. Robinson, pp. 121-122.

62. For a different view, see, e.g., Cherniss **5**, esp. pp. 142-144. In spite of disagreeing with Cherniss' view that the methods described in the *Phdo*. and the *Rep*. are essentially the same, I note that my ultimate conclusions would not be affected by accepting that view. For my ultimate point is that the method as expounded in the *Rep*., whether or not it is also expounded in the *Phdo*., leaves problems open which are then tackled in the *Phdr*. (Ch. V, sec. 1), with the result that the method of hypothesis turns out not to have provided the sort of satisfactory starting point which Plato needed (see Ch. IX, secs. 1 and 2).

CHAPTER IV

The Republic: Forms, Hypotheses, and Knowledge

The *Republic* has generally been regarded as the high-water mark of Plato's philosophical career. At one time it was thought to have been his most mature work, the culmination of his philosophical reflections.[1] More recently it has been agreed to be a product of the middle part of his life, but the notion that it is a sort of culmination has persisted. One school of thought holds that it marks the fruition of the theory of Forms which had been developing from his earliest works, and that it is this theory which he then begins to reexamine and criticize in his later works.[2] Another view holds that his later works do not show any recantation of the doctrines of the *Republic*,[3] but those who hold to this view often think nevertheless that the *Republic* is the dialogue in which Plato collected most of his important ideas together, and that much of the work that followed it was devoted to examining special facets of his theory.[4] On both views, then, the *Republic* tends to be regarded as a high point. I myself am of the opinion that after the *Republic* and a few other works that were written in the same period, Plato did reconsider his views and change some of them in notable respects, and I shall be betraying this opinion from time to time in what follows.

There is, nevertheless, some reason to be wary of the view of the *Republic* under which it is supposed to show a fully matured and worked-out doctrine, later to be reexamined. The reason for caution is not that Plato did not later reconsider the ideas of this dialogue. I have just said that I think that he did. Rather, the reason is that although the *Republic* contained much that Plato later wished to examine anew, it does not contain a doctrine that is in all respects completed, and I think that Plato realized this. The most important part of the theory that remains without anything approaching final polish is its epistemologi-cal part. Although the *Republic* does contain some grand and ambitious pronouncements on topics having to do with knowledge and the like, there is much in it that is left sketchy, and about which Plato makes no claims of definitiveness. In particular, the crucial epistemological pas-sages in books V-VII show a number of ideas that are unelaborated and programmatic, but do not appear—unless one reads very deeply bet-ween the lines indeed—to be backed up by any completely detailed and developed treatment of the problems at hand. For our purposes, the central case in point here is Plato's treatment of what he sometimes calls "dialectic," which, as we shall see, poses many of the epistemological issues with which he is confronted and which he goes on in subsequent dialogues to discuss more fully. But it is not that at the time of the writing of this work he thought that he had solved them and only later realizes that they needed more attention. Rather, he shows every sign of realizing already that there is more to be said about them. In 532d-533a, he explicitly excuses himself from pursuing the topic of dialectic further than he has, on grounds of an inability to settle the pertinent questions, and there is no reason not to take him at his word.[5]

If one reflects on the nature of the *Republic*, it is not too surprising that Plato should have intentionally left unexplored a good deal of the epistemological territory which is mapped out there. The main con-cerns of the dialogue, after all, lie elsewhere, and there is no reason why he had to range further than was necessary from the central areas of political philosophy and ethics on which he was concentrating. This is by no means to say that Plato was not serious about the metaphysical and epistemological views which he expresses there. It is just that there was a great deal to say, and Plato could be expected neither by us nor by himself to say it all at once.

If one recognizes that Plato consciously left important things unsaid in the *Republic*, certain other facts fall more readily into place than they otherwise would. Whatever second thoughts Plato may have had in later dialogues about his doctrine of Forms as it was expounded in the *Republic*, and in other works of his middle period such as the *Phaedo* and the *Symposium*, it is well known that he never openly voiced any outright recantation. This fact has frequently seemed to be evidence for the claim that he did not in fact change his views in any significant respect, but it is not. For one thing, there was much that he retained in his later period, and it was quite reasonable of him to regard himself as still working within the same theory as before. In addition, however— and this is where the foregoing remarks come in—we can now see that he must later have regarded himself as still working on issues that the *Republic* had not purported to settle once and for all. If we take him to have thought at one time that the *Republic* had tied everything up into a neat package, then it becomes considerably harder to understand why he did not more openly proclaim that he had changed his mind. If, on the other hand, we do not attribute that view of the *Republic* to him, then we can readily understand why no such proclamation appeared to him to be required.

In addition to the *Republic*, I shall treat here also of two other dialogues which I believe to have been written in the same period as that work. One of them is the *Symposium*, which many agree to have been produced either a little before or a little after the *Republic* (it does not matter for my purposes which came first).[6] The other is the *Timaeus*, over which controversy has raged.[7] I believe that it too was written around the time of the *Republic*, in spite of the traditional view that it came toward the end of Plato's life. Little that I shall say, however, depends much upon the *Timaeus*, which deals only tangentially with the problems that chiefly concern me here.

1 The Knowability of the Forms

One of the central epistemological doctrines of the *Republic* is that whereas sensible things can be the objects merely of "belief" or "opinion," it is only Forms that can be "known."[8] We have seen the genesis of this view in the *Phaedo*, in the claim that our apprehensions of Forms are "true" and "accurate," and in the connection of that claim with Plato's views about unqualified predications. But the *Republic* expounds the idea far more fully.

It is in the *Republic* that Plato's metaphor of "looking to" and "seeing" and "viewing" the Forms comes into its own.[9] Although he does not believe that what is involved is literally sight,[10] he does want to claim that it is possible to do something *like* seeing Forms, and that it can be done somehow in greater or lesser degrees. Sometimes, as in the allegory of the cave (514ff.; cf. 518d), he talks as though people often fail to "see" the Forms because they are, as it were, "looking" in the wrong direction (though he does seem to believe that every human being is capable of "seeing" the Forms). At other times the picture is different. It is as though we might "see" the Forms, but only under circumstances in which, or through a medium because of which, it would be impossible to perceive them clearly, as though—to use a figure that Plato tends not to employ, but that conveys the idea—there were a mist between us and them which we had to penetrate in order to apprehend them.[11]

By contrast with Forms, sensible objects are what we habitually heed, but at the same time they are thought to be unilluminably dark to our view, as though our apprehension of them were blocked by a mist which is somehow part of the objects themselves, and through which there is no penetrating.[12]

What is the cash value of this notion that sensible objects are ineluctably obscure whereas Forms are not? The origin of this view, as I have suggested, lies back in the *Phaedo*, and is taken up again in the *Republic* and the *Symposium*. The knowability of the Form of Justice, for example, arises from the fact that it is unqualifiedly just, does not have to be said to be just in this or that respect or relation, and never in any respect or relation fails to be just. This means, as Plato sees it, that when one judges that the Form of Justice is just, one is never in any danger of having to say that it is also unjust. Thus, he thinks, we can say flatly that the claim that Justice is just is true, and that the claim that Justice is unjust or not just is false. Something sensible that is just, on the other hand, is also unjust (in different respects or relations, of course), and accordingly, he thinks, the judgment that it is just is false, because the judgment that it is unjust is also true. How could the judgment that it is just fail to be false, after all, if the judgment that it is unjust is also true? So both judgments must be false (as well as true). Of course he realizes that we get no formal contradictions here, because the appropriate qualifications can be added.[13] But because he does not insist on *always* adding them, he is able, in a manner which we have seen (cf. Ch. III, sec. 2), to conclude that there is something wrong with judgments about sensible objects, and that they are not true. But because he not unreasonably wants to say that a judgment that expresses knowledge must not be false, he not surprisingly decides that the only judgments that can express knowledge are the judgments about the Forms which stand in no need of qualification. Had he insisted on *always* adding what he thinks of as qualifications when he is talking of sensible objects, he would no doubt have realized that once judgments about sensible objects are qualified, they stand in no further need of qualification.[14] But his preoccupation with the simple predications is strong enough, as we have seen, to prevent him from attending to this fact.

It is tempting to say that this is the *whole* content of his belief that Forms are knowable and that sensible objects are not. But this idea would be inaccurate, and the preceding paragraph does not give us the full story. For it is evident that Plato himself does not regard the claim that the Forms are "clear" to the mind as a *mere* shorthand for what I have just set forth. Rather, he thinks that the Forms have some sort of clarity which can be apprehended by the mind, and which *explains* the fact that unqualified statements can be made about them.[15]

This metaphor is of course compounded by Plato's view that sensible objects are more or less poor replicas of Forms (cf. Ch. III, sec. 2). As *Phaedo* 73ff. shows, this idea is also based on the ideas about qualified and unqualified predication which appear there.[16] For as we have seen, it strikes Plato as quite plausible to say that what is qualifiedly equal, e.g., can be said to resemble, though imperfectly, the thing that is unqualifiedly equal. What diminishes the aptness of this claim to us, of course, is our awareness of the initial difficulty inherent in Plato's idea of qualified and unqualified predications. But once the idea is established, it contributes in its own way to the view that Forms are knowable and sensible objects are not. For it is easy to think that there is something somehow epistemically superior in models over copies,[17] and even if it is not clearly explained by Plato what that something is,[18] the notion takes hold and adds to the general epistemic prestige of the Forms.

2 Obstacles to Knowledge of Forms

When Plato claims that Forms are "knowable," he obviously means just that: that they *can* be "known," not that everyone in all respects *does* "know" them.[19] Thus, we have observed him suggesting different ways in which one's knowledge may fail, such as the idea that the appropriate organ of apprehension might be somehow occluded, or that it might be, as it were, turned in the wrong direction (sec. 1, *init.*). Although he might admit that his use of visual language in describing our knowledge of Forms could be misleading, he plainly does not think that it is totally so (cf. n. IV-10), and he takes quite seriously the idea that our inability, as things are, to be completely knowledgeable about Forms is due to some sort of hampering of the soul by the bodily apparatus.

But Plato has more in mind than *simply* the desirability of our "viewing" the objects of knowledge. For he plainly wishes the Forms, properly viewed, to play a substantial role in our cogitations about the philosophical problems that confront him. As we saw (Ch. III, sec. 6), Forms are supposed to figure, however dimly and imperfectly, in our intellectual activity even before we have reached clarity about them, and they are supposed to correspond in some sense to the words which we use and the thoughts which we entertain.

The main argument of the *Republic* illustrates these facts. It is devoted in large part to developing a notion of justice which will explain, among other things, why it is that (as Plato firmly believes to be the case) being just is part of what is genuinely good for a human being. The notion of justice that Plato develops is a rather technical one, bound up in and framed by the concepts that are part of his own theory of the human soul, according to which each part of the soul should in some sense fulfill its own function. But Plato does not think of this notion of justice as tied only to his theory and unrelated to justice as ordinarily conceived. Rather, he suggests that the more common account of justice, that it is "doing what is one's own" (τὰ ἑαυτοῦ πράττειν),[20] is an "adumbration" of the same justice of which his own view is a more refined account.[21]

Clearly, Plato also thinks it possible to err in such matters.[22] Prominent in book VII is the idea of the need to gain a correct conception of the good, leading to the injunction to distinguish the Form of the Good from all other things (534b8-c1, διορίσασθαι τῷ λόγῳ ἀπὸ τῶν ἄλλων πάντων ἀφελὼν τὴν τοῦ ἀγαθοῦ ἰδέαν).[23] Elsewhere, too, Plato suggests that it is desirable not to confuse or conflate distinct notions, though it is all too easy to do so.[24] In fact, book VII has given a prominent place to this idea, in the course of a rather elaborate argument concerning the appropriate educational curriculum for the rulers of the ideal city (521ff.). Having asked what disciplines have the tendency to turn the soul toward what is knowable (521c-d), Plato's first answer mentions arithmetic and the discipline of calculation (525a9, c1). The reason for this answer is based in what we have seen already of Plato's views about sensible objects (Ch. III, sec. 4; Ch. IV, sec. 2). For example, the same things in the sensible world which are seen by sense to be large are also seen to be small (compared, presumably, to different things). When something like this happens, the soul in its perplexity calls in "calculation and thought" (525b4, λογισμόν τε καὶ νόησιν), which are capable of distinguishing between the Form of the Large and the Form of the Small (c13), in a way in which sensation could not succeed in doing (c3-4).[25] Thus, the person's attention is turned upwards, so to speak, to the intelligible and away from the sensible. But why is calculation, or arithmetic, involved here? Because Plato views the problem posed by sensible objects as a question of telling whether one has on one's hands, in largeness and smallness, one Form or two (b7, c1), and arithmetic is the discipline that "distinguishes one, two, and three" (522c5-6). So gaining knowledge of the Forms importantly involves the avoidance, somehow, of confusions or conflations of one Form with another

(524c7, οὗ συγκεχυμένα ἀλλὰ διωρισμένα).²⁶

That Plato could hold these views is fully in accord with what we should expect from someone who adopts his stance. The Forms are not dependencies of our minds; they are in the world outside of us, supplying matters of fact for us to be right or wrong about (cf. Ch. I, sec. 3). There is a right and wrong about a definition, which must in some fashion be true to the facts about a given Form, and there must equally be a right and a wrong about the apprehension of Forms and about whether or not one is in one way or another confused about them, just as we all think—at least in unreflective moments—that there is a right and a wrong about whether we are accurately seeing, counting, and identifying by their positions or other characteristics, the peas that are lined up in a pod. No doubt the world of Forms is more complicated, but the principle is in relevant ways the same.

But beyond his description of the way in which sight can apprehend both largeness and smallness in the same sensible object, Plato gives relatively little explanation of the failure adequately to distinguish Forms. It is uncertain, for example, whether he has in mind cases like those in which one apprehends a certain thing and mistakes it for something else, or like those in which one sees a shadowy figure in the darkness and fails to discern that it is two people standing close together rather than a single person, or cases of some other sort. That he has in view something like the second sort of case is suggested by his comparison of the Form of the Good to the sun, when he indicates that the Good in some manner *illuminates* intelligible things (508-509), so as to make it possible for us to know them (sec. 4), but the point is not certain. Plainly he thinks that it is possible in some sense to be mistaken about what the Good is (e.g., 562b9, ὃ δημοκρατία ὁρίζεται ἀγαθόν; 555b9-10), but the exact mechanism of these mistakes is left unspecified, as when he drops the suggestion that it is possible to confuse, as it were, a Form with things which partake in it.²⁷ What we learn, however, from the idea that these errors can occur is that the effort to gain knowledge of Forms involves more than simply the training of the mind's eye on them so as to be able blankly to view them. It also involves, in some sense or other, the *recognition* or correct *identification* of, and the avoidance of certain sorts of confusion about, the Forms that one has in one's ken.

3 Science and Dialectic

The problems surrounding Plato's notion of dialectic and his "method of hypothesis" are numerous, and many of them are acute. In the *Republic*, moreover, there are exceedingly difficult passages dealing with these matters, particularly those concerning the sun and the Divided Line at the end of book VI, and the allegory of the cave at the beginning of book VII.

Among the issues arising in these passages, the most central for our purposes is Plato's attack on the state of science in his day, as he viewed it. Plato's notion of science, of course, is intimately bound up with his notion of knowledge, and therefore with his contention that there can be knowledge, strictly so-called, only concerning Forms. From this perspective, it is disciplines such as geometry that seem to him most worthy of sustained philosophical attention, and accordingly it is upon geometry itself that he turns his most direct scrutiny.

It is well known that his attack on the then current state of that science is twofold.[28] In the first place, he takes geometers to task for relying on unsupported assumptions or axioms, for which they are unable to provide any grounds. In the second place, he maintains that it is a fault of their procedures that they rely on sensible figures such as those drawn in the sand, whereas what they should be talking about are not those sensible figures but rather certain geometrical entities which are apprehended, not by the senses, but by the mind.[29] An outstanding problem of interpretation concerns the connection between these two criticisms.[30] Plato seems quite clearly to think that they are connected, and indeed that the reason why the geometers of his day must rely on unproved axioms is precisely that they do make use of sensible illustrations. But it is not clear why he thinks that this is so. In addition, there is another difficulty. It is the commonly accepted—and correct—view that Plato proposes to remedy the former defect of geometry by establishing a science, which he calls "dialectic," which can somehow be used to establish the axioms which geometers have left unproved.[31] This new science, however, is apparently regarded by him as itself an axiomatized body of statements, with its own theorems and, more importantly, its own axioms. The question therefore arises what superiority Plato saw in this new science of dialectic over the old science of geometry. Because they both seem to contain unproved assumptions, why should the unproved assumptions of geometry be any the worse, for being unproved, than the unproved assumptions of dialectic? The usual answer to this question, and an answer that is obviously on the right track, has been to say that the superiority of the assumptions of dialectic lies in the fact that they are explicitly about Forms and not about sensible objects.[32] But then the question arises, why this fact should make them better off? If they are still unproved, then they are still unproved, and *that* defect of them—if it is a defect—still remains no matter what their putative subject matter may be.[33]

Although Plato's position cannot, I think, be vindicated, it can be more thoroughly understood.[34] The key lies in his belief that predicates apply to sensible objects only defectively or with qualification, in the manner which we have seen, whereas they apply to Forms unqualifiedly. The same holds for geometrical predicates, such as "(is a) triangle," and the like. Exploiting this clue, let us consider a theorem of Euclidean geometry such as (1) "Every triangle has interior angles equal to two right angles." Now from the fact that "triangle" applies to sensible objects qualifiedly at best, Plato seems to infer that no sensible object is precisely a triangle, in that, for example, its sides are not perfectly straight, or do not actually meet, or the like. This inference and its conclusion are both problematical in various ways, but let us not pause over that matter.[35] The next point to notice is that Plato seems to think that geometers want such theorems as this to be, as it were, true statements *about* the sensible figures which they draw on wax or in sand, where this requires that there *be* sensible figures which are strictly triangular and have interior angles equal to two right angles. But it is on this point, Plato thinks, that they go wrong. There are no sensible triangles, in the strict sense of "things that are unqualified triangles," but geometers are committed to the view that there are. Thus one of their claims would be best expressed, not by (1),[36] but by something like (2) "Triangles have interior angles equal to two right angles," where this means—though the geometers might not put it in just this way— "There are sensible triangles and they have interior angles equal to two right angles." This, in Plato's view, is false. But there is, he thinks, a correct analogue of this statement which purports to talk of nonsensible objects, which might be framed (3) "The Triangle has interior angles equal to two right angles."[37] This statement, so construed, seems to him to be subject to none of the difficulties that infect (2).

What does all of this have to do with Plato's contention that geometers use hypotheses in a mistaken way? Simply that he thinks that built into their statements, as they construe them, are assumptions to the effect that sensible objects really satisfy the conditions laid down by the geometrical predicates.[38] Whereas (2) itself would be taken to be at best a theorem rather than an axiom of geometry, any assumption with which a geometer starts will, like (2), have packed into it a false assumption to the effect that some sensible objects do satisfy geometrical conditions without qualification. When geometry is done in the way in which Plato regards as proper, however, it will be free of such false assumptions.[39] The phase of dialectic that deals with geometrical objects will instead make statements explicitly about Forms. And whatever assumptions might be packed into the dialectician's talk (to the effect that there are such objects as those whose existence he is presupposing) will be true.[40]

Once geometry is purified, two other things become possible. First, it becomes possible to give a *logos* or "account" of the objects that it assumes to exist (533b-c, e-534c), in the sense of a definition of them. Second, it is likewise possible to demonstrate, on the basis of statements of dialectic, the purified analogues of the statements which geometers have heretofore had to take for granted. (As various commentators have observed, it is not obvious that Plato distinguishes clearly between these two things.)[41] On the latter point, Plato does not show us just how such a demonstration might look,[42] but what makes one possible is, of course, the fact that our purified geometrical axioms are, unlike the old ones, unqualifiedly true and hence susceptible of demonstration. On the former point, the idea is simply that as long as geometrical talk purported to deal with sensibles, then—as an instance of a quite general point about definitions which we have already seen (Ch. III, sec. 4)—no definition can be adequate. For Plato already has reasons for thinking that proper definitions must be explicitly about Forms.

There is a sense, then, in which geometry can be saved from the plight in which it finds itself.[43] It can be saved by the abandonment of sensible images and of the habits of speech that make it seem to be a science of sensibles. Geometers, in Plato's view, have not been entirely on the wrong track. Rather, their mistake merely lies in encouraging a mistaken construal of what their statements were about.[44]

Does this account not leave Plato in just as bad a state as before? For if the geometer employed unproved assumptions, does not the dialectician still do so? It must be granted that in this respect Plato has presumably made little progress, though there is a bit more that we can do, in the next section, to understand his position. As we shall see there, the important feature of his view is evidently the idea that whereas the assumptions of geometry *need* to be proved, the assumptions of dialectic somehow do not need to be proved (and, perhaps, cannot be).

But in another way the above interpretation puts Plato's argument in a better light, in that it shows that his complaint against geometers was not simply that they employed unproved assumptions but rather that by their faulty casting of geometrical statements they blocked themselves from seeing that accounts of geometrical expressions, and demonstrations of geometrical assumptions, are conceivable, and mistakenly committed themselves to statements which purported to talk about the sensible world.

4 Dialectic and the Good

The science of dialectic is invoked by Plato in an attempt to solve certain basic epistemological problems which had been raised by his talk of the method of hypothesis in the *Meno* and the *Phaedo* (Ch. III, sec. 7). Leaving aside the details of manifold exegetical difficulties, we can summarize the earlier developments as follows.[45] By the time of the *Phaedo*, Plato had settled upon a way in which various important disputes could be at least provisionally resolved. One would advance a proposition as a hypothesis, and go about testing it by seeing whether it had any consequences that were obviously absurd.[46] Once this was done, if two people were still in disagreement over the hypothesis, the proponent of it would cast about for a "higher hypothesis" which would entail the original hypothesis, and he would test this new hypothesis in the way in which the original hypothesis had been tested, by examining its consequences. If his interlocutor accepted the higher hypothesis, then the dispute would end and the interlocutor would have to accept the original proposition. If the interlocutor still did not accept the higher hypothesis, then the search would start for a still "higher" hypothesis which the interlocutor might accept and which would be tested in turn. This process would then go on as long as was necessary to produce agreement.

But of course agreement might not be reached in this way, and it appears that in the *Republic* Plato undertook to expand his method to remedy this defect and arrive at a means by which eventual agreement might be assured.[47] The idea seems to be that if the original hypothesis were indeed true, then after obtaining "higher" and "higher" hypotheses (each entailing its predecessors) by what Plato calls the "upward path," one would eventually arrive at an "unhypothesized beginning" which, by a "downward path," could then be seen to entail all of the preceding former hypotheses, including the original one over which the dispute first arose. Plato's view in the *Republic* is apparently that this unhypothesized beginning will in fact serve as a starting-point from which all of the knowable truths (which he takes to concern only Forms) could be deduced, and will thus—to reverse the metaphor—be a sort of foundation for all scientific knowledge.[48] It will be from this beginning, for example, that all of the geometrical truths, once properly formulated, will be derivable. Plato holds the further view that this beginning will have to do with the Form of the Good, and will presumably be a proposition or set of propositions about that Form.[49] He also talks in a manner that has led many interpreters to think that one's knowledge of this beginning or foundation of science will involve some sort of "direct acquaintance" with the Form of the Good, which would be required for the rest of one's knowledge to be properly grounded.[50]

There is much in this scheme of things that has puzzled commentators, and it raises a number of questions which, though they must be kept apart, have not always been distinguished. One is the question why this unhypothesized beginning should have anything to do with the Form of the Good rather than something else. Another is the question why Plato thought that there was such a foundation of knowledge at all. Another is why he thought that all knowledge could be founded on such an apparently slender basis as he seems to claim, and how he could have thought that a proposition, or even a set of propositions, about some single Form could possibly yield the geometrical truths and all of the rest as consequences.[51] Still another question arises over how one could tell, at any given point, that the foundation had been reached, and why disputes might not arise over any alleged foundation. Yet another question—and now we are coming closer to our main concern—is: What does the "seeing" of the Form of the Good have to do with the allegedly obtainable certainty over the proposition or propositions about it which serve as the foundations for other scientific claims? All of these are questions that have standardly arisen over this part of his doctrine.

Let me now raise some further questions which arise out of the considerations that have occupied us heretofore. Although Plato's remarks in this connection are highly figurative, he seems to suggest that for a person fully to know any other Form, he must first come to know the Form of the Good, because this seems to be the outcome of his view that what there is to be known about other Forms can be genuinely known only after one has derived it from the unhypothesized beginning. But knowing a Form consists, in part, in being able to view it with the mind. If this is so, however, then Plato appears to be saying that we cannot view other Forms, at least with full clarity, until we have viewed the Form of the Good.[52] Now why should this be so? It appears at first as though Plato is saying that what occludes one's view of the other Forms will be removed or penetrated only after the penetration or removal of what blocks one's view of the Form of the Good.[53] But one wonders why other Forms might not come clearly into focus before the Good does.

But we have oversimplified Plato's point in a way that is crucial. Recall that the task is not merely to apprehend or "view" Forms, and in particular it is not to apprehend or view just any Form on which you happen to stumble. Rather, it is to apprehend the Form or Forms that you set out to view and to recognize it or them as such. It is this fact that makes the use of the word "intuition," often deployed in discussing these issues, misleading and unsatisfactory, because, like some of Plato's own words, it tends to make one think of nothing more than a sort of blank mental gaze.[54] But we have seen that Plato cannot, in the *Republic*, be thinking of the epistemological enterprise as simply an indiscriminate Form-viewing expedition.[55] We should take this fact into account when we interpret the role of the Good in the theory of knowledge expounded in this dialogue.

When we do so, we can see that in all likelihood it is not simply that the Good must be clearly *apprehended* before any other Form can be, but rather that it must be *identified* or *recognized as* the Good before any other Form can be recognized with assurance as the Form that it is. The idea would be that in Plato's view adequate identification of any other Form must be carried out by knowing, so to speak, the relationship in which it stands to the Good.[56] It is plausible to suspect, moreover, that the reason for this idea would be as follows. The Form of F, he believes, is, as it were, an unqualified F, or something which is unqualifiedly F. But we know that he passes from this idea to thinking that it must therefore be a nondefective or, in this sense, a perfect F (Ch. III, sec. 2). But his notion of goodness is such that he can think of the idea of a "perfect F" as close to, if not the same as, the idea of a "good F." And by this line of thought, it is not at all unnatural that he should arrive at the conclusion that the adequate identification of any Form must be carried out by knowing, so to speak, the relationship in which that Form stands to the Form of the Good. To understand what it is to be the Form of F, then, is to understand what it is to be an unqualified, and thus nondefective, and thus perfect, and thus good, specimen of an F.[57] This view may involve for Plato, as some have suggested, the idea that the understanding of what it is to be an F requires an understanding of what ultimate purpose, or good, it is that an F is for.[58] But however this may be, the idea remains that in some sense the proper recognition and identification of each Form requires knowing something about how it stands to the Good.

The Good is accordingly somewhat like the point of origin in a

Cartesian coordinate system, by reference to which each point in the system is located and identified. We may illustrate the idea with the example of Justice, which is central to the *Republic*, and has already been alluded to (sec. 2). We begin with a tentative and rough view that justice has to do with "doing what is one's own" (370a-b, 433a-b). This view is refined and elaborated in the discussion that follows. But it is regarded as reasonably well established only when it is shown how the idea of doing what is one's own can be fitted into the notion of what it is to be a good man and a good city. This occurs with the establishment, at the end of book IV, of the way in which doing what is one's own can be seen as making possible the appropriate division of labor within the ideal city (433-434), and also harmony within the individual soul (443c-444a), which are respectively claimed to be essential to a good city and a good man (449a, 433c-d). Full certainty in this matter would of course have to await further discussion of the Good itself, and a determination of what it is (534a-c), but this earlier stage of Plato's account shows us clearly enough the structure of the argument as he views it, and the way in which the understanding of a notion can seem to require reference to the Good.[59] Once the relationship has been ascertained, thenceforth one can presumably recognize and identify a given Form without difficulty, by means of that relationship of it to the Good.

Thus, an important part of dialectic will consist of statements expounding the relations of various things to the Good. But these are presumably not the only sorts of statements that Plato admits into that science. For his comparison of dialectic to geometry suggests, at least, that some statements are to be derived from others by something like logical deduction.[60] There is considerable difficulty in understanding just how he means these deductions to proceed, and how statements about one Form could be deduced from statements about another, and in particular from statements about the Good. And there is also further difficulty about how such deductive procedures are to be connected with the apprehending of Forms. In this latter connection, one is reminded of a somewhat parallel uncertainty in Plato's earlier works, in which we noted that he sometimes seems to think that we gain information about Forms by apprehending them and then, as it were, examining them in order to ascertain facts about them, whereas elsewhere he apparently indicates that we might, having obtained a correct definition, deduce further information from it. (Ch. II, sec. 1).[61] But in spite of these problems, the outline of his view is fairly clear.

If we recognize other Forms by means of their relations to the Good, then how do we recognize the Good?[62] Plato gives us little to go on, and it is no accident that just before the crucial remarks in 534a-c about the connection between dialectic and the Good, Plato warns us of the difficulties involved in the issues that he is discussing, and of the need for further treatment of them (532d; cf. Ch. IV, introd.). In his comparison of the Good to the sun (507-509), he harps on the idea that the Good is somehow the "brightest" object accessible to knowledge, but it is unclear how much weight he puts on it. He is perhaps supposing that we could recognize the Good, if we try to apprehend it, *as* the "brightest" object there is; but even if we suppose that we understand the requisite notion of brightness, it is not plain why, when one thinks that what one is viewing is the brightest thing there is, there is not always the danger that something else is brighter. In 534b-c he seems to hint at some more substantial definition, but it is unclear what it would be like, or out of what materials it would be constructed. Plato does not pursue these matters. He knows that he is moving over very difficult ground, and that he does not have it entirely under his control.

5   Forms and Dialectic

The epistemological ideas of the *Republic* are a direct response to the problems that have arisen in his theory of knowledge from the time of his earliest works. Notwithstanding the fact that it contains gaps, and the fact that it is primarily devoted to an account of Justice, the dialogue is nevertheless the outline of a method of investigation from its start to its completion and is meant to illustrate the way in which Plato now believes that a serious inquiry should proceed. There is a central hypothesis concerning Justice, that it has to do with "doing what is one's own," which is elaborated into an account of what such a thing could have to do with goodness in a man and in a city, and which is then said to need to be fixed ultimately by means of an account of the Good itself (sec. 4). In such a manner as this we must be supposed able to carry out, *mutatis mutandis*, Plato's general program in the theory of knowledge.

Plato began with a conviction that there are facts for us to be right or wrong about, somehow independent of popular usage and common opinion, which we must try to find out about for ourselves. He determined that the subject matter of such discoveries must, for various reasons, be the Forms whose susceptibility to unqualified description was later to be described in the *Phaedo*. But the engine of discovery was not built yet. The earliest works were undecided about methods of investigation, about how it might legitimately begin, and about the respective roles of definition and the apprehension of Forms; and the same uncertainty broke out into the open in the paradox of inquiry in the *Meno*, which was laid to rest by the somewhat hasty palliative of the theory of recollection. But in the same work the notion of a hypothesis appeared, which promised to supply a more satisfactory account of the way in which our investigations might in principle be inaugurated, and the method of hypothesis was expounded further in the *Phaedo*. Aiming to develop and extend earlier ideas, the *Republic* takes certain machinery from the earlier dialogues for granted. It exploits, as we have seen, the idea of a sort of mental "apprehension" or "viewing" of the Forms; and it assumes also that definitions play a crucial role in philosophical and scientific investigation. Most importantly, however, it extends the role of the method of hypothesis and suggests that it leads ultimately not to mere provisional agreement, but to a result somehow more fixed and certain, depending in a crucial way on the Form of the Good. It is by expanding this idea that Plato would be expected to clarify his epistemological enterprise, to show where our inquiries might begin, and how they could be completed. It is true that questions must arise about his program. Prominent among them are those directly concerning the Form of the Good,[63] the way in which it is to be apprehended and recognized, the way in which a definition of it is to be obtained (as 534b-c suggests that it can be), the way in which these two things are related to each other, and the precise way in which they might engender or support further knowledge. But in spite of these questions, Plato has nonetheless given a sketch of the whole of his method, in accordance with which his theory of knowledge and Forms might be built to completion.

We must now see what becomes of his plan. For it is appropriate to note at this point that whatever ideas of the *Republic* subsequent dialogues may continue to accept, their emphasis and direction, within the sphere of the theory of knowledge, are quite different in important respects. Two notable examples: later discussions of dialectic do not make the Form of the Good carry the sort of weight that it did in the *Republic*, and Plato's account of dialectic itself is cast in importantly different terms. We must now see more of these differences, and of the effects which they exert upon his undertakings.

Notes

1. Thus Schleiermacher, p. 32. There were problems in reconciling this view with the internal evidence of the *Timaeus* and the *Critias*, and with Diog. Laert. III.37, which suggests that the *Laws* was Plato's last work (though it certainly does not *say* this; see Owen **1**, p. 335, n. 1).

2. The recent impetus for this view has been provided by Owen **1**.

3. In reply to Owen see Cherniss **7**. This issue has been made to revolve recently around the question of the chronological place of the *Timaeus* among Plato's other works, as it is generally felt that because that dialogue is so plainly allied doctrinally with the *Phaedo* and the *Rep.*, a late date for it would *require* saying that Plato's theory changed little from the middle of his life to the end. The placing of it near the time of the *Rep.*, therefore, removes a barrier to saying that it changed. But of course an earlier date does not, of itself, require us to say that it changed (see Cherniss, p. 341). What makes it desirable to say that there was a change is, given the *possibility* of placing the *Timaeus* earlier, the content of the *Cratylus*, *Parmenides*, *Theaetetus*, *Sophist* and *Polit.*

4. Thus, for example, Shorey **5**, vol. I, pp. xxiv-xxv, and Jaeger, vol. II, p. 85.

5. It seems to me that this interpretation is the most commonsensical that one could ask for. Shorey's manner of viewing the matter is for the most part correct (**5**, vol. II, p. 200, n. *a*), but he does not grant to the problems confronting Plato sufficient difficulty, and to Plato's desire to solve them sufficient meticulousness, to allow him to suppose that Plato is really still in the midst of his epistemological ruminations and does not know what to say.

6. What matters most for my purposes is that the *Symposium* is before the *Phaedrus*, which in turn is after the *Republic*. It seems as certain as such things can be that *Symp.* 193a gives a *terminus post quem* of 385 *B.C.* for the work; see Bury, pp. lxvi-lxvii and *ad loc.*, and Dover, pp. 2-9. Still, some—including Bury, *ibid.*—have wished to place the *Phaedrus* yet earlier. Sufficient answer is given to that view, it seems to me, by Robin (his **1**, p. iii), but I think there are further reasons, too, for thinking that the philosophical position of the *Phaedrus*—even aside from the use there of the method of collection and division—is more sophisticated than that of either the *Symp.* or the *Rep.*; cf. Ch. V, introd. (See also Hackforth **2**, pp. 3-5 for a survey of some other arguments for placing the *Phdr.* after the *Rep.*; and see Dover, pp. 16-20, for the removal of other difficulties.)

7. See Owen **1** and Cherniss **7**.

8. See esp. 475e-480a; for criticism of a different view of this passage, see n. IV-9.

9. See for example *Rep.* 475e4, 476b7-8, 479e7-8, 484c-d, 500c3, d4, 511a1, 526e1-4, 540a8-9; *Symp.* 210e*sqq.* It has been suggested that this way of talking is not to be taken seriously. Thus, for example, Cross pressed such a view, but he was adequately answered by Bluck **2**. More recently, Gosling **1** has interpreted *Rep.* 475ff. in a way that would support Cross's account, maintaining that that passage does not make Forms out to be the province of knowledge, or sensible objects to be the province of opinion, in the way in which more traditional interpretations would maintain. Gosling's mistake is to claim that because Plato must be arguing in such a way that his opponents, the φιλοθεάμονες of the passage, would accept his premises (which is correct), therefore the passage cannot be "relying on" the distinction between Forms and sensibles (pp. 121-122). What Gosling's argument fails to take account of is the fact that the real argument against his opponents begins in 479a, where it is established that because sensible objects have predicates true of them only in a "qualified" way, whereas Forms have the same predicates true of them "unqualifiedly," Forms and sensibles must be different. This is an argument that Plato regards as beginning with assumptions which are not question-begging and which should be accepted by his opponent. It having been agreed (on grounds given in 477e6-7—which are again non-question-begging) that *episteme* and *doxa* are different *dynameis*, and also (477c-d) that different *dynameis* have to do with different objects, Plato can conclude (given that Forms are ὄντα and sensible objects are "between τὸ ὄν and τὸ μὴ ὄν," because of the difference in the way in which predicates apply to them) that it is reasonable to say that *doxa* has to do with sensible objects, whereas *episteme* has to do with Forms. What this shows, then, is that the traditional interpretation allows Plato to push his argument through without begging the question against his opponents. But once we see that this is so, there is no objection to saying that 476c-d distinguishes between *dynameis* by the objects with which they deal. (Gosling's objections to this claim seem unconvincing anyway—pp. 124-125—because the use of the singular "ἐκεῖνο" in 447d1 is hardly sufficient to cancel the plain implication of d1-5, that a distinction is being drawn between "ἐφ ᾧ ἐστι" and "ὃ ἀπεργάζεται.")

Still, there is this apparent difficulty in the argument (which Gosling's interpretation does not help to eradicate), that whereas 477d1 gives the impression that difference of objects and effects is *the* criterion of distinctness of *dynameis*, it turns out that Plato's reason for saying that *episteme* and *doxa* differ is (and must be if his argument is not to be question-begging) that the former is, while the latter is not, infallible. But this fact does not help Gosling's position, because the view in question is one that Plato has all along thought obvious, quite independently of the theory of Forms (cf. *Gorg.* 454d; *Meno* 97d-e), so he would not regard its use as a premise here as unfair. That being the case, we can regard this difference between *episteme* and *doxa* as a difference in effect (ὃ ἀπεργάζεται), so that Plato will indeed be using the criterion of distinctness of *dynameis* which d1 announces.

10. *Rep.* 507b, 508b-c, 509d4, 529b, d-e; *Phdr.* 247c6-8. It is less clear that

Plato does not regard the experience of intellectual apprehension as, phenomenally described, a "visual" experience. One does not, to my knowledge, observe him trying to combat this idea, and some of his remarks positively encourage it (e.g., *Rep.* 514ff.; *Symp.* 210-212).

11. This notion appears in the *Phaedo*, in the course of a myth, at 109d2-5, 8-e6, 111c1-3, as well as briefly in 82e2-4 (in 83a4ff., however, "διά" takes on a different sense; cf. n. III-10). In other places Plato uses a rather different figure, which nevertheless has the same effect, of picturing us as having the Forms in view in a sense, yet being unable clearly to make them out. This is the figure according to which when one ascends from the cave into the sunlit world of intelligible objects, the light is at first too bright for one to be able to discern things (515c-516b, 532b-c, 518a1-3; cf. *Soph.* 254a8-b1). Another figure that allows a Form to be apprehended with less than maximum clarity is that trope according to which the "eye" of the soul must be "cleaned" of bodily accretions; see 527d-e with *Phdr.* 250c4-6, and *Gorg.* 523d3. His way of discussing Justice, treated in sec. 2, is in a similar vein, inasmuch as it suggests that while we have, so to speak, a dim apprehension of Justice, we need to get it more clearly in view (see also 368c-d, where it is said that we shall see Justice more clearly if we see it writ large; note esp. d4). Likewise, *Phdr.* 250b-c suggests that one may perceive a Form only poorly because one's relevant "organs" are somehow too weak or "dark." (To this point the dispute over the exact meaning of "ὀργάνων" in 250b4 is irrelevant; see Hackforth **2**, pp. 94-95 with Hermeias *ad loc.* For even if it alludes also to "arguments" or to "rules"—cf. Robin **2**, p. xcvi, n. 2—the notion here being employed is one of an organ of sense: see d2 and, for this use of "ὄργανον" in Plato, *Rep.* 508b4, 518c5.)

12. In the *Rep.* see, e.g., 475e-480a (esp. 478c), 514a-517e, 509d9, 518a-c. See also *Phdo.* 109b7, 110c-e, 111a. The metaphor here is again mine, in part: Plato tends to think of sensibles as "dark" or "unclear."

13. See n. III-26, and esp. *Rep.* 436e with Vlastos **8**, pp. 14-15.

14. Unless he thinks, for some reason that he never betrays, that we somehow *cannot* add all of the necessary qualifications.

15. See, e.g., 478c, 479c-d, 518c9. This is not to say that Plato spells out the distinction between the two ideas, but only that he shows no sign of believing that the clarity of the Forms *simply consists in* the fact that they admit unqualified predication. It is the "reality" of the Forms—the fact that they are *par excellence* ὄντα—that has the better claim to consist in the fact they admit unqualified predication; cf. n. III-25 and Vlastos **8**. (There is of course more that could be said about Plato's notion of ὄν than is directly relevant to our present purposes.)

16. This does not mean, however, that Plato always regards it as so based. The point of this remark is something that cannot be explored fully here, namely the fact that even when Plato is not explicitly entertaining the idea that Forms are, as it were, unqualified samples of characteristics of which sensible objects are qualified samples, he still tends to view sensibles as imitations or copies of Forms (at least before his later period; cf. Owen **1**, pp.

318ff.). See Ar., *Met.* 990b15-17 with Owen **2**, and note Aristotle's apparent suggestion that such entities as may be argued for by the λόγος ἐκ τῶν πρός τι are not subject to the Third Man Argument.

17. On the inference from the claim that *X* imperfectly resembles *Y* to the claim that *X* is a copy of *Y*, see n. III-23.

18. It has not been explained by others either. It is often true that if you want to know something about *X* (or about *F*s), then you are better off looking at *X* (*F*s) than at a picture of *X* (*F*s). But counterexamples are easy enough to come by, and, more important, there are plenty of things about pictures of *X* (*F*s) which you can learn better, if at all, from the picture than from examining *X* (*F*s). This point is, of course, related to a similar one which Plato later saw about pictures, in *Soph.* 239d-240c (cf. Austin **4** Ch. VII). Notice, too, that this view of the epistemic inferiority of pictures is surely linked by Plato (though it is really quite distinct from it) with the view of the ontological inferiority of pictures, as it appears in the interpretation of Lee.

19. For instances of the idea that knowledge of Forms can be a matter of *degree*, see *Rep.* 476c2-4, 479e1-2, 484c6-d1, 479a1-3, 480a1-4, 514a-517b, along with *Symp.* 210-212, *Phaedo* 65d-66a, 67c. But it is not clear precisely what Plato means to say. In the passages cited from the *Rep.*, for example, he seems to suggest that some people do not have any apprehension of Forms at all, but if this is so, then there is a conflict between this view and the notion, which we saw in the *Phaedo* (cf. Ch. III, sec. 6), that everyone who uses his senses has some kind of apprehension of Forms. (Whereas we might try to disarm 476c2-4, 479a1-2, and 480a1-4 by distinguishing between apprehending Forms and believing that there are Forms, and by saying that in these passages some are said to fail merely to do the latter, the other two passages are not similarly tractable.) Secondly, although Plato does seem clearly to allow different ways in which knowledge of Forms can be a matter of degree, he does not take pains to mark the different ways off from each other. As we shall see *infra*, he sometimes speaks as though the less fortunate see the Forms less clearly than the more fortunate, whereas at other times it seems that the former are not *as close* to seeing the Forms as the latter (e.g., *Phdo.* 65e4), or that they are somehow not looking in the right direction (*Rep.* 514ff., *Symp.* 203e4-5, *Phaedr.* 249d).

20. See 370a-b, and also 374a-d, 394e, 423c-d, 433a-b, with Shorey **5**, vol. I, p. 328, n. *d*.

21. See 443c. This is part of the matter raised by Sachs.

22. This notwithstanding the fact that 477a might seem to betray the view that only "what is not" (τὸ μὴ ὄν) can be the object of ignorance. In fact, what it must mean is that (only) "what is not" is incapable of being known.

23. That λόγῳ here means "by means of a definition" is made virtually certain by the fact that λόγον must mean "definition" in b4, and it is unlikely that Plato would change senses of the word so quickly without warning. See also n. III-58, and esp. Thompson, *loc cit.* For the significance of this fact, see sec. 5.

24. See 402b2, c5, and possibly also 515b4-5 (though on the text here see n. III-53). In a related vein Plato suggests (454a*sqq*.; cf. 382b-c) that it is possible to fall into merely apparent disagreement, when two people, whether by design or not, are using words with an eye to different things. Note esp. b6-7, and also compare the phrase in a5-7, διὰ τὸ μὴ δύνασθαι κατ᾽ εἴδη διαιρούμενοι τὸ λεγόμενον ἐπισκοπεῖν," with Plato's language in the *Phaedrus*, discussed in Ch. V, sec. 1.

25. The mechanics of thought envisioned in the passage are somewhat unclear, in ways which do not matter much for our purposes. For example, it is the soul (ψυχή) that is made to "call over" calculation to solve its problem, as presumably sensation itself would not be perplexed by the spectacle of the same thing's being both large and small; but it is clear neither what "part" or "faculty" of the soul this might be, nor that Plato's theory of the soul leaves room for the idea that the soul "as a whole" could somehow do this. That it is Forms which are the subject matter of the activity of "calculation and thought" here is plain both from c13 and e1, 6, and from the whole point of the passage, which is to discover disciplines that are conducive to knowledge of Forms.

26. Though Plato makes little of the point, 524e6 suggests that part of what calculation does, as part of its job, is to ask questions about the Form of One itself. (Note that here as elsewhere we do not have the modern distinction between "pure" and "applied" arithmetic; the contrast between the terms "ἀριθμητική" and "λογιστική" might seem to hint at this distinction, but the use of the two terms is not maintained, as 525c1 and 526b5 show.)

27. The suggestion is present in 476c5-d3, esp. d1-3, and in 534b9-c2. It may be in 515b5-c2, esp. b8-9 (though the textual difficulties in b4-5 render reasonable certainty impossible, and the language of the passage is relatively loose anyway), and perhaps also in *Tim.* 49b-50b, if part of the idea there is that we ordinarily mistake the receptacle, or parts of it, for the Forms which are somehow reflected in it. The same idea had appeared already in *Phaedo* 109c-d, e-110a, though in the context of a myth.

28. See Robinson 1, pp. 103-104, and Hare 2, esp. pp. 21-22, 24-27.

29. See esp. 533b-c, but as we shall observe in a moment (see 526a1-7 and 510d6-7, e7-511a1), the story is a bit more complicated than would be suggested by a simple contrast between what geometers are talking about and what they should be talking about.

30. See Robinson, p. 154.

31. See 531d9, 532a2, b4, d8, 533a1-10, 534e2-535a1, with Owen 7, esp. pp. 139-145, Robinson 1, pp. 198-201, 175-176, and Hare 2, pp. 30-31. 30-31.

32. See Robinson and Hare, with 527b3-8, 525d5-8, 510d7-8. There seems no reason to accept the once popular view that the "Divided Line" (509d-511e) introduces the "intermediate," "mathematical" objects, a belief in which was attributed to Plato by Aristotle in *Met.* I.9, XIII-XIV, *passim*. See against this view Robinson, pp. 181, 190-192, 197-201; Fogelin, pp. 376ff.; Shorey 5, vol. II, p. 164, n. *a*, p. 171, n. *h*, p. 206, n.*a*, and reff. therein; Sidgwick 1. In

favor of the view see Adam, vol. II, pp. 156-163, and his note on 510c; and Wedberg. Robinson, pp. 193ff., is worried about the fact that, as he thinks, Plato seems in the Divided Line to mark out four sorts of objects. He thinks that if Plato had carried this suggestion further, then he might indeed have posited mathematical objects "between" Forms and sensibles; but he thinks that Plato did not carry the suggestion through (p. 194). Now if Fogelin's interpretation is on the right track (as I think it is), then there is no problem here, and Plato's hint of four sorts of objects is, for straightforward reasons, misleading. But it is not at all clear that the passages that Robinson cites (p. 193) really show any fourfold classification of objects. They are 510b2, 511c3-6, 534a5-7. The first tells us how to cut the *part of the line* representing *noesis*, and can well be taken to be carefully avoiding the suggestion of a division of objects. If there is a division of objects in 511c, the passage pointedly avoids saying that there is no overlap of the objects of *dianoia* and the objects of *noesis* (or *nous*), and d1-2, 3-4 decisively return to a contrast between geometers and dialecticians and their respective *abilities*. Likewise, 534a fails to rule out overlap, and leaves the division of intelligible objects undescribed (see Shorey **5**, *ad loc.*).

33. Cf. Robinson, pp. 172-176.

34. The following interpretation is basically similar to that of Wedberg, pp. 53-62, and fits neatly with much of what is said by Fogelin. (The main point at which I take exception to his interpretation has to do with his claim in pp. 372-378, that somehow the Form of the Good "has no place" on the Line of 509-511. The evidence that he provides is insufficient to support this view, and his argument depends heavily on a notion of what it is for the sun to "reign over" the visible world which, at the very least, needs to be argued more fully, and which ignores Robinson's arguments, pp. 181-190, against assuming too strict a parallelism among the figures of the Sun, the Line, and the Cave. One thing that militates against attributing too special a position to the Good is the fact that in 534b-c we are said to need a *logos* of it, as of everything else; but cf. the following section, and n. IV-62.) The crucial point of Fogelin's interpretation (see esp. pp. 379-381) is that the objects with which geometry deals are just sensible objects, but sensible objects treated as images of Forms. This can easily be taken to be another way of putting the interpretation offered here.

It seems, moreover, that one difficulty that Fogelin finds in his own interpretation can be removed. On p. 382 he says that he does not see how the allegory of the Cave can "represent the idea that one and the same thing can both have an image and be used as an image." But why is this idea not represented by the claim that the objects whose reflections appear on the wall of the cave are themselves copies of objects in the outer world? So the moral is that when you are in the cave, you cannot tell that statues are copies (all you realize is that the shadows are their copies), but when you emerge into the light you become aware that they are.

35. See Owen **2**, p. 311, on the fact that the "defectiveness" of sensible objects is viewed by Plato in different ways for different cases. See also Ch.

III, sec. 2, and *Rep*. 525d-526b, 529c-530a, *Ep*. VII, 342a*sqq*., with Wedberg, pp. 49-50. Note esp. 529c-d, where there seems to be a contrast between, e.g., motion along an exactly circular path and motion along a path that is not quite exactly circular; and also 530e-531a, on exact *vs.* inexact musical intervals. (On a similar matter, see Ar., *An. Post.* 76b39-77a3.) As was remarked in Ch. III, sec. 2, Plato's move from saying that a thing is *F* with qualification to saying that it is *F* defectively is a dubious one (cf. n. III-23). Likewise, there is a considerable difference between the way in which something *inexactly* triangular is only defectively (or qualifiedly) a triangle, and the way in which something large *compared* to another thing could be thought of as only defectively (or qualifiedly) large. The tendency to assimilate these sorts of cases is an unnatural feature of Plato's theory.

36. Not, that is, if you take "Every *A* is *B*" to be compatible with there being no *A*s. But if you take "Every *A* is *B*" to imply "Some *A* is *B*," in the manner of Ar., *An. Pr.* 25a17-18, then the geometers' claims can indeed be expressed by statements of the form of (1).

37. Cf. n. IV-32, along with "the square itself" and "the diagonal itself" in 510d7-8.

38. More strictly, Plato takes geometers somehow to be talking about sensible objects (that is, they phrase their statements as though they were about sensibles), while at the same time thinking (or at least, trying to think: "ζητοῦντες" in 510e3) about Forms; see esp. 510d5-7, 525d-526a (where the mathematicians are pictured as realizing that they do not, after all, want to be dealing with sensible units), and possibly 533b8-c1 (cf. n. III-53).

39. 525d-526b shows plainly Plato's view that the statements of mathematicians of his day could not stand up under the observation that the sensible objects that they seemed to be talking about did not fit the specifications that were being imposed on them. For Plato there represents the contemporary mathematician as insisting that you not regard as divisible what he takes to be a unit, and as then admitting (526a6-7) that what he really wants to talk about are not sensible.

40. See esp. 511c1-2.

41. See Hare, pp. 22-24, for a related observation. More directly on the point, however, is the fact that "λόγος" in 533c2 on the one hand, and in 534b3, 4, 9, c3 on the other, seems to carry quite different senses: something like "justification" in the former case, and something closer to "definition" in the latter.

42. Indeed, he quite certainly is aware that he does not know how one would look, at least with any clarity (cf. Ch. IV, introd.).

43. This interpretation, then, presses home the account that is given more tentatively by Hare **2**, pp. 30-31, and Robinson **1**, pp. 199-201. Notice, too, that we can overcome an obstacle that Robinson, pp. 198, 200, 103-104, sees in the way of his interpretation. He is afraid that 510b5 and 511a4, when they say that geometry is "forced" to use hypotheses, may be saying that there is something irredeemably wrong with geometry. But in both of those passages

this constraint on geometry is explicitly tied to the fact that they use images (510b4-5, 511a6-7). On the present interpretation, it is clear why geometry can be redeemed by the realization that Forms are its proper subject matter and the consequent abandonment of the idea that it must use images. In addition, the present interpretation yields a clear account of what Plato means when he says that dialectic "removes" (ἀναιρεῖ) hypotheses (533c5). This remark has seemed puzzling, even to Robinson, who gets close to the correct interpretation of it when he says (p. 161) that what dialectic does is to remove the "hypothetical character" of, e.g., geometrical axioms. Plato does mean this, in part, but he also means—what makes his phraseology more understandable—that dialectic will cease to cast those axioms in the way in which the geometer ordinarily casts them and will instead adopt a different, less misleading, manner of putting them.

44. This interpretation does not entail saying that Plato regarded reformed mathematical science as being *the same as* dialectic. For good reasons for rejecting this view, see Shorey **5**, vol. II, p. 169, n.*f*.

45. Concerning this general line of interpretation I am in agreement with Robinson, Ch. VIII-X.

46. As Robinson argues (pp. 29-32), Plato seems to regard this sort of "*elenchus*" as the derivation from a statement of a *self-contradiction*. On the connection of this way of so regarding it with other features of Plato's early doctrine, cf. n. I-70. (At *Rep.* 487b6-7, he talks as though the consequences of a proposition could contradict that proposition itself—apparently even if the proposition were not self-contradictory.)

47. For an argument for this interpreation, see Robinson, Ch. X (cf. n. III-62).

48. Cf. also Owen **7**, pp. 139-145.

49. See 510b6-9, 511b7-c2, 517b8-c1, 519e9-d1, 526e1-4, 532a5-b2, 533b-e, along with Robinson, pp. 159-160, 176; Shorey **5**, vol. II, p. 110, n. *a*; and Adam's note on 510c. On the idea that a proposition is involved, cf. *infra*.

50. Thus, Robinson, pp. 172-177, calls this account of Plato's doctrine the "intuition" interpretation. Shorey denies that the Form of the Good plays quite this role, noting that in 534b8-c5 Plato does not say that he who does not know the Good knows no other Form but only that he knows "no other good (thing)" (ἄλλο ἀγαθὸν οὐδέν). But the comparison of the Good to the sun in 507-509 certainly suggests (esp. 508e1-509a5, b6-8) that the Good is what makes possible knowledge of any knowable thing. Moreover, the line of interpretation offered in this section, *infra*, allows us to accommodate the passages cited by Shorey, by observing that in a substantial sense all of the Forms are good things, as intended in 534c5, in the sense that they are good or nondefective specimens of their kind.

What, then, of Forms associated with predicates that might seem ineluctably "bad" (cf. Vlastos **8**, p. 8, n. 1)? If there is a paradox here, it is not one that Plato ever faced (unless the *Sophist*, with its account of "what is not," including its privative sense, should be viewed as a treatment of it). Note that on some views, Plato would be accused of failing to distinguish the notion of goodness-of-a-kind, and perhaps the notion of perfection, from other sorts of goodness; see e.g., Geach **1** and Hare **1**.

A quite different account of Plato's reflections about the good is given by Irwin, esp. pp. 763-772. On this account, Plato's view arises out of a certain diagnosis of a problem that had afflicted Socrates (or Plato in the early dialogues) about how to specify the final good independently of the actions that we seem to take in pursuit of it. Irwin believes that Plato answers this problem by maintaining a view under which there is no "independent standard" (p. 770) for the correctness of one's total moral view, but only a kind of internal "coherence" (p. 771). There seems to me little reason, however, to believe this conclusion, which runs counter to the general tendency of most of Plato's thought. It is true that the method of hypothesis begins merely as a way of gaining, *inter alia*, consistency (Ch. III, sec. 7), but Irwin does not disarm the evidence that the *Rep.* is going farther (esp. the talk in 533c about the desirability of turning ὁμολογία, consistency, into knowledge; cf. *Crat.* 436c-d). It is likewise dubious that Plato diagnoses Socrates' difficulty in the manner that Irwin supposes he did (and supposes that it should be diagnosed), and it is equally dubious that the treatment of "ascent" in *Symp.* 209ff. is an account merely of "mutual adjustments between desires and beliefs" (p. 765).

51. There is no evidence that Plato ever exploited the idea of packing a great deal into a single proposition by conjoining many smaller propositions into a larger one.

52. *Rep.* 505a6-7 appears to go against this claim, but it is provisional, and is quickly disarmed by c2-4, e1-3, and 506a6-7.

53. Alternatively (cf. sec. 2), the idea is that one's "mental gaze" will turn in the direction of the other Forms only after it has turned in the direction of the Good. Analogous questions can be raised about this assumption, and what I shall say will, *mutatis mutandis*, apply to it.

54. Cf. n. III-18, and Ch. VIII-IX. For the same reason we cannot explain matters by a simple invocation of one of the contrasts between "knowledge of" and "knowledge that," or between "propositional knowledge" and "knowledge by acquaintance" or between "savoir" and "connaître" or "wissen" and "kennen" (cf. n. II-29).

55. See sec. 3. For the possibility that he takes a different view later on, see Ch. VIII, sec. 3. It is interesting to note that in *Tim.* 71dsqq. we seem to have the idea that a mantic can *apprehend* Forms but lacks the ability to *identify* or *recognize* the particular ones that he is apprehending. I think—although the point cannot be argued here—that Plato believes something similar about poets.

56. A possible qualm about this account would have to do with the fact that this doctrine might seem to make "relational entities" of all other Forms, in the sense of Ch. III, sec. 3. But there is some considerable reason for saying that Plato accepted this consequence. For remember that he says not only that the Good makes knowledge of other things possible but also that it gives

"being" to all other things (509b6-8). The present interpretation handles this fact nicely, since other Forms turn out to depend on the Good for their "being" in the same manner that sensible objects depend on Forms for theirs (see esp. n. III-36). (Further material on this issue is to be found, perhaps, in Aristotle's *De Bono*, and in the many scholarly discussions of it, but the matter is cloudy.)

57. For this idea see Hare, pp. 35-36.

58. See Sidgwick **2**, pp. 38-40; Shorey **1**, p. 227; Ross **2**, pp. 41-43; Shorey **5**, vol. II, pp. xxxv-xxxvi and 106, n. *a*. (There is a difficulty, perhaps, in the fact that Plato may have admitted what we might call "bad Forms," such as the Form of Injustice; see Vlastos **8**, p. 8, n. 1.) (This talk of "relations" and "reference" to the Good is, of course, impressionistic, though perhaps it could be made more precise.)

59. The central position that Plato gives quite generally to the Good shows that it is no accident that the account of Justice can be seen to fit this general pattern. It is not simply that Plato wants to show that Justice is a good. It is that every Form must be seen in its relation to the Good.

60. First, Plato has generally pictured the progress of a dialectical argument as proceeding by deduction (see Robinson **1**, p. 105). Second, it would appear that Plato regarded geometry, e.g., as proceeding by deductive steps, and he seems to think that the relation between the unhypothesized beginning is the same as the relation between the geometer's hypotheses and the statements that he derives from his hypotheses (though I know of no place where he actually says this).

61. In particular, he does not clarify the matter in 510-511 or in 532-534. Indeed, it would have been difficult for him to see its point, if he was as prone as he seems to have been to regard his "hypotheses" indifferently as *statements* of science and as *objects* (Forms) with which science deals (see n. IV-41 and Robinson **1**, p. 103, and Hare **2**, pp. 22-24).

62. From the popular view that Plato makes the Good out to be in some strong sense "transcendent," it is easy to conclude that whereas there may be specifications of the other Forms in terms of their relations to the Good, there should be no specification of the Good itself. This part of the view, however, jibes with what we have seen, since there is a sense in which, for us, the Good would not be specified (in the sense, that is, in which the location of the origin of a Cartesian coordinate system might be thought of as unspecified). On the other hand, it seems unmistakable that in 534b8ff. (cf. also 532a6-b2), Plato does say that there will be a *logos* of the Good distinguishing it from everything else (cf. n. IV-23). (Nor is *Symp.* 211a7 counterevidence, because it plainly does *not* say that there is no *logos* or knowledge of the Beautiful; cf. Bury *ad loc.*) There is no contradiction here, of course, because Plato has not committed himself to the view that everything specifiable must be specified by reference to the Good or by reference to something other than itself; rather, there is just a mystery over what sort of *logos* of the Good there could be. The mystery has led some (e.g., Shorey **5**, vol. II, p. 206, n. *d*) to question the idea

that the Good stands at the head of each piece of "downward" hypothetical reasoning. But although it may be hard to see what sort of *logos* Plato might hope to provide for the Good, his reason for thinking that there is one is probably in part plain common sense: the reflection (*Laches* 190c, e.g.) that if you can recognize a thing, then you ought to have some way of describing it. (What he is not here insisting on—and what has raised problems for him in the *Meno*—is that one have a description or specification in hand *before* one can recognize the thing.)

One is tempted to say, in reply to the question how the Good, or a correct definition of it, is to be recognized, that we simply have to know that when there is disagreement over some relevant issue, then one party or another must simply not have a clear or correct view, or account, of the Good. But this reply is insufficient, because the actual absence of disagreement is no guarantee that it will not arise, and Plato is aiming at more than merely such provisional conclusions, and at more than mere consistency (see n. IV-50). Disagreement, whether it is between opinions of two different people or between two opinions of the same person, shows that something is wrong; but agreement is no guarantee by itself that everything is right, in the sense that Plato wishes (cf. Ch. IX, sec. 2).

63. For important lines of debate, see Shorey 1, esp. pp. 231-239. Because I am not certain of the force of his denial that the "unhypothetical beginning" is to be taken in an "ontological" sense (p. 231), I am uncertain whether my conception of that notion is the same as his. Nevertheless, I do agree with his contention that there is nothing importantly "mystical" at work (p. 230). There is much that is unclear, in a fundamental way (this Shorey would probably deny), but there is no reason to think that Plato is content with the unclarity.

CHAPTER V

The Phaedrus: New Problems of Language and Method

The *Phaedrus* is an easy work to misevaluate and to misunderstand. It has generally been accorded importance as the first dialogue in which Plato unveils a new method to be used by dialectic, namely the method of "collection and division," which plays a considerable role in later works.[1] But the method is not very carefully explained in the *Phaedrus*, and this fact, along with the fact that the dialogue contains much that is obscure, have made those who prefer philosophy to be clear and straightforward tend to neglect this work. There is, however, rather more to be extracted from the *Phaedrus* than this attitude might encourage one to look for, as one can see when one realizes the extent to which the *Phaedrus* is responding to problems that have arisen in the course of Plato's previous work.

One of the signs of this fact is that in the *Phaedrus* Plato starts to take a harder look than he had at the nature of language, and at the puzzles which it might put in his way. He is becoming dissatisfied with the simple picture, taken for granted in the *Phaedo* and the *Republic*, of the relationship between words and Forms (Ch. III, sec. 5) and begins to question it, realizing that in many cases it will be unsatisfactory to say simply that a given predicate, say "*F*," corresponds to the Form of *F*, and undertaking to construct a view that allows for greater complexity.

This fact ought to make us feel confident of the idea that the *Phaedrus* was written after the *Republic*.[2] This idea was already almost certain anyway, because the *Phaedrus* resoundingly introduces the method of collection and division, of which the *Republic* and earlier dialogues made no use;[3] but the following pages will show the reasons for this methodological innovation, and the certainty of the chronological order will accordingly become greater. Another chronological point will also become clearer. By the time we have finished discussing the *Cratylus* in the following chapter, it will be clear that that work came after the *Phaedrus*. The reason why we may be sure of this claim is that although the *Phaedrus* makes important strides in raising questions about language and its connection with the Forms, the *Cratylus* delves into these issues more deeply, in a way which makes it implausible to think that the *Phaedrus* was written after the investigations of the *Cratylus* had taken place.[4] In fact, once we see the main thrust of the *Phaedrus,* it will be easy to see why the *Cratylus*, if it was written soon afterward, should have taken up the issues that it did. The *Theaetetus*, often grouped with the *Phaedrus* as a sort of companion-piece, clearly goes well beyond both the *Phaedrus* and the *Cratylus* in dealing with the epistemological issues which arise in all three of them.[5]

We can set the stage for our discussion of the *Phaedrus* by noticing some fairly obvious facts. In the first place, the view of the *Republic* and earlier works, that one's mind has an ability to "view" Forms, and that this ability is highly desirable, is much in evidence in the *Phaedrus*. Indeed, more is made of it in this work than in practically any other (e.g., 247-248, 249e4-5, 254b5-7).[6] In the second place, the *Phaedrus* is one of the three dialogues (the others being the *Meno* and the *Phaedo*) in which the doctrine of recollection plays a major speaking role.[7] The view of the *Phaedrus*, like that of the *Phaedo*, is that such recollection takes place to some extent in everyone—not just in fully mature philosophical activity, but in judgments made by ordinary people at ordinary times.[8] Finally, the *Phaedrus* retains Plato's longstanding concern to discover definitions, and the view that they are crucial to his epistemological enterprise.[9] We have, in sum, the ingredients of the problems with which we have been occupied.

1 The Method of Collection and Division

The new method of collection and division in the *Phaedrus* is a response to a set of problems which has already made its appearance in the *Republic* in a tangential way and is now expanded and viewed in a more systematic light. We have already seen that the *Republic* calls on the art of calculation to avoid the conflation of distinct Forms which are jointly and simultaneously exhibited in sensible objects, and in so doing recognizes the possibility of a certain sort of conceptual confusion (Ch. IV, sec. 2). The *Phaedrus* shows related worries concerning the possibility that different Forms may somehow be confused with one another, and also the possibility that different people may call to mind different Forms in response to the same word. This preoccupation is clearly in evidence in 260ff., (esp. 260b, c, 261c-262a, 263a-c; see also 237b7-c2, 275d7-e2).[10] It is problematical, however, just what role the problem has in the discussion of that passage. For example, does Plato think that mistaken judgments of ordinary predicative form (such as "That raven is white") are caused by one's somehow mistaking one thing, such as a Form, for another (e.g., whiteness for blackness)? One might thus take 260b as saying that a man who falsely believes that a certain object is a horse when it is actually an ass may in a sense be mistaking the Form, Ass, for the Form, Horse. It is certainly not clear that Plato thinks that all such false beliefs are caused by this sort of mistake,[11] but it is not unlikely that he thinks that some of them are, and it is plain that he is concerned with the possibility of some sort of mistaken identification.[12]

Concern with mistaken identification plays an important part, too, in Plato's discussion of the official subject matter of the *Phaedrus*, namely love. The *Phaedrus* contains a number of disparate and confusingly related accounts of what love is, and Plato traces much of the confusion and disagreement to a failure to see. that the word "love" may be used to correspond to quite different things (237b-d, 263d-e, 265e-266a, etc.).[13] In addition, Plato suggests that madness (μανία) also is, as it were, not a single thing, but that there are a number of things that go by that name (this is clear by 244a; see also 265e-266a). It is the confusion of different things that are called "love," and also of different things that are called "madness," which, he thinks, are responsible for conflicting views about whether love, and madness, are good things or not (cf. 260c). It is equally clear that, according to Plato, the method of division (I shall call it this for short, instead of "the method of collection and division"; cf. n. 28) is being used to try to avoid this confusion (265e-266a).

Before we go on to see what the method of division is and how Plato expects it to help him, let us pause to consider the relationship between the *Phaedrus* and the other dialogue that has much to do with love, the *Symposium*. It has often been observed that the discussion of love in the *Symposium* is less complex than that which we find in the *Phaedrus*.[14] What we can now see is that the *Phaedrus* attempts to diagnose and cure some of the difficulties that plagued the discussion of love in the other work. The *Symposium* contains a number of conflicting accounts of what love is and what it is like, capped by a final account by Socrates which is obviously meant to be superior to the ones that precede it. But the *Symposium* does not attempt, as the *Phaedrus* does, to explain how this confusion and disagreement over love arose. All the more reason, then, to regard the *Symposium* as the earlier work.

Now let us see what the method of division, along with the companion method of collection, amounts to. It is expounded only briefly in the *Phaedrus*, in 264e-266b. Collection is explained first, as the procedure

> . . . in which we bring a dispersed plurality under a single form (εἰς μίαν ἰδέαν), seeing it all together: the purpose being to define so-and-so, and thus to make plain whatever may be chosen as the topic for exposition . . . (265d3-5).[15]

Division is then explained as follows (e1-3):

> [It is] the reverse of the other, whereby we are enabled to divide into forms, following the objective articulation (κατ' εἴδη διατέμνειν κατ' ἄρθρα ᾗ πέφυκεν); we are not to attempt to hack off parts like a clumsy butcher . . . .

This is the substance of the account, which is followed by an example of the method, taken from what has gone before. From this and what Plato says elsewhere about the two methods, we can piece together the following rough idea of what is going on, simplified so as to focus on our main concerns. First, we somehow specify a broad class of things that we are talking about,[16] under which we presumably know in advance that there are important subclasses. We then divide this broad class into those subclasses, giving a specification of each. This division is carried on in stages: first we divide the original broad class into two or more subclasses; then we divide the subclasses; then the subclasses of the subclasses; and so on until we reach the end of the division, which Plato takes to be a juncture at which the classes can no longer properly be divided. The idea is that by the end of this process of division, we shall have reached subclasses that are of particular interest to whatever discussion it was in a particular case that precipitated the use of the two methods.

There are questions to be raised at virtually every stage of this account of the methods, and whereas I do not propose to discuss all of them, there are a few salient points that must be mentioned. In the first place, although for convenience I have talked as though what are involved are classes, and although Plato often talks in this way too, such a manner of speaking is inaccurate. Plato does not have anything quite like the modern notion of a class or set. Rather, in spite of his occasional class-like talk, he gives every sign of thinking that the entities involved in collection and division are Forms (note "ἰδέαν" and "εἴδη" in 265d3, e1), and that Forms are not classes.[17] But this idea of his leads to a second problem, which arises over the question what it can mean to "divide" a Form, and what it can mean to divide a Form into other Forms. This problem leads us straight into some important issues in Platonic metaphysics, which have exercised commentators since Aristotle (cf. n. 17). Fortunately, however, these issues need not impinge on our discussion. Last, there is a difficulty over both what Plato means by "following objective articulations," and also what method he has of telling that a division has come to an end. The latter of these last two problems can be left aside here.

The former, however, is more important to us. It leads us straight into a Platonic version of the doctrine of "natural kinds." If we use talk of classes, the idea is that not every way of partitioning a class yields genuine subclasses, but rather that some subclasses are genuine and some are not. We saw this idea much earlier, in the view that not any and every random group of things has a Form corresponding to it, but that only some groups do, and that it is the existence of certain Forms that apparently explains why certain groupings are legitimate and others are not (cf. Ch. I, sec. 1). In the *Phaedrus*, however, this idea gains an explicitness which it did not have before; and the explicitness remains in subsequent works. In the *Statesman*, for example, it is denied that the class of non-Greeks is a genuine group (262c-e). This is not to say that Plato gives any clear criterion for determining what is a genuine class and what is not. In fact, he seems to think that it will generally be obvious.[18] This is a disputable contention, but we need not examine it here.[19] What concerns us is simply that he holds this view, and that it plays a role in his cogitations on the matters with which we are occupied. If we switch from talk of classes to talk of Forms, the important fact to see is that not everything that might appear to be a genuine Form really is one. There could not, for example, be a Form such as the Form of Barbarian, and anyone who thought that there was would be regarding as a unity, or unitary thing, something which is not so, and thus would be incorrect.[20] Moreover, Plato makes it clear that he thinks that anything that cannot be reached by a division according to natural "articulations" is a bogus entity.[21] It is the function of dialectic, as he now conceives it, to eliminate one by one the notions of such bogus entities and to make us see which things are the genuine units.

It is at this point that we begin to perceive the relevance, as Plato sees it, of the method of division to the effort to avoid confusing different Forms or concepts. Plato here regards such mistakes as much like literal fusings or conflatings of entities which do not, in fact, go together to make up a genuine unit. We have seen that the method of collection and division is supposed to help us avoid the problems that led to conflicting views of love in the early part of the dialogue. There, love was argued to be both a good and a bad thing, and Plato is now claiming that the conflict arose because we did not keep two sorts of love separate from one another (265e-266a, esp. a3-5 vs. 6-7). What he has in mind is that when we were puzzling over this conflict and were inclined to accept both that love was a good thing and that it was a bad thing, we were somehow combining the two distinct kinds of love into one, and making a judgment of value about this—as it were—conflated entity. The cure for our puzzlement was to see that this entity was bogus, and that it was composed, in our minds, of two distinct and separate things which we had wrongly tried to weld, so to speak, into one. But, Plato claims, they cannot be thus welded, because there is in actual fact a boundary between them which his method will eventually reveal.

The same idea shows itself in works other than the *Phaedrus*, and is not an unnatural one. It is easy in English as in Greek, when one wishes to express the idea that X and Y are identical with each other, to say that they "are one," and it is likewise easy to say that they "are two" when one means that they are nonidentical. But although "X is identical with Y" and "X and Y go together to make up a unitary object" are quite different forms of sentence, "X and Y are one" (or "X is one with Y") can easily be used in the sense of either. Plato's phraseology sometimes straddles this borderline, as at *Statesman* 258c5-6, e8-11, 259c1-2, 262a-b, d4-6, 263c10, and *Philebus* 26c1-2, e6-8, 57b9-c1.[22] In like manner, we saw that in the passage of the *Republic* where we saw Plato considering the confusions engendered by sensible objects (522ff., on which see Ch. IV, sec. 1), he already showed the tendency to regard these confusions as similar to conflations of two things into one.[23] One important reason for this tendency was undoubtedly the fact that in that passage his mind was on the idea that two contrary attributes, such as largeness and smallness, could cause confusion to our sight because of being mixed together, as it were in the same sensible object (note συγκεχυμένον in 524c4 and συγκεχυμένα in c7). Plato's picture of the matter need not be that one has one's apprehensions of two Forms literally mixed or superimposed with each other as one views them. His account does not become that fixed or vivid, and his manner of speaking can in large part be simply a reflection of the idea that a single word may be ambiguous in its general use and correspond to more than one thing. Still, the fact that he does speak in this way must have had its effect, and it makes intelligible the fact, otherwise somewhat odd, that the method which he introduces as a device for avoiding conceptual confusion is described by him as a method of cutting things according to their natural articulations.

But much more important than his particular manner of thinking of the matter is the fact that in announcing the new method as the chief tool of the dialectician, Plato is exhibiting an important shift of attention, if not an outright change of view. We need not decide whether he continues to accept the central ideas of the *Republic* concerning dialectic, namely the method of hypothesis and the notion that the Form of the Good may be invoked to gain more than merely provisional conclusions (Ch. IV, secs. 4-5). For even if he does, he makes no use of them in the campaign against the confusions that the method of division is intended to combat. Rather, the new method is left to function quite on its own.[24]

The importance of this fact is considerable, though it cannot be fully assessed until we have seen the later development of Plato's epistemological views (see esp. Ch. IX, secs. 1, 2). In the first place, the claim in the *Republic* that the Form of the Good illuminates the intelligible world, and the further things that Plato said in that same vein, fell short of being an explanation of how one might actually avoid mistakes or confusions. The new method is meant to make good that deficiency. Even more far-reaching in its effect, however, is the fact that the eclipse of the method of hypothesis, which now ceases to figure explicitly in Plato's reflections on method, itself leaves an important gap. A crucial feature of that method was that it provided the beginnings of an account of how our investigations into Forms and definitions could begin, and we saw that such an account was for Plato an urgent need.[25] But the method that replaces it provides no general substitute for it.[26] In narrowing his attention to focus on a particular problem and in thus neglecting to elaborate the broader account of the relationship between the goals of investigation and its starting points in hypotheses—an account that the earlier method gave promise of supplying—Plato is laying aside a problem of vital importance to his philosophical enterprise.

2 New Views on Language

Plato's attempt at a systematic attack upon conceptual confusions involves what is in effect a recognition of the importance of problems of ambiguity in the use of words.[27] Moreover, since the methods of collection and division have as their aim to establish definitions, they involve the recognition that the same term, in its customary employments, may have more than one definition. Thus, the effort to avoid conflation is seen by Plato as an aspect, though a newly emphasized one, of the old quest for definitions. What is missing is of course any clear way of telling whether or not a definition is correct, though the methods might be of some help in making distinctions and noticing ambiguities.[28] Still, the realization of the importance of the fact that a term may be ambiguous, or have different definitions, or correspond to more than one Form, is of obvious importance. It marks a change from Plato's earlier days of tending not to think about ambiguity in a sufficiently thoroughgoing way, or to ask in detail what issues this notion might raise in connection with his own methods (Ch. II, sec. 2). It likewise marks a change from his tendency in the *Phaedo* to think that the correspondence between Forms and terms is unproblematical, as though all there were to say is that a term corresponds to its own Form. Words, as he now emphasizes, may deceive us.

It must appear no accident that the most famous, or notorious, part of the *Phaedrus* has been the section toward the end of the work devoted to—as it has been taken—an attack on written language (274b-278e). Some interpreters have been inclined to take Plato as signaling to us here that we are not to take his voluminous writings quite seriously as evidence for his philosophical views.[29] What better evidence they might hope to have is, of course, a problem. Other commentators, while rightly resisting this interpretation, have tended to throw up their hands at this point, and the result is that much in the passage remains obscure. What we have already seen, however, enables us to understand Plato's motives in writing the passage and to comprehend how it arises in a natural manner out of his earlier reflections and the problems that they face.[30]

Until the *Phaedrus*, Plato has for the most part paid little heed to certain problems that confront one who is trying to cast his mind from a term in his language to a Form that corresponds to it. With the emergence of the preoccupations described in the previous section, this neglect begins to cease. In particular, Plato can now realize plainly that if two people are attempting to communicate with each other, problems can be raised by ambiguity, and that if it is afoot, there may be nothing gained by telling someone simply to "look to the Form of *F*," since what comes to his mind may be the wrong thing. In the *Cratylus*, Plato will start to wonder more deeply what it is, in the first place, for a term to correspond to a Form. For the moment, however, he still accepts that notion, but starts to see it as a defect of words that they do not, as it were, clearly show us what Forms they correspond to. It is these worries that lead to the discussion at the end of the *Phaedrus*.

What is the nature of his complaint about language as he states it in this dialogue? His complaint appears at first to be directed merely against written language, but that is only part of the story. He says that there is no way in which, for example, one can cross-examine a book to find out what it really means, and he also says that the use of writing tends to discourage the use of memory. But it is clear that he is praising by contrast not *all* spoken words, but only words which are spoken by one who "knows" and which are spoken "with knowledge" (276a, c3-4, e; cf. 275d1, 277b5-6, d1-2). He also maintains here that what is necessary is long and arduous training, thus clearly implying that the mere spouting of a stream of oral verbiage is not at all what he is encouraging (277e8-9). Rather, what we need is knowledge of Forms, the ability to apprehend them and to recognize the ones we are after. He gives reasons why he thinks that writing is a poor tool in the achievement of this end, but writing *per se* is not his primary target. As applied to his own written work, his moral can only be that, for example, the mere ability to recite his dialogues, or to pull them off the shelf and read them, is no insurance against the most egregious lack of that knowledge of Forms which he recommends.[31] For in the midst of his attack on ignorant and unproductive uses of writing, he takes care to point out that written work can be an aid to memory, provided that it is used to stimulate oneself fully to rethink those matters with which it deals (276d1-5).

What the *Phaedrus* reveals, therefore, is a considered view, based on earlier and more recent reflections, of the pitfalls of language, of the dangers of ambiguity, and of the lively possibility that one's words will be misunderstood. Beginning in this work, Plato's attention to these problems exerts an ever greater influence on his epistemology.

Notes

1. See, e.g., Hackforth **2**, pp. 134-136, esp. 135, n. 1; Ross **2**, pp. 80-82; Robinson **1**, pp. 52, 70, 162-165, 280.

2. See Ch. III, sec. 6, and Ch. IV, sec. 6. On other arguments for dating the *Phdr.* after the *Rep.* see Hackforth, pp. 3ff., and the references therein. Robin's chronological association of the *Phdr.* with the *Tht.* is for the most part sensible (see his **2**), but it leaves out of account the matters that induce me to order them as I do.

3. See e.g., the remarks of Hackforth, p. 135, n. 1.

4. Consider, for example, 238a-b. It adopts a view quite the same as the one in *Phdo.* 102-103, that objects simply "get their names" from characteristics which they have (Ch. III, sec. 5). The rest of the *Phdr.* will show something of why this is too simple a picture, but the *Crat.* pounces on this matter from the start and discusses it at length. Thus the remarks of 238a-b would look extraordinarily primitive to anyone (including Plato) who had the *Crat.* in mind, and it would be very difficult to see why Plato would have written them as they are. Furthermore, at 275d4ff. he suggests in a very brief and offhand way that language is similar to painting; but the *Crat.* investigates at length the idea that words resemble the objects they are about, and if he had already discussed that idea one would expect him here to say a bit more about it. Analogous remarks apply to "ὀνόματα τιθέμενοι" at 244b7.

5. It seems to me quite clear that the *Parm.*, about which there will be little said here, comes after the *Phdr.*, after the *Crat.*, and, most probably, after the *Tht.* The arguments advanced by von Arnim for dating the *Phdr.* after both the *Tht.* and the *Parm.* are hardly cogent (esp. pp. 192-197, 202-205). I shall not attempt here to say much about how the *Parm.* fits into the scheme of things, since it has little of importance to say directly about the epistemological aspects of the theory of Forms (thus, the matter raised in 133a-135b is a corollary, bearing on the notion of knowledge, of a claim about the relationship between Forms and particulars, but its main interest lies outside the area of our concern.)

6. As in earlier works, Plato is not always meticulous in marking the contrast between apprehending a Form and bringing a definition to mind. A grammatical difficulty offers itself as a part of the reason (though only a part of it). Recall the remark in n. II-31 on the contrast between *quid* and *quod*, and note that in 237c1-5, d1-2, 238e2, it is possible to read Plato as saying either that what we "look to" (ἀποβλέπειν) is a definition or that it is the object that is defined (in this case, love). Indeed, the words "ὃ μὲν δὴ τυγχάνει ὄν . . . εἴρηταί τε καὶ ὥρισται, βλέποντες δὲ δὴ πρὸς αὐτό . . ." (238d8-9) were cer-

tainly ones which could lend themselves to the confusion in question, because the underlined phrase could be read either as a relative clause or as an indirect question, and therefore Plato could be saying that we should "look to *that which* . . ." or that we should "look to *what* . . ." (cf. Smyth, sec. 2668). The former suggests the idea of looking to the object, while the latter suggests the idea of looking to the answer to a question, i.e., to the definition given in answer to the question "What is so-and-so?" (Indeed, Smyth also suggests, 2668a, that Greek might generally be a bit hazy about the relevant grammatical distinction in such contexts, and also notes, in 2668d, that serious ambiguities may arise in the use of such constructions.) It is possible (though perhaps more difficult because of the presence of "αὐτό") to see the same lack of clarity in many of Plato's uses of the phrase "αὐτὸ ὅ ἔστιν," as at *Rep.* 532a7, b1. The confusion of the relative clause and the indirect question is not as trivial or as difficult for philosophers to make as one might think; see Austin **3**, pp. 64-65.

7. Plato's words are a bit equivocal in one respect, since he does not make totally clear here whether to recollect a Form is to call up some sort of memory-image of it or to perceive it (however dimly) anew and recognize it as what one has seen before (cf. n. II-38). The former view is probably given by 249-250, esp. 249b6-c1, and the latter is perhaps present in 254b5-7 (though the wording is hardly unambiguous). For similar indecision see *Rep.* 484c7-d1. For discussion of the appearance of the notion of recollection after the *Meno*, see Hackforth **3**, p. 77; Bluck **4**, pp. 47-61; Cherniss **3**, p. 69, n. 53; Gulley **1**, esp. pp. 200ff. Henceforth I shall simply say "view" instead of "view or recollect," except where the difference is important.

8. See 249-250, esp. 249b6-c1, e4-5; cf. Ch. III, sec. 6. (This notion is, of course, connected with what I called the "semantic" consideration for the existence of Forms.) It is true that 250a comes very close to suggesting that less fortunate people have no memory of the Forms left at all. But it does not quite say so: note the qualification "ἱκανῶς" at a5. And in 249b-c Plato clearly is thinking that the ability to use language and classify things at all must require some sort of apprehension of the Forms. (I take it that as Hackforth argues *ad loc.*, Heindorf's addition of "τό" and Badham's emendation "ἰόντ'" in 249b7 are necessary.) As earlier (cf. Ch. II, sec. 5), Plato wants to suppose in effect that there are two sorts (or degrees) of "recollection," one which is required for the ordinary man's use of language, and the other of which is required for being able to "know what such-and-such is" and to give a definition of it, but he never takes the time to sort these two uses out from each other very explicitly (though he had made a bare start at *Meno* 97-98).

9. See 237c-d, 238b-c, 277b-c, noting "ὅρος" and "ὁρίζεσθαι", as well as the use made in the later *Soph.* and *Polit.* of the method of division in constructing definitions.

10. The vocabulary of Forms occurs at 265d3, e1, where Plato is summing up the purpose of the method of collection and division. Some would say that Plato has radically changed his view of the nature of Forms by the time of this

work, perhaps in response to such difficulties as appear in the first part of the *Parm*. But even if the *Parm*. was written before the *Phdr*. (cf. n. V-5), or the ideas expressed in it had already come to Plato's mind, the consequences of the changes made as a result would not affect our concerns. Cf. Ch. VII, introd.

11. In 262b2-3 we get what is apparently a quite different way of viewing at least some false belief (cf. Ch. VII, sec. 4, however, and note that the existence of these two different ways of looking at false belief could be the cause of there being two different ways of treating it in *Tht*. 187-200).

12. Something like this point is noted in passing by Zeller **2**, p. 625.

13. I do not, however, claim to be able to smooth over in this way all of the various apparent anomalies in the construction of the dialogue (cf. Hackforth **2**, pp. 8-12, 133, n. 1, 136-137).

14. See for example Robin's **2**, pp. iii-iv.

15. Hackforth's translation, as *infra*.

16. For discussion of further issues (including the question whether all the objects are collected before the dividing has begun), see Hackforth **1**, pp. 142-143, and **2**, p. 132, n. 4.

17. The latter point is clinched by the difference in identity-conditions for Forms and classes (or sets—I shall not distinguish): whereas classes a and b are identical just in case they have the same members, it is not the case that Forms F and G are identical just in case they are, say, partaken of by the same things. On this last point, see n. I-77, along with Cohen, pp. 170-171 and Moravcsik **3**. But one must be careful not to go too far, as Moravcsik seems to do when he says (p. 339) that "set theoretic notions are simply irrelevant to Plato's purposes." For although he is correct that the notions associated with collection and division are not purely set-theoretic, Plato often talks about them in a manner that indicates that he has on his mind, in a somewhat unclear way, a notion like the notion of a set. This fact, indeed, appears in much of the vocabulary of the method, e.g., in the term for "collection" (συναγωγή; 266b4, cf. 265d3-4), and in the terms "εἶδος" and "γένος" as there employed (265a9, 271d2, e.g., and further reff. in Moravcsik, pp. 328-330.) (One must be wary, however, for there are snares even in the Greek word most suggestive of "class," namely "γένος": it could carry the meaning of "family or national group," indeed (cf. Ar., *Met*. 1024a29-36), but remember that such a group has, as it were, an internal structure, which a mere class in our sense does not. The word "εἶδος," of course, is much less suggestive of set-theoretic notions; cf. Gillespie.) In addition, however, there are hints of the idea of a straightforwardly physical part-whole relation (e.g., in the notion of cutting in 265e1-3), though of course Plato does not mean that to divide a Form *is* literally to cut it. And thirdly there are various other notions, of a—vaguely speaking—intensional character (Moravcsik **3**, pp. 339ff.).

There is no reason to believe that Plato had a very clearly worked-out idea of the relationships involved, e.g., the relationship between *possessive art* and *art* (*Soph*. 223c6), or in general between one of his Forms and another Form from which the former is obtained by division. We know, indeed, that Aristotle sometimes conceived the relation between a species and a genus as a quasi-set-theoretic one (e.g., *Top.* 121b25; *Cat.* 3b21-23) while other times regarding it in a manner which would seem more likely to be intensional, at least in a vague sense (e.g., *Met.* 1037b10ff.). There is therefore not too much reason to expect fixity on the issue from Plato. If he mixed features of the part/whole, the member/class, the included-class/incuding-class, and the contained-concept/containing-concept relationships into his own ideas about Forms at this stage, then that is only to be expected. For he was, after all, beginning the whole discussion of these issues. Moreover a number of his views on the topic come through with some fair clarity (Moravcsik, pp. 339-341—who, however, claims things to be somewhat clearer than they are).

What justifies the use of set-theoretic talk in my exposition, however, is that in many cases there are set-theoretic relations that parallel the relations involved in collection and division. For example, if you "divide" Form *F* into *G* and *H*, then you can be sure that the things that partake in *G* and *H* will be proper subclasses of the class of things that partake in *F* (cf. Moravcsik, p. 335). Soon, however, it will become important that we are not dealing with classes.

18. He also thinks that there is no routine procedure for carrying out a collection or a division (*Phileb.* 16b5-c3, and Robinson **1**, pp. 69-73).

19. Some recent discussions are: Price, Ch. I; Quine **11**; Goodman **2**.

20. *Polit.* 262a-263e (the example is in 262d) shows the importance of the idea of unity (cf. *infra*.); see also Moravcsik **3**, pp. 339-344. On the notion of "natural kinds" in connection with division, see Skemp, pp. 66-82.

21. Thus, a kind such as *barbarian* could not be so reached (*Polit.* 262d), though its correlate, *Greek*, might conceivably be reached by division.

22. The same straddling can be observed in Aristotle: see my **1**.

23. Note the language of 524b10-c1, 4, 7, and see also *Legg.* 757a-b.

24. See 266c1 with Hackforth **2**, p. 135, n. 1, and Robinson **1**, pp. 122-165. The problem would not be remedied by the presence of clear signs (or even explicit statements) that Plato still held to the method of hypothesis. What would be needed would be an explanation of precisely how it was to be connected to the new method. (For this reason, hints that the method of collection and division is already present in earlier works will also not touch the real problems of method.)

25. See Ch. I, sec. 4, and Ch. II, secs. 4, 5, for the need, and Ch. III, sec. 7, and Ch. IV, secs. 4, 5, for the beginnings of the account.

26. Lest there be mistake, notice that this is not to say that the method *could* not have been developed into a substitute or so linked to the method of hypothesis as to allow them jointly to supply one (cf. n. V-24). Note too that the use of hypotheses in the *Parm.* is quite different and does not further the ends of which I am now speaking.

27. For a brief discussion of the notion of ambiguity in connection with division, see Ackrill **2**. Plato does not have the sort of technical terminology

which might have encouraged him to talk of ambiguity explicitly. He does have a term that is pertinent here, namely "ὁμώνυμον," but it is used not of expressions (as is our term "ambiguous") but of (groups of) things labeled by the same expression, and means "having the same name"; see Owen **2**, p. 301.

28. See for example the criticisms of Ryle **1**, pp. 141-142, and **3**, pp. 135ff. In defense of Platonic division, see Ackrill **2**. In *An. Pr.* I.31 and *An. Post.* II.5, Aristotle argues that division is not a method of *demonstration* (it is not clear whom he is arguing against because Plato does not seem to have believed that it was); unlike Ryle, however, Aristotle does seem to have thought that division was a good heuristic device (see *An. Post.* 96b25-97b6). Plato's emphasis on division rather than collection (see Hackforth **1**, pp. 26, 142-143) fits with the fact that Plato's main aim is to avoid ambiguity and confusion. The point of collection is to make sure, if one can, that the full range of things that might be being conflated is under explicit examination. Thus, if the effort were to avoid conflating whales with fish, division would do no good if one's initial collection of things among which to make divisions (265d3-5) included no mammals. But of course there is no clear-cut method offered to ensure that one has spread one's net widely enough (short of trying to include everything—here we encounter issues directly related to Aristotle's adaptation of the ideas in the *Phdr.*).

29. In recent times a view of roughly this character has been advocated in, e.g., Krämer esp. pp. 80ff. *Contra* Vlastos **5**.

30. Note well that I am not assimilating the remarks about language in the *Phdr.* and words on the same topic in *Ep.* VII, 341b*sqq*. Although they are often associated, and thought to be saying much the same thing, we shall see in Ch. VIII that they are quite different from each other (and also from *Symp.* 210e, which is also often yoked together with them).

31. See Hackforth **2**, pp. 163-164.

CHAPTER VI

The Cratylus:
Language and Reality

Seen in isolation, the *Cratylus* is easy to misconstrue. And it has indeed usually been seen in isolation. Not that commentators have ignored connections between it and other dialogues, of which there are many. It is rather that they have not seen the main topic of the *Cratylus* to be as closely linked as it is with some of Plato's central preoccupations.[1] Vaguely put, the main topic is language, and because language is not the chief issue of any other dialogue, people tend to think that it is as if Plato in the *Cratylus* were taking time out from his usual interests.[2]

But the *Cratylus* is not an isolated work in the philosophy of language. It is a treatment of problems having to do with language that arises directly out of crucial themes in Plato's epistemology and metaphysics. It is a natural development of the line of thought that we have seen coming to the fore in the *Phaedrus*, which in turn was a response to difficulties that were latent in Plato's doctrines from the start. In the *Phaedrus*, Plato had started to see that there was something problematical in the idea that we can simply pick a term and say that there is a Form that "corresponds" to it. In the *Cratylus*, Plato pushes this observation further, saying in more detail what was problematical in this notion of correspondence, and asking what it might amount to.

The *Cratylus* asks at the start whether the connection between "names" (ὀνόματα) and the things that they name is "natural" or "conventional."[3] Plato's term "name" does not correspond to any single technical term in contemporary philosophical discourse, and we shall see that the views that underlie his use of it are complicated and

131

subject to some difficulty. And at the end of the dialogue it will turn out that on his view only Forms can strictly be named. But let us connive with him in employing the term, and see what he does with it. In asking, then, whether names are "natural" or "conventional," he is in large part asking whether, when we say that a term is the name of an object, we are alluding to a relation that holds between the name and the object independently of how the name is used in a particular language or by particular people, or are rather dealing with a relation that is dependent on particular linguistic practices, habits, or behavior. In holding to the conventionalist view, Hermogenes is claiming that the relation is thus dependent; in propounding the "naturalist" view, Cratylus is maintaining that it is not. For most of the dialogue, Plato plays these two views off against each other, until in the end, as we shall see, he arrives at a view that is distinct from both of them. In adopting this third view he does not, as will emerge, extricate himself from all of the problems that had surrounded his views about predicates and Forms, but he significantly deepens his understanding of them and goes far beyond the simple picture of the *Phaedo*, under which one can say simply that a predicate is a name of a Form, and leave it at that.

1 The "Conventionalist" and "Naturalist" Views of Names

Commentators have generally been puzzled by the line of argument in the *Cratylus* because they thought that it showed a puzzling divergence.[4] Plato starts out criticizing Hermogenes' conventionalist account, giving arguments that seem intended to show that the naturalist account must be correct. Then, toward the end of the dialogue (roughly from 427e), he seems to turn around and argue against the naturalist view. Although he does not adopt the conventionalist position which Hermogenes had been pushing, he has seemed to sympathize sufficiently with it to puzzle his interpreters and make them wonder what his final view is. Some find him ultimately on the naturalist side, whereas others see his conclusion as containing elements of both of the two apparently opposed positions.[5] All of these interpretations, however, find difficulties in seeing how he can end up adopting, whether in whole or in part, views that he seemed to regard himself as refuting. The truth, as I have said, is that he really adopts a third view, which is neither strictly conventionalist nor strictly naturalist, as these two views had been construed. To see this fact, however, we have to look more closely at his versions of, and his arguments against, conventionalism and naturalism, to understand how he could have found yet another view to prefer to both of them.

Stripped to its bare bones, the conventionalism advocated by Hermogenes is, as I have said, the doctrine that whether or not a given expression is the name of a given thing is determined solely by the usage of those employing the term, and that by adopting the proper usage, one can make any expression the name of any object one chooses. This claim, Hermogenes contends, holds whether the usage in question is that of a single individual or of an entire community. Plato is little concerned at this point with the question how a single individual could forge anything that could be called a convention, or a language, in isolation from the linguistic habits of his fellows,[6] and so he does not raise the sort of objections that some contemporary philosophers might bring against such a possibility.[7] Nor is Plato interested at all in the sort of conventions of language which have played a part in contemporary discussion, having to do with the notions of "truth by convention" or analyticity or the like.[8] It is easy to see that such notions find no place in the *Cratylus* (cf. also Ch. I, sec. 3). Nor does Plato care whether or not the conventions involved in his discussion are anything like explicit conventions or agreements. For his purposes they may perfectly well not be conventions in any very literal sense, but can rather just as well be habits of speech (see 434e4-5).

That Plato is not here concerned particularly with conventions in the literal sense, nor with anything more than the claim that the relation of namehood is solely dependent on the usage of the speaker or speakers in question in a particular instance, is plainly shown by the argument that he mounts against Hermogenes' version of conventionalism (385b-390e). The strategy of that argument is relatively straightforward: the claim is that Hermogenes' conventionalism entails what can be called "Protagoreanism";[9] but inasmuch as Hermogenes quickly finds Protagoreanism unacceptable, it is maintained that he must reject his conventionalism.[10] What is Protagoreanism? It is the claim, later to be examined more thoroughly in the *Theaetetus* (cf. Ch. VII, sec. 1), that there is no saying that any statement is true or false *simpliciter*, but rather that whatever a person believes is the case "for him" (385e-386a). This doctrine, and the question what precisely it comes to, raise many difficulties, but we may legitimately cut through many of them in order to see just what is at stake in the present argument.[11] The idea is, roughly, that if there is no choosing one language over another, and no ground for saying that a certain language is the best language, then there is no ground for saying, as it were, that there is a particular way that is the way things in fact are. There are, so to speak, no facts that we can try accurately to report in words; rather, how things are depends, in a sense, on what language you pick. Thus, if I try to report a state of affairs by means of uttering the sound "The cat is on the mat," while you adopt a convention under which these vocables are labeled false (because they are, as we would say, used to mean something different), then there is no saying that the cat either is or is not on the mat; rather—the claim is— whether the cat is or is not on the mat depends on what language you adopt.[12]

This example, although simple, raises more philosophical questions than we can discuss here. What Plato starts out with is the observation that on Hermogenes' view the sentence "The cat is on the mat" may, in one acceptable language, be true, whereas in another equally acceptable language it is false. The moral, as has been noticed,[13] is that rather than dealing with a predicate "true," we must instead regard ourselves as requiring the use of predicates of the type "true-in-*L*," where "*L*" holds the place of an expression referring to a particular language. But this, one wishes to say, does not mean that how the world in fact is depends, in any problematical way, on which language you choose. We can perfectly well say that the world is the way it is and would be that way no matter how we spoke (with the exception, of course, of facts about our habits of speech themselves). We all believe that what is "dependent" on language is not how the world is, but simply how to say how the world is, so that this sort of conventionalism does not by itself entail Protagoreanism in any objectionable sense. Whether this unreflective "realist" belief can be justified is another matter. Plato, however, shows no sign of entertaining the idea that the term "true" should be relativized to a language, and so he does not have the task of showing that such a relativization does no damage to the belief in a world somehow "independent" of language. Rather, he combats Hermogenes' position, and his own realistic tendencies take him in another direction, as will appear (see esp. Ch. IX, sec. 2).

Another point to notice about the conventionalism that is at issue in the *Cratylus*, and also about the doctrine of naturalism which is opposed to it, is that they both have directly to do only with the relation between "names" and various objects in the world. No account is taken of other features which might be claimed to attach to languages, and to make a difference to their acceptability.[14] The emphasis on naming is established early by the initial examples (e.g., whether or not "Hermogenes" is the name of Hermogenes, 383b), and it influences Plato's discussion in ways which show up both in the *Cratylus* (cf. sec. 3) and in later works. But we should not fail to notice at this juncture that as the emphasis on the relation of namehood shows, Plato's concern in the *Cratylus* is closely related to a matter that has occupied us, the idea of a correspondence between general terms and Forms. For it will turn out that the relation of namehood includes this relation of correspondence, and indeed that the cases of namehood that he thinks most important are those involving precisely general terms and Forms (sec. 4).

The doctrine of naturalism that Plato plays off against conventionalism is precisely the view that the relation between names and what they name is independent of the way in which names are used by any given person or persons, or in general of the way in which people talk. That this is the position of the character Cratylus is made plain by him thoughout the dialogue. (This does not mean that the doctrine posits a *unique* correct name for a given object; indeed, the naturalism on whose behalf Socrates temporarily argues in 385b-390e explicitly allows for a plurality of correct names for a single thing. The claim is that certain expressions name certain things no matter how the names are used, or what opinions people may have about what they name; but this claim leaves room for saying that the same thing may have more than one name.)

What is notable about the discussion of naturalism, however, is that Plato does not argue explicitly against naturalism *per se*, but rather against a particular version of it, which he proposes as the most plausible of those which come to mind. This is the view that the relation between a name and what it names is a relation of *similarity* or *resemblance*.[15] (It is to be noticed that Plato here conceives of similarity as holding among things independently of people's ways of talking or thinking. Although there are objections to be raised to it, it is not a surprising one to find Plato adopting. He shows the same belief in his view that sensible objects resemble Forms in some objective way quite independent of what we might happen to perceive or believe.)[16] It is against this version of naturalism that Plato argues. The reason why he adopts this strategy is that he sees that if naturalism is to be made plausible, or indeed clear, then it must be fitted out with some account of just what the usage-independent relation of namehood is supposed to be; without that addition, its only claim to our attention is that it seems, however unclear, to be the only alternative to conventionalism,

which has been discredited by 390e. Thus, in 391a-b and again in
422b, Plato points out that the task confronting the opponent of
Hermogenes' conventionalism is to show what a plausible naturalistic
account of the relation of namehood might consist in, and Hermogenes too is made to say that it is the lack of such an account which
is chiefly responsible for his scepticism about Cratylus' naturalistic
claims (427d-e). Accordingly, Plato can think that if he disposes of the
only reasonable naturalistic account of namehood that has been offered, then he has successfully disposed of naturalism, at least until a
better version is proposed (427e1-3).

But this argument against the resemblance version of naturalism is
not Plato's only way of undermining naturalism. As we shall see in the
following section, Plato argues *independently* for a third view and
thinks that his arguments for this view show it to be superior to any
version of naturalism likely to come along.

Cratylus turns out to be remarkably stubborn against Plato's attacks
on his position, and it is not until late in the dialogue that Plato seems
to think that he has been satisfactorily dealt with. The final argument
that is directly concerned with the resemblance version of naturalism
occurs in 432a8-d4, where Plato argues that it would be absurd to
suppose that *wholly exact* resemblance should obtain between name
and nominatum, and thus that something beside mere resemblance
should be said to constitute the relation of namehood.[17] Cratylus
drops this version of naturalism at this point (c7-d4). From here on,
he merely asks how some names of a thing can be better than others
(433b7-10), a question that Plato attempts to answer by means of his
own rival view, which will be expounded in the next section.

Preliminary to our examination of Plato's own view of namehood, a
further point about the arguments against Cratylus deserves attention. Plato wishes to claim against him that a certain sort of misnaming
is possible, in order to allow a place for false statement. His way of
supporting this claim hinges on a distinction which he insists on drawing between the resemblance of a term to an object and someone's
application of a term to an object (429b-431e—note esp. "διανεῖμαι",
"προσφέρειν", and related expressions). Socrates is made to press
Cratylus to accept the contention that a term may be in some sense
applied to a thing even if it does not resemble it as closely as does some
other (432b*sqq.*). Cratylus is nevertheless still inclined to think that
what makes an expression properly called a name is not that it is
somehow applied to a thing but rather that it resembles a thing, and
thus that whatever expression may be *applied* to a thing, a *name* of a

thing is only an expression that resembles it (429b-432a). But finally Cratylus does accept the *distinction* between the relations of resemblance and application,[18] and once he does so, the issue in the dialogue is simply which of these relations ought to be thought of as the relation of namehood. But Cratylus will not yet give up the view that it is resemblance that is namehood, and so Socrates must fall back on the argument mentioned in the preceding paragraph, that the possibility of exact resemblance shows that namehood cannot be simply resemblance. But even aside from this final argument, Plato still has reasons for holding that the important relation between expressions and objects, and the relation that should be said to be namehood, is not similarity but, as we shall see, something else.

2 Plato's View of Names

The key to understanding Plato's own view of names in the *Cratylus*, and the way in which he disagrees with the conventionalist and naturalist accounts, is to see what he thinks is the purpose of names.[19] This is also the key to seeing how the *Cratylus* is connected with the works that precede it. We have observed in the chapter on the *Phaedrus* that Plato has begun to be sceptical about the view that words are such satisfactory "guides" as he had been inclined tacitly to suppose that they were. That is to say, in connection with the Forms, that he had begun to see that there was something problematical and incomplete about simply thinking that terms correspond to Forms and enjoining us simply to try to fix our minds, in the case of each predicate which interests us, on the Form to which it corresponds. The *Cratylus* presses the problems which he sees arising here and makes an attempt at setting matters straight.

Plato's preoccupation with how words can help us to know Forms is clearly evident in the final pages of the *Cratylus*, where Socrates is made to dispute Cratylus' contention that somehow by means of names one can come to know objects that are named (435e-439b). Cratylus' suggestion is that once we know what names are like, we can without difficulty tell what the objects that they name are like,[20] and it is this claim, in part, that Plato wishes to dispute. He wishes to say, first, that determining what names are like is an unreliable way of telling what their nominata are like, and, second, that there is a better way of telling what objects are like than by examining their names. The fact that he makes these claims, and also the fact that he makes them at the end of the dialogue in the course of expounding what are patently his own views, make evident the epistemological import of the work. Plato is talking about names in order to see what connection there is between names and knowledge.

It also becomes apparent at the end of the dialogue that he is primarily concerned with the bearing of an account of names on his views about Forms. For the last couple of pages are as clear an announcement as one could wish that the Forms are, properly speaking, the only things that can be named (cf. also 397b-c), just as they are, properly speaking, the only things that can be known. The latter view is of course familiar from the *Phaedo* and the *Republic*; the former view, and Plato's reasons for holding it, will emerge in due course (sec. 3). But we can already see that Plato's discussion of namehood here must be pertinent to the questions that we have asked about the nature of the "correspondence" between general terms and Forms.

Plato's view, which he emphasizes throughout the *Cratylus*, is that the purpose of names is to help us distinguish among things and tell us what things are like (e.g., 388a-c, 422d-e, 424a-b, 428d-e, 432e-433b, d-435a, 435d).[21] What he wants a name to do is to help us separate out certain things from others, so that we may consider them and learn what there is to be learned about them.[22] Part of what this requires is that when a name is used, it should make one somehow "think about," or otherwise "apprehend," an object (e.g., 434e-435a). It is from this claim that Plato's own account of names takes its start.[23]

Plato repeatedly emphasizes that this job is not done satisfactorily by the names which are in ordinary use. This point begins to emerge in the long middle section of the dialogue which is devoted to giving various etymologies, since one of the things which this section tries at great length to show is that any likely etymological account must admit that expressions have been altered, e.g., for the sake of euphony, in such a way as to conceal their import (414c-d, 421d). The point becomes clearer when the resemblance view of names comes up for examination later. Here Plato explicitly maintains that the resemblance between *actual* names and their respective nominata is rough at best, and that for this reason it is risky to rely on those names for an indication of the features of the objects named. He says that in a fully satisfactory language, on the other hand, names would much more closely resemble their respective nominata. The point of this contention is that in such a language each name would resemble its nominatum more than any other name would, and thus there would be a minimization of the confusions that arise in actual languages, in which a name may very well not resemble its nominatum as much as something else does, or as much as it resembles something else. What he is plainly after, in this talk of a perfect language, is a perspicuous one-to-one correlation between names and other objects, so that (at least as long as one could gauge resemblance accurately) there would be no doubt about which name named which thing.

It is very important to notice that Plato is *not* here saying that for a perfectly constructed language, the resemblance view of namehood *would hold*.[24] For although in a perfect language namehood and a certain sort of resemblance might coincide extensionally, he plainly wants to deny that for an expression to be a name of an object *is simply* for the two to resemble each other (432a8-d4; cf. sec. 1).[25] Rather, for an expression to be a name of an object is for it to make a person think of that object, since that is what Plato thinks it is the purpose of names to do.[26] For this job to be optimally done, moreover, is for us to have a language in which we can be sure that each expression will make all of us think of one and only one thing, so that there will never be a case in which one person uses a name trying to make a second person think of a particular thing, only to find that that second person has gone off and thought of something else or has failed to think of anything at all.[27] This is the end that a perfect language would achieve, and resemblance is merely a means by which this end might best be reached. The reason why Plato thinks that resemblance would be a good means to this end is simply that he thinks that there are objective similarities in the world to which we are all capable of responding, and that we naturally tend to pass from apprehending a thing to thinking about what is similar to it.[28] But he fully recognizes that convention or custom can also induce an association, as it were, under which an expression can tend to make us think of a thing quite consistently even if it does not resemble that thing (434e-435a). Convention too can thus serve as a means of achieving the purpose that names should serve, even if, given the variability of our customs, it does the job less well than resemblance would. Once again, however, the goal is to have a consistent scheme for getting others to think of the objects of which we want them to think.[29]

This goal being so overridingly important, Plato views it as supplying the *raison d'etre* of names, and as the dialogue proceeds, discussion of it comes to dominate the dispute between the view that names are established by nature and the view that they are set up by convention. The idea is first broached in 388a-c, when it is claimed—without opposition—that a name is an instrument (ὄργανον), and in particular an instrument for teaching and for distinguishing between things (the phrase διακριτικὸν τῆς οὐσίας in c1 harks back to the discussion in the *Phaedrus* of the method for avoiding conceptual confusion; Ch. V, sec. 1). By 433-435, it is clear that the naturalist and conventionalist accounts of naming have been superseded, since both of these accounts are being assessed by the standard of whether or not they show how names can serve this ultimate purpose. On this score, both are found wanting (see esp. 435d*sqq.*). This is the reason why he sets aside naturalism without arguing against it (sec. 1), and also the reason why, even though he sympathizes with the idea that we should use names resembling their respective nominata, he nevertheless does not support—and ineed argues vigorously against—the resemblance account of namehood. To the extent that Plato here intends to present a positive explanation of what the "correctness" (ὀρθότης) of naming consists in,[30] it is that whatever one might say further about it, names must be such that speaker and hearer are free from confusion, and both think of the same things.[31]

Modern philosophical consideration of language has made this view seem in many ways an oversimple and unsatisfactory one, and in fact it produces difficulties for Plato himself (Ch. VII, sec. 5). But as those who have attacked it have seen, it is probably the most natural view of language for a person to adopt. For it is easy to think that the words that we utter run parallel to a train of ideas about various things, and that successful linguistic communication consists in someone else's thinking of the same things, when he hears the words, as we do when we speak them. Moreover, Plato's earlier views have encouraged him in this picture of the way in which language works. The semantic consideration for the existence of Forms (Ch. I, sec. 1) involved the idea that such objects could be used to explain the meaningfulness to us of individual words, and was easily joined to the idea that the explanation lies in a connection between the use of the word and an apprehension of a Form (Ch. I, sec. 4; Ch. III, sec. 6). It is hardly a step from these ideas to the views of the *Cratylus*, which can now be seen as in effect consolidating the position which, in an unformulated way, Plato had been occupying all along.

3 Naming, Describing, and Other Issues

Of the many issues that the *Cratylus* raises, I shall deal in particular here with 1) Plato's continued neglect in the *Cratylus* of the distinction between two functions of expressions, denoting and describing; 2) his notion that the things in the world can be analyzed, as it were, into simple or atomic constituents, and the effect of this notion on some of his remarks about language; 3) certain remarks that he makes about statements and their truth and falsity.

The first matter has to do with the way in which Plato thinks that names might help us not only to think about other objects, but also to tell—as I have been putting it, following Plato—what they are like. It is abundantly clear that Plato thinks that a name may do more than simply direct our attention, as it were, to an object, but may also in some sense contain some information about features which the object possesses.[32] This point is intimately connected with a matter on which we dwelt briefly some time back, namely the fact that he views his Forms as "self-predicative" (cf. Ch. III, introd.). We remarked when this matter was first broached that part of the reason why he holds this view is that he sometimes fails to distinguish between saying that a thing is (in the sense of "is identical with") the Large and saying that it is (predicatively, as we might say) large. Along with the failure to make this distinction clearly goes another failure, the failure to distinguish between an expression that simply denotes or refers to an object, and that describes that object. We need not pause here over the exact nature of this distinction.[33] It is enough for our purposes to illustrate both it and Plato's mistake by saying that at least before his latest works, he tends to think that because the expression "large" can, in his view, be used to refer to the Form of the Large, it must therefore also describe that object, so that our referring to the object by means of that expression forces us to say simultaneously that that Form is itself a large object. (It is, of course, unqualifiedly large, unlike any sensible object, but I pass over that complication here; cf. Ch. III, sec. 2). In the *Cratylus*, he on the whole continues to be caught in this confusion.

I say "on the whole" because Plato can on occasion distinguish between something that merely serves to make us think about an object and one that describes that object. For example, in the *Cratylus* he observes that we may get someone to think about a thing by pointing at it (422e), and he presumably would not say that to point at a thing is to describe it. Nevertheless he is otherwise not, as we shall see, as alive to this distinction as we might hope him to be.

In his discussion of the resemblance theory of names (i.e., the theory that namehood just *is* a sort of resemblance), Plato consistently seems to think that the way in which an expression names an object is by exhibiting features of that object, and it is as if he believes that a name, by its very construction, encapsulates a description by which the object may be recognized. We might compare this view to a modern view, that a referring expression must either be, or somehow mean the same as, some singular description of the Form "the such-and-such," where "such-and-such" holds the place of a predicate (perhaps conjunctive or otherwise complex) which is true of that object, and that object alone, which the referring expression denotes.[34] Thus, the expression "Aristotle" might be claimed to mean the same as "the student of Plato who taught Alexander the Great," at least for some people on some occasions. Plato's view at this point is a little like such a view, except that he regards the description as capturable, at least in a properly-formed name, from the etymology, or the physical make-up (cf. *infra*) of the name itself. Another difference, moreover—and an important one—is that Plato does not require that the encapsulated description must in all cases apply to one and only one thing, the bearer of the name, or that such a requirement be made explicit by the use of the definite article "the" (as in *the* student . . ."). Thus, the term "Baker" might serve to denote some person, Baker, a baker, without our having to say instead "*the* Baker," or to claim that he is the only Baker (baker). Plato's remarks, however, about what a perfect language would be like, do suggest that he thinks that in such a language the description encapsulated in a name would be true of one object uniquely. But even here he does not say (although he may take it as obvious, since Greek very often places the definite article in front of what we call proper names) that this uniqueness of application should be signaled by the use of "the."

However this may be, Plato seems not to be openly distinguishing here between two functions, referring and describing, which an expression may perform. But he is not thus far *barred* from making this distinction, as we can see when we recall what his view is of the purpose of names. For remember that Plato does not himself accept the resemblance theory of names and is thus free to believe that even if a perfect system of names would resemble their respective nominata, and thus encapsulate descriptions of them, nevertheless a name *can*, by custom, standardly make us think of a thing that it does not resemble, and of which it therefore does not encapsulate a description. If he took advantage of his freedom to say this, then he could be on his way to distinguishing, if not between referring and describing, at least between "making one think about" and describing. He is still committed, however, to the view that the reason *why* we would want to think about a thing is to acquire knowledge about it. But this view by itself is obviously not tantamount to a confusion between referring and describing.

At the end of the dialogue, however, in 439b-440e, Plato does say some things that suggest that he has not seen his way clear to making this distinction. This passage, on which more later (sec. 4), indicates that he believes that only Forms may properly be named, and his reasons seem to have to do with the idea that the term "beautiful," for example, cannot be reliably used to make one think about a thing, unless the thing is in all respects and at all times—i.e., unqualifiedly (cf. Ch. III, sec. 2)—beautiful. Now he presumably means to claim that *no* term can be thus reliably used except under that proviso, but he does not attempt to rebut the claim that even if a predicate such as "beautiful" cannot be reliably used to make one think of a thing that is only qualifiedly beautiful, nevertheless one might thus employ some *non*descriptive term to the same end. This is not to say that that claim would seem to him to stand up under his attack or that it would actually do so. It is only to say that he does not give the claim a run for its money and therefore does not show full awareness of the contrast on which we have been dwelling.

The second matter I wish to discuss concerns Plato's ideas about simple and complex names. A part of the resemblance view of names is the claim that certain names are atomic, and resemble atomic objects, whereas other names are complexes of atomic names, and resemble complex objects.[35] As Plato explains it, the resemblance of a complex name and a complex object consists simply in the fact that the atomic constituents of the name resemble atomic constituents of the object. A perfect name is implied to be one in which each element resembles just one constituent of the object, and such that each constituent of the object has an element of the name which resembles it (433a5-6).

Plato says relatively little about the nature of these simple and complex objects, and the question arises how far we are to take this idea as an expression of his own views. We have seen that he does not accept the view that namehood simply is a sort of resemblance, so it is possible that he also does not accept the accompanying distinction between simple and complex names and objects. On the other hand, his argument is directed explicitly only against the resemblance theory, and neither against the atomic/complex distinction itself, nor against the idea that in a perfect language complex objects would be named by names whose elements named elements of the object.[36] Hence, it is also possible that these are ideas that Plato does accept on his own behalf. A related passage, *Theaetetus* 201d*sqq.*, which we shall take up later (Ch. VII, sec. 5), does not settle the question definitively, but it does make it likely that Plato did at least tentatively accept these ideas, or at least saw no clear alternative to them.[37]

The same conclusion is also indicated by Plato's treatment of sentences (λόγοι) in the *Cratylus*,[38] which is the third matter on which I wish to touch here. Moreover, his treatment of sentences illustrates his emphasis on the notion of naming, and his neglect of other roles that expressions play. Although he does not believe that all expressions are names, and speaks in addition of "phrases" (this is here probably the best translation of "ῥήματα")[39] and sentences, he makes no use of the possibility that such expressions might function in some way differently from names. He accordingly treats a sentence as though it were a sort of compound name, whose function is the same as that of any other sort of name and serves to induce one to think about some sort of compound object, say, a "state of affairs" or the like. It should be emphasized that he does not say very much in this vein about sentences and does not use any expression such as "state of affairs" for the sort of objects that sentences might make us think about. What shows him starting to slip into the view that there are such things is simply that he does not here distinguish between the sort of compounding that gives rise to a name and the sort of compounding that gives rise to a sentence (431b-c, 432d-e).[40]

Although the idea that a sentence is a sort of name, or at least some sort of referring expression, might be defensible,[41] it can in certain circumstances run into trouble. For it is an easy—though not necessary—step from this idea to the view that what makes a sentence meaningful is for it to refer to some state of affairs. But it is also then natural to think, in addition, that what makes a sentence true is likewise that it refer to a state of affairs. The result of these two views, however, is that truth and meaningfulness for sentences then coincide, and there cannot be such a thing as a false but meaningful sentence. It is interesting in this connection that although Plato does get into trouble over the explanation of how a sentence can be false, both in the *Cratylus* and in later works, the difficulty that arises over falsity in the *Cratylus*, at least, is not plainly of the sort I have described. At 429c-d, Cratylus objects that it is impossible to speak falsely because to do so is to "not say what is" (τὸ μὴ τὰ ὄντα λέγειν).[42] It is true that the objection here *may* be that a false statement would have to fail to name any state of affairs and would thus be meaningless, but the argument is not fully enough developed for us to be at all sure that this is so (on the problems over falsity in the *Theaetetus* and the *Sophist*, cf. Ch. VII, sec. 4).[43]

But however this argument be best interpreted, Plato still shows a tendency elsewhere in the *Cratylus*, as I have noted, to treat sentences as names of a sort and not to explain them in some other way. Moreover, the only account of sentences that he gives is in terms of the notion of compounding (σύνθεσις), and he offers no alternative. This fact should lead us to believe that even though he does not accept the resemblance view of names, he does accept the notion of a compound which figures in that view.

4   Names and Forms

The final pages of the *Cratylus*, as I have said, maintain that only Forms can strictly be named. The line of thought that leads Plato to this conclusion is the same as one that we have seen already, in accounting for his belief that only Forms can be known (cf. Ch. IV, sec. 1). It is Plato's view that no predicate, of the sort that concerns him, can be true of a sensible object at all times and in all respects. Thus, the only thing to which the predicate "beautiful," e.g., can apply unqualifiedly is the Form of the Beautiful (cf. also 397b7-c2). When we take into account Plato's failure to distinguish between an expression's referring to or naming an object and its being true of, or describing, an object, then we can see that he would naturally be led to say as well that the word "beautiful" cannot strictly or unqualifiedly name anything but the Form. Indeed, Plato here links the view that only Forms can be named with the view that only Forms can be known (439e-440b), in a way which supports the claim that his treatment of naming here ought to be parallel to his treatment of knowledge earlier.

In his view, the difficulty in the idea that a sensible object can be adequately named is as follows. As 433a5-6 shows, a perfect name of an object is one that would put us perfectly in mind of the object (especially by resembling it greatly) and all of the features that it has. The word "beautiful," for example, might (if it properly resembled beauty) put us in mind of a beautiful sensible object for a time, but it would never put us in mind of all of the features or attributes possessed by the object. If, however, we tried to construct an elaborate compound name of this sensible thing, we would have to include words which would make us think of many other features of the object, and not merely its beauty.[44] But the attempt to construct such a complete name (as one might put it) of a sensible object is doomed to failure. For Plato believes that each sensible is constantly changing, in the sense that between any two distinct moments, no matter how closely spaced, the object has altered in some respect.[45] But this means that an utterly complete name of a sensible object can, in his view, properly name that object for no stretch of time at all. A Form, on the other hand, can be properly named, because Plato thus far thinks that every attribute that a Form has is possessed by it for all time (and otherwise unqualifiedly).[46]

One should not overlook the relationship between the view that Forms can be named and the earlier line of argument in the dialogue, for it will bear importantly on our examination of the *Theaetetus*. Another way of looking at what we have just seen is to say that for Plato it is the Forms which, by being the objects of which we can (satisfactorily) think, serve as the objects that can be named; so that if there were no Forms, there would be no names (439d8). But Plato clearly takes it that the view that there are Forms and the Protagoreanism that was summarily rejected earlier (385-390; cf. sec. 1) are incompatible, so that if Protagoreanism turned out to be true, then his claim here that there are Forms, thus construed, would have to be rejected. Nor can Plato claim that in 439-440 he has, by arguing that there are Forms, succeeded in showing Protagoreanism false, for such an argument would be question-begging. It would be question-begging because it *assumes* that naming (389d8-11) and knowledge (e7-440a), in senses that would be rejected by the Protagorean, are possible. Moreover, in the earlier argument against conventionalism as an explanation of naming (385-390), the falsity of Protagoreanism was likewise, in effect, simply assumed.[47] But if the falsity of Protagoreanism is contested, then conventionalism as a theory of namehood has not been ruled out. But if it has not been ruled out, then Plato cannot in 439-440 now assume a view of naming at odds with conventionalism and expect to be allowed to use that view as a premise in an argument indirectly supporting the denial of Protagoreanism. For if he did that he would be assuming that Protagoreanism is false in order to prove that it is.

I think that in fact Plato is not trying to argue in this illegitimate manner and that he realizes that he needs to argue further. For I think he exhibits in 440b a clear realization that all that he is showing is that there are Forms, *if* knowledge, in the sense in which he takes the word, is possible. But I do not think that he claims here to *prove* that knowledge, or naming in the sense in which it requires such nominata as Forms, is possible. I do not think, therefore, that he can be claiming to have disproved Protagoreanism. And if he has not done that, then he has not disproved conventionalism concerning names either. Where does Plato attempt to dispose of Protagoreanism? In the *Theaetetus*. So we shall see the thread of the argument in the *Cratylus* picked up there (see n. VI-10, and Ch. VII, sec. 1).

From the beginning of our discussion, one of the questions concerning us has been the question what the "correspondence" between Forms and terms amounts to. With the revelation at the end of the *Cratylus* that, strictly, only Forms have names, we become aware that the questions surrounding namehood here are in large part the very ones that surrounded correspondence. It is now time to bring that fact to the fore, so as to tie the preoccupations of this chapter to earlier ones.

The *Phaedo* presented the correspondence between terms and Forms as though it were something unproblematical (Ch. III, sec. 5), and by and large the *Republic* followed suit. The *Republic* did, however, record the fact that a sort of confusion of different Forms was possible, and this fact was then pursued in the *Phaedrus* (Ch. IV, sec. 1; Ch. V, sec. 1). But once the *Phaedrus* had recognized the importance of the fact that terms may not necessarily guide our minds unerringly to the Forms to which they correspond, the way was open for the *Cratylus* to ask what this correspondence really consisted in. The answer was, appropriately, that it consisted precisely in the ability of terms to guide our minds to Forms and to enable us to avoid confusing them, in the manner in which actual terms in actual language so frequently and lamentably fail to do. The need, then, is for a language in which terms actually serve this end.

These new developments put old questions in a different light. In a certain sense, the crucial problems are not now questions such as "What is holiness?" or "What is justice?" or efforts framed simply and naively as "the effort to apprehend (or look to, or view) Holiness" or "the effort to apprehend Justice." It is problems of this sort that were predominant in earlier dialogues, serving as their thematic backbones. Now, however, we cannot so confidently think that the terms with which we start, "Holiness," "Justice," and the like, are straightforwardly and unambiguously tied to particular Forms in a way which irrevocably fixes the subject matter of our old, naively framed investigations and searches for definitions. In fact, after what the *Phaedrus* and the *Cratylus* have said about the ways in which words can mislead us, the question arises why a definition—which is after all made up of words—should be more perspicuous or informative than a term such as "Justice" or "Holiness" itself.[48] This question must therefore be added to the others that we have posed about the role of definitions (cf. esp. Ch. I, sec. 4). Moreover, now that the *Phaedrus* has vigorously pressed the issue, we have to recognize that you and I may not be using words to correspond to the same Forms or may both be in various ways confused. Thus it becomes necessary, as a general matter of method, to wonder whether the Form that you associate, so to speak, with a certain term is the same as the one that I associate with it, and to ask how we might reach agreement in this respect, how definitions would figure in our efforts to do so, and how we might tell whether we have succeeded or not. Thus, subsequent dialogues tend by and large to be more overtly methodological, dealing with these and allied questions.[49]

Notes

1. Sometimes this mistake has led to an early dating of the *Crat.*, as in the case of Taylor **3**, pp. 75ff. Although he does not make this mistake (indeed, he sees much of the point of the dialogue; cf. nn. *infra*), Kahn places the work relatively early but his dating gives far less point to the work than does our association of it here with the problems in the *Phdr.*, and although he voices worries about misidentification (p. 173, n. 27), he does not show what its motivation would be at an early stage of Plato's career. Moreover, two further difficulties that Kahn encounters (p. 176, and the top of p. 163) are eased if the *Crat.* is placed after the *Phdr.* and read in the light of the latter's preoccupations. For other arguments for an early date, see Luce **1** (with references there on the whole controversy), and Calvert. In support of the present dating, cf. Owen **1**, pp. 315, n. 2, and 323, n. 3 (though with reference to the latter citation, notice that *Crat.* 439d need not be read as pushing its point as far as Owen takes *Tht.* 181-183 to be doing). Although I shall make certain points about this issue in the notes *infra*, I cannot cover the controversy adequately here. Still, the following points can be briefly made. First, a simple contrast between "transcendent" and "immanent" cannot possibly handle all of the complexities of the issues motivating the theory of Forms (cf. n. I-23) and will not support the weight of argument for an early date placed on it by, e.g., Ross **4** and Calvert, pp. 32-33. Second, although stylistic considerations weigh slightly toward an early dating (see Luce, but cf. Owen, *ibid*.), they do not do so decisively enough to outweigh strong counterevidence from the content (as Ross saw). Third, as I shall argue in nn. VI-45 and VI-30, *infra*, the

evidence that Plato is unsure about certain points concerning Forms is better handled by placing the *Crat.* after *Phdr.* and just before the *Tht.* Fourth, it is wrong to argue for an early date by supposing (as does, e.g., Luce, p. 149) that if the work is not early then it must be late enough to jibe perfectly in content with the *Tht.* and the *Soph.*, and then to show that it does not do the latter. Plato's works cannot be divided *simply* into "early" and "late."

2. It also goes without saying that he is not speculating *simply* on the historical origins of language. If he were doing that, then he *would* be taking time off.

3. This opposition is of course a crucial one in Greek thought. For some conjectures about the way in which it lies in the background of the *Crat.*, see Kahn, pp. 154ff., who posits certain Eleatic influences. But much more likely than these to have been of direct concern to Plato are the Protagorean issues which are explicitly mentioned in 386c*sqq.* (though of course Protagoras can have been influenced by earlier thinkers in some ways compatible with what Kahn says). Note in particular the fact that in 383a (and see 385e4, not neglecting the force of "καί" in "καὶ τὰ ὄντα," which points up the contrast with "ὀνόματα" in e2). Hermogenes' view about names is presented—not merely as entailing Protagoreanism (see sec. 1), but *also*—as an *instance* of it. It is here that we should look for the immediately relevant suggestion that names incorporate a view of reality, rather than (except perhaps indirectly) in Parmenides (cf. Kahn, p. 156).

4. For settings of this problem, see Robinson **5** and Kahn, p. 152.

5. Thus Taylor **3**, p. 78, and Kahn, who advocates an interpretation that is in certain respects similar to mine; cf. *infra.* Robinson **5** seems to place Plato finally on the side of nature, but in **6**, p. 122, he sees Plato discarding the nature view in favor of the convention view (which he finds in *Ep.* VII; cf. Ch. VIII, sec. 3). Friedländer, vol. I, pp. 196-215, seems to adopt a quasi-conventionalist interpretation of Plato's position.

6. For Hermogenes' indifference, not attacked by Plato, over whether or not a group or an individual is involved in setting up a linguistic convention, see 385a, d-e, with Robinson **5**, p. 109. At 434e-435a the indifference becomes more pronounced, when ουνθήκη and ἔθος (roughly, convention and habit, though "ἔθος" can have the overtones of "convention") are assimilated, and a person is spoken of as making a convention with himself (435a7-8). (Or does 435a10-b1 express a reservation?) This indifference is mirrored in the fact that it is sometimes not clear whether Plato has in mind, in speaking of the "application" (θέσις) of a name (390d8; cf. 384d2, 393a1, and "τίθεσθαι" at 393a1, 396a1, c6, 401a5, 411b5, c10, 414c4, 429b7, 10, c1, 4, and elsewhere), the initial bestowing of a name on a thing—the dubbing of the thing, as it were—or the mere use of an already established name. But one cannot say flatly that Plato is confused over this matter, since the question whether names are natural or conventional involves for him the question whether dubbings are necessary or have any point, for if names are established by nature, then no dubbing is

necessary to establish a connection between name and object, and a dubbing contrary to nature would be of no effect. Cf. n. VI-29.

7. It begins to look as though Plato is putting Hermogenes into the position of thinking that there can be a "private language," in the sense in which private languages were rejected by, e.g., Wittgenstein **3**. On this point cf. Weingartner, pp. 18-21. (Weingartner rightly observes that Hermogenes' view would mean that there are no names at all, in the sense in which Plato wants there to be names [cf. sec. 4].)

8. To say that a feature of a language is somehow established by convention is not yet to have a notion of *truth by* convention (cf. Quine **7**), and Plato never makes use of such a notion (cf. n. I-75).

9. Not only that: it is an *instance* of it; cf. n. VI-4. I take here no position on whether the view that Plato puts indirectly into the mouth of Protagoras was actually subscribed to by him. Cf. Ch. VII, sec. 1.

10. This may seem too brisk a statement, as 386-390 does contain something which might be called an argument against Protagoreanism. But not only is it perfunctory, as Luce has noted in his **1**; it is also rather clearly question-begging. For it assumes that a sort of expertise is possible in the craft of naming, which a Protagorean would wish immediately to reject. (For this reason, it seems to me that too much is made of the argument by Weingartner, pp. 27-28.) Moreover, this fact does not go unnoticed by Plato. In the *Tht.* he makes Protagoras *redivivus* object vigorously to this sort of *petitio principii* (166a-168c) and then counters the objection by two further arguments against Protagoreanism (169d-171c, 171d-179b) which, whatever their flaws, are certainly far more sophisticated and cogent than anything in the *Crat.* or in the earlier part of the *Tht.* We may suppose, therefore, that Plato realized at some point that the Protagorean position had not been adequately dealt with in the *Crat.* (cf. Ch. VII, sec. 2). We may also see in this course of events a further argument for placing the *Crat.* chronologically just before the *Tht.* (cf. sec. 4) and supposing that the latter picks up where the former left off.

11. One of the difficulties is revealed by noting a potential difficulty in deriving Protagoreanism from Hermogenes' conventionalism. For if we say that conventions can hold only within a group and not just for an individual, then conventionalism could entail at best merely that what is believed true in a given language it true "for" the speakers of that language (or true in that language). But we have seen that Plato allows conventions to hold for lone individuals (cf. n. VI-6). I have gone along with Plato on this point in my remarks below, leaving it open in my talk of "truth-in-a-language" whether a single individual can be said to have his own language.

12. The situation is of course different if we are talking of "propositions" or "statements" instead of "sentences" (in the sense of strings of sounds), but Plato is manifestly talking of the latter. (In fact, one can see his own view as, in effect, an insistence that we talk about the former instead; cf. sec. 2). For some remarks on Hermogenes' sort of conventionalism, and the claim that it is innocuous, see Putnam, p. 32.

13. See Church, and Quine **4**, pp. 134-135.

14. I have in mind various features of the sort that are frequently discussed in contemporary philosophy of language, such as various sorts of simplicity, ease of computation (e.g., drawing inferences), and the like.

15. This is a little too simple, in a way that is, however, harmless to our present efforts. In 432, e.g., it is more as though the naming relation were being said to be the picturing relation (though perhaps the two are only thought to be analogous), which would in turn be taken by the naturalistic view as the relation of resemblance. But once picturing is shown to be a distinct relation from resemblance (432b-d), and naming and resemblance are likewise shown to be distinct, the naturalist view as it originally arose is treated as disposed of (at least until someone can present a better version of it).

16. For some objections see for example Goodman **2**. For Plato's attitudes on this and related matters, see Ch. I, sec. 1; Ch. V, sec. 1; and Ch. IX, sec. 2.

17. The reason is stated to be that if we had something *exactly like* Cratylus, we would have not a name of Cratlyus alongside Cratylus himself, but "two Cratyluses" (432c5). Plato's manner of speaking here supports the view that he does not clearly distinguish between singular and general terms (cf. sec. 3). It also shows a way of thinking about sensible particulars that Aristotle is later anxious to combat (e.g., *Cat.* 1b3-5; *Met.* 1040a27-b4).

18. He accepts the distinction at least as early as 430c1. What he is disputing about later (e.g., at d8-e2) is not whether there is such a distinction, but whether in the light of the distinction we can say that there is such a thing as incorrect application in the case of names (he admits it for pictures). By this time Socrates has him on the ropes, but in 431e-432a he makes a final effort and does not give in until 433 (cf. *supra*). (His final effort in 431e-432a is to urge, using a claim about spelling to provide examples, that misapplications are not misnamings.)

19. This fact has been seen by Weingartner, pp. 18, 29ff., and by Kahn, pp. 153, 159, 163, n. 16. Weingartner's interpretation is similar in spirit to mine, especially in that he sees (though he does not develop) a link between the *Crat.* and the concerns of the *Phdr.* (p. 35; cf. *infra*, n. VI-30, and sec. 4). Kahn's interpretation is also in many ways akin to mine, but he concentrates too little on the link between the employment of names and the identification of Forms. Anagnostopoulos is correct in seeing that there is a connection between the enterprise of the *Crat.* and the problem of inquiry in the *Meno* (cf. Ch. VII, sec. 5).

20. "What they are like": Plato uses varied terminology here, without much attempt at precision. At 422d3 and 439d5 we have "οἷόν ἐστι"; at 423e*sqq.* we have "οὐσία"; at 389c1 and elsewhere we have the notion of "φύσις"; and at 389c6 we have a notable phrase (which shows that Plato is not emphasizing any distinction between "οἷόν ἐστι" and "φύσις"), "οἷον ἐπεφύκει." Although at one point Plato is particularly interested in the οὐσία of named objects (see n. VI-21), he is not generally too anxious to explain just what sort of information

one might expect a name to supply, or fail to supply, about an object. (Cf. Ch. I, sec. 2; Ch. II, sec. 1.)

21. This office is assigned to dialectic at 390c11 (cf. *Phdr*. 266c1 and Ch. V, sec. 2). Cf. also 393d3-4, e2-3, 6-7, 396a4-5. Here there is an added feature, that a name should somehow convey the οὐσία or φύσις of a thing (cf. 423e). There is no need for our purposes to enter into this matter here. But notice that the examples in 423e show that there is no notion here of any "essence" or the like of a sensible object. Since one of his examples is "the οὐσία of a color," he has in mind, e.g., the thing that is mentioned in answer to the question "What is yellow?" (Cf. also 429c4 with Schanz's bracketing of c5.) Plato does not believe that sensible objects, as we ordinarily think of them, have "essences" in any important sense (cf., with reservations, Hackforth **3**, pp. 154-155, and Prauss, pp. 67-98; see also my **1** and **2**. See *contra* Lorenz and Mittelstrass, whose general scheme, while suggestive, seems untenable as an interpretation. Robinson **6**, pp. 127ff., denies that Plato realizes that what namehood is depends in some sense on what names are for. His argument for this view is that in 388b and elsewhere, Plato's description of the function of a name confuses denoting and describing. But the fact that Plato makes this confusion (cf. sec. 3) does not mean that he does not see a connection between the nature of naming and the function of names.

22. Cf. n. VI-20. Prauss, pp. 122, claims that this enterprise in unnecessary, but his reason for thinking so is obscure, because the fact that at *Rep*. 524c Forms are described as διωρισμένα and κεχωρισμένα does not rule out the possibility of their being confused—a possibility about which we have seen Plato already worried.

23. Cf. Berkeley, Introd., sec. 19: ". . . it is a received opinion that language has no other end but the communicating of ideas . . ." Cf. also the presupposition underlying the views of Gorgias (or whoever it may be) in Sext. Emp., *Adv. Math*. VII.83-87 (cf. also [Aristotle], *De Melisso, Xenophane, Gorgia* 980a19-b22).

24. Vs. e.g. Kretzmann, p. 137. It is thus wrong to think that Plato slips back and forth between thinking of actual and thinking of ideal languages.

25. That is, he can think that even if, for such a language, "is a name of" and "resembles" in "such-and-such a way" have the same extensions or apply to just the same pairs of expressions and objects, nevertheless—as he sees it—the *notion* of namehood is not the same thing as the *notion* of (such-and-such a sort of) resemblance. Cf. n. I-77, and *infra*.

26. See 434e7-8, 436a3-8, 438a8-b3, 439b6-8. In the latter three passages, notice the use of "ζητεῖν" (along with "μανθάνειν"), suggestive of the same sort of searching which we saw most clearly in the *Meno* (Ch. II, sec. 4).

27. How does Plato suppose that we know which Form, say, a person is thinking of? He does not raise the issue here, but see Ch. VIII, secs. 2-3.

28. See 433d7-e2, 434a1-2; of course Plato realizes that convention can overcome this natural tendency (cf. *Phdo*. 73c-74a).

29. It is now possible to see a further reason why Plato does not pause to distinguish between the bestowing of names and the use of a name already bestowed (cf. n. VI-6). For what Plato is most concerned with is whether or not the use of a name will make one think of the proper thing (which we might take to be—though Plato does not go into this matter here—the thing that the person speaking intended you to think about; cf. Ch. VIII, secs. 2-3), and it is of no concern to him whether the "association" between the name and the thing, which leads one to think of the thing when presented with the name, was established by some sort of dubbing or not.

30. Cf. 389d6-7, 383b4-7, and notice that in giving his account of name-hood, Plato does not mean simply to be making a *proposal* about how we should use the word "name" nor to be describing ordinary usage. I believe that Kahn, p. 162, is substantially correct in saying that the Form of Name suggested in 389b-390e can be thought of as "the general sign relation . . . as required for the formulation and communication of truth in words." But Plato is not quite so clear about the matter, since he does not say explicitly what would have been helpful there, that this Form is, as it were, a relational Form (cf. n. III-16), and he does not make clear just how we are to think of particular names as "partaking" in this Form. As Kahn observes, however, Plato is not much interested here in working out the metaphysical status of the Form of Name; rather, he brings it in primarily to make clear that he thinks that *there is* a *correct* account of naming. Still, the difficulties that Plato encounters here provide a further argument for placing the *Crat.* after the *Phdr.* Calvert observes (pp. 33-34) that not only in connection with the Form of Name, but in connection with other Forms as well, Plato seems to be pointing hesitantly at something like a distinction between genus-Forms and species-Forms. This fact is taken by Calvert as a sign of an early groping after the theory of Forms, but it makes far more sense if we notice that this very distinction comes to the fore in the *Phdr.*, in connection with division, and it is there that Plato is forced to deal with this matter (about which earlier dialogues have nothing explicit to say of any consequence). The gropings of the *Crat.* (and I think that they are genuine, notwithstanding Shorey **4**, p. 268, n. 5) become thoroughly understandable, since we can suppose that Plato has not worked the matter out (if we are to believe Aristotle, *Met.* VII.13, e.g., he never did). Cf. n. VII-1.

31. Plato does not attempt to give a fully developed and elaborated account of naming, but it seems clear that he does not have in mind the idea that, say, N names X for a given pair of people on a given occasion just in case the speaker intends that the hearer think of X when the speaker utters N. The notion of intention does not figure in Plato's exposition. Whether it would have if he had elaborated his account is another question.

32. Cf. Robinson **6**, pp. 130ff.

33. It is singular terms that have the role of referring to objects or denoting them, as I view it, whereas general terms describe or are true of them. For some remarks on this distinction, see e.g., Quine **8**, pp. 95-100. (Of course, a

singular description, such as "the house that Jack built," may contain or encapsulate general or descriptive terms, but its denoting in the relevant sense does not arise from those terms alone, since "*a* house that Jack built" is descriptive but it is not a singular denoting phrase.) Notice that not only is the singular/general distinction tied up with the denoting/describing distinction, but the identity-statement/predicative-statement distinction is of a piece with both of them. This fact emerges when we consider the factors that led Plato into the "self-predicative" view of Forms (cf. Ch. III, introd.) For example, to understand that "Large is large" may be either an identity-statement or a predication requires an understanding of the fact that the second occurrence of "large" may be either (respectively) a singular or a general term, which in turn requires understanding that "large" may be used (respectively) either to denote or to describe the Form of the Large. In the *Parm.* and the *Soph.*, Plato may have begun to be aware of these contrasts (cf. Owen **1** and **11**.) For another instance of the same sort of confusion, see n. VI-34.

34. For such a view, see Frege **2** and Russell **3**. (There is, of course, the complication, which I pass over, that Russell did not think that singular descriptions have denotation on their own, as it were, since he thought that they could be contextually eliminated.) For an opposing view, see e.g., Donnellan. It does not occur to Plato here to remark that there might conceivably be singular terms that denote but do not contain any encapsulated general or descriptive terms (i.e., terms such as some have thought various sorts of proper names to be; cf. Russell **5**). Thus, it does not occur to him that the semantic function of denoting and that of describing are different. This fact dovetails with what we saw in n. VI-33; cf. also Kahn, pp. 172, 156, 166; Luce **2**; Lorenz and Mittelstrass, pp. 5-6.

35. Obviously this cluster of ideas is related, as many have noticed, to ideas developed by Wittgenstein in his **1**.

36. But 422c-d shows that he does not think that the naming of a complex object by a name that is complex *simply consists in* the naming of the elements of the object by the respective elements of the name, because holding this would require, contrary to what he wants (cf. 435e2), that there be *another* account of what the naming of a simple object consists in. (Notice that although I say "respective elements," because this is what this view presumably necessitates, there is no inkling of just how he would explain this idea. What, for example, would be the effect of transposing two letters in a name? This is an instance of the problem that he is getting at in *Tht.* 203csqq., e.g., and instances of which often worry Aristotle, e.g., at *Top.* 150b22ff. and *Met.* 1035a14ff.).

37. This does not mean that Plato thought that he knew just how to break things, or names, into their constituent atoms; see 425d, 439b.

38. This translation of "λόγος" in the *Crat.* is disputed by Prauss, pp. 43-46, 58-60, in my opinion mistakenly. On pp. 43-46 he is too ready to think that Plato could not have made the mistake of ascribing truth to both sentences

and ὀνόματα—a mistake that is by no means unnatural, expecially given the fact that the notion of truth, which attaches to sentences, is closely connected to the notion of being *true of* an object, which we have seen Plato attaching to his names. On pp. 58-60, he places more weight than it can bear on the claim at 396a2 that the two names of Zeus are together "just like a *logos*" ("ἀτεχνῶς . . . οἶον λόγος"), and draws from it an account of *logos* which is dubious and goes beyond the evidence that 396a2ff., even on his interpretation, would provide. Moreover, the use of "λόγος" at b7 shows that in a2 Plato merely means that the combination of the two names of Zeus, though indeed just like a *logos* in Plato's view, is nevertheless just *like* a *logos*, and there is no reason to take Plato as saying that it *is* a *logos*.

39. See 399b1, 7, 425a1, 431b2-6. I do not believe that Plato's use of this term in the *Crat.* should be assimilated to his use of it in the *Soph.* (262a*sqq*.), and I therefore think it misleading to translate it by "predicate," or the like, as Oehler does, p. 59, n. 1. In addition, the translation is made implausible by Plato's failure in the *Crat.* to distinguish between denoting and describing (cf. n. VI-33). For an argument that supports the translation "phrase," see Prauss, pp. 54-58.

40. Cf. also 385c and 431a-c, where both sentences and names are said to be capable of being true or false (cf. n. VI-38).

41. We see a certain form of it in Frege's view in **2** that sentences are expressions that refer to or denote, though of course he believes that there are only two possible denotations for them, namely the True and the False (truth and falsity). In this way, Frege's view avoids the difficulty that I go on to mention, because it allows a false sentence to be meaningful and nevertheless refer to something (namely, the False). The effort of Kahn, pp. 174-175, to find a place in Plato for a Fregean distinction between sense and reference runs afoul of Plato's confusion, of which we have seen signs and which Kahn recognizes (p. 172, in saying that Plato does not distinguish between proper names and general terms.) One symptom of Kahn's difficulty is that within the "extension" of a Form he places two quite different sorts of things: 1) other Forms "contained" within it (e.g., as Bravery might be "contained" in Virtue), and 2) particulars that participate in it. But it is one thing to be *a virtue* and another to be virtu*ous*. (For a recognition of this problem, cf. Moravcsik **3**.)

42. At 385b5-10 the matter is put differently, as in *Tht.* 189 and in the *Soph.* For our purposes here these niceties do not matter (cf. Ch. VII, sec. 4).

43. For a case against seeing states of affairs at work in the argument of *Tht.* 188-189, see McDowell **2**, pp. 198-202, though on pp. 235ff. something like states of affairs (in the loose sense which I am employing) do seem to be in the picture.

44. This line of interpretation fits with (but does not require) the idea that Plato sometimes thought of sensible objects as somehow bundles of properties; cf. n. III-34. It is tempting to connect this idea with Plato's discussion of simples and compounds (sec. 4), but Plato gives us too little information to

allow us to do so. One consideration discouraging such a temptation is that he might well have meant the compounds and simples there in question all to be Forms, so that sensibles would have no place in the scheme. We shall, I think, never be certain.

45. I do not think that he believes that each sensible object constantly changes, in the stronger sense that between any two distinct moments it has altered in *all* respects. Cf. n. III-20; Ch. VII, sec. 1; and my **1**, p. 190. It seems likely that in his early and middle periods, Plato was not as precise as he might have been in thinking out just what he meant by saying that the sensible world is utterly subject to change. Calvert has maintained (pp. 38, 43) that in 439-440 Plato is uncertain about the doctrine of the mutability of sensible objects and is unclear about it in a way in which he is not in the *Rep*. But in the light of the evidence that we have seen of the way in which the preoccupations of the *Crat*. fit well after the *Phdr*., these uncertainties and unclarities are better explained by supposing that Plato has now come to realize that his earlier imprecise claims about mutability need to be better spelled out. He does not capitalize on this realization in the *Crat*., and so he pursues the matter further in *Tht*. 181-183 (see Ch. VII, sec. 2, and my *loc. cit.*).

46. See n. III-36, along with Owen **8**. I say "thus far" because this view seems to come under attack in the *Soph*.; see Owen, *ibid*., pp. 336ff.

47. For the qualification "in effect" see n. VI-10.

48. The ideas about letters and syllables, which is indeed introduced in the *Tht*. in a manner suggesting this response (201ff. and Ch. VII, sec. 5), appears on the scene in totally different garb in the *Crat*. (424c*sqq*.; cf. 425d).

49. The pertinent dialogues are the *Tht*., *Parm*., *Soph*., *Polit*., *Phileb*. Of course, Plato does continue his efforts to establish definitions, esp. in the *Soph*. and *Polit*., but the emphasis on the illustration of the points of method that I have discussed is greater than it had been earlier (which is not, of course, to say that it had earlier been absent).

CHAPTER VII

The Theaetetus: Knowledge and Definition

One must count the *Theaetetus* an important dialogue, whether or not one believes that it records a turning-point in Plato's career. One must also regard it as puzzling. For those who think that Plato did not substantially alter the doctrines expounded in the *Phaedo* and the *Republic*, it is hard to explain why the *Theaetetus* does not follow the lines of those dialogues more closely.[1] For those, on the other hand, who think that Plato did change his views and find in the *Theaetetus* some pieces of evidence for that view, it is nevertheless a task to say why this work does not announce more openly the overthrow, or at least the need to reexamine, earlier doctrine.[2] To both of these broad classes of interpreters, the *Theaetetus* should seem somewhat isolated: it asks for an account of knowledge, but it does not say whether it is building on or tearing down the work that went before it.

The reason is that it does neither. In its quest to say what knowledge is, it is pressing further an investigation of the problems that had surrounded Plato's epistemological views from the very beginning, which continued to be present in muted form in the middle dialogues, and which had begun to seem more urgent in the *Phaedrus* and the *Cratylus*. It does not reject outright the views of the middle period (the *Phaedo*, the *Republic*, the *Symposium*, and the *Timaeus*) because although Plato may now be having some doubts about those views, in important respects he is still working within his old theory. It does not reiterate those views, on the other hand, because Plato now sees ever more clearly that there are some serious difficulties that plague not only the account of knowledge which that theory contained, but any account of knowledge which is roughly similar to it. I have already argued that the *Republic* does not claim to give a complete and finished theory of knowledge, that Plato was at the time fully aware of that fact (Ch. IV, sec. 1), and that he has continued to work on issues that the middle works admittedly left undeveloped (Chs. V and VI). The *Theaetetus* should, I believe, make us continue to cleave to this view of Plato's development, and to the idea that he did not view his middle works as presenting an epistemological dogma which had to be accepted or rejected *in toto*, but rather as a theory that left, or even raised, further problems to be investigated. So it is not so much that later dialogues overthrow earlier thought; rather, they continue work on issues that Plato has all along meant to investigate more deeply.

In the foregoing, of course, I speak of epistemological matters, and not of the full range of issues with which the theory of Forms deals. Thus, I am here neither asserting nor denying that by the time of the *Theaetetus*, there had been a change in Plato's views on various metaphysical issues, such as the question whether Forms are self-predicative (cf. Ch. III, introd.), and various other matters having to do with the mutability of sensibles and the stability of Forms.[3] Although I think that those questions can (and ultimately must) be tied to the matters that concern us, they are to a fair extent independent exegetical problems which we may safely leave aside here.

The *Theaetetus*, as we shall see, goes back to some basic questions that had occupied Plato since the beginning of his career. Not surprisingly, therefore, it contains a number of apparent allusions to earlier works, and to arguments that were standard in them. It starts with a request by Socrates for a definition of knowledge, and when Theaetetus responds to the request by presenting some examples of knowledge (146c-d), he receives a rebuke from Socrates which harks back to some of Plato's earliest works.[4] In addition, the ending of the dialogue, with an announcement by Socrates that he must go off to defend himself against the charge that Meletus has brought against him (210d), might also seem to harp on themes from earlier times, when Plato devoted so much time to portraying Socrates. Perhaps it is fanciful to see in such passages conscious reminders of old issues, but the content of the dialogue, as we shall see, does bear out the claim that in this work Plato is asking basic questions about the foundations of the doctrine which he has expended so much energy in developing and expounding, and about the legacy he had received from Socrates.

1 The Line of Thought in
the First Part of the Dialogue

For my purposes, the *Theaetetus* can be seen as falling into two parts, the first ending at 186a12 with the final refutation of the claim that knowledge (ἐπιστήμη) is sensation or perception (αἴσθησις), and the second beginning at 187a1 with the examination of the problem of false belief and running to the end of the work. To the second part I shall return later, trying to show both what its central concerns are and how they are connected with those of the first part. It is that first part that we must take up now.

It is no easy task to follow the line of thought of the first part and to see its continuity. The reason is that it touches several ideas, and Plato does not make explicit how he thinks they are connected with one another. With a little work, however, we can make things fall reasonably well into place. Here, then, are the main ideas which have to be taken into account. (1) There is a contention that may be described as "Protagorean" (cf. Ch. VI, sec. 1), that whatever any given person believes is in some sense "true for him," that no belief is ever to be preferred to any other on the score of truth or anything like it, and that consequently nobody can be said to know about any matter better than anyone else who has an opinion about it. (2) There is a claim that in some sense knowledge is the same thing as *aisthesis*,[5] an identification that is Theaetetus' first full-scale response to Socrates' request to say what knowledge is (151e1-3), and which is finally refuted in 184b4-186e12. (The Greek word "αἴσθησις" is ambiguous as between "perception" and "sensation",[6] so I shall generally use its transliteration.) (3) There is an account of the workings of *aisthesis* that is gradually expounded from 152d2 to 157c3, and that never receives any explicit refutation. (4) There is a view, linked to the account of *aisthesis*, according to which everything is in some sense in constant change or flux. This view is first put forward at 152d7ff. and appears to be refuted in 181b8-183c4 (with a preface to the refutation in 179d1-181b7). I say "appears to be refuted" because, as will emerge, the doctrine that is refuted here seems to be importantly different from the view concerning flux which figures in the account of *aisthesis* from 152d7 on.

These four points are the main ones with which I intend to deal here. It is not that there are no other issues arising in this part of the dialogue; there are others indeed, and of great complexity and importance. Nor do I intend to cover even these four points in complete detail; rather, I shall take them only as far as we need to in order to understand the main course of Plato's argument and to see what emerges from this section to be used in the second part of the work.

The first fact to be noticed, which is perhaps the most important for the understanding of the drift of the dialogue, is that although (2), the identification of knowledge and *aisthesis*, might seem to be the most important target of Plato's attack in this part of the work, the Protagorean contention, (1), is of at least as much concern to him. We have already seen it before. We saw it in the *Cratylus*, where it was explicitly laid out but where its falsity was simply assumed, in effect, as a premise in the argument against linguistic conventionalism (Ch. VI, sec. 1).[7] In the *Theaetetus* Plato now has the opportunity to make good the lack there of any rebuttal of it. But it is not hard to see that whether Plato had explicitly associated it with the actual Protagoras or not,[8] the Protagorean contention was in an important way his adversary long before the *Cratylus*—as early, in fact, as the earliest of his works. For we saw him convinced from the start that there are truths that are independent of human belief and that are to be discovered without reliance on hearsay or other such defective sources of information (Ch. I, introd. and sec. 4). But if all there is to holding a true belief, in the most substantial sense of "true" allowable, is simply holding the belief—that is, if *anything* that you believe is "true for you" and there is no more to be said about truth—then obviously Plato's conviction would be entirely undermined, and he would no longer be able to maintain that some judgments are to be preferred to others as better reflecting how things actually are.[9]

The Protagorean contention, (1), and the identification of knowledge and *aisthesis*, (2), are intimately connected, and it is not entirely clear how Plato means them to stand to each other. Thus, he might think that the latter is the most likely way in which the former might be supported, or he might think the reverse.[10] But however that may be, he does attack the two claims separately and realizes that they are distinct. First, he argues against the Protagorean contention, ultimately introducing two main arguments against it. One of these is what has been called "the table-turning argument," in 169d-171d, which purports to show that Protagoras must himself regard his own contention as not true (175c5-7). Next, there is a piece of reasoning having to do with judgments about the future (171d-179c, including a digression). Second, in 184b-186e, Plato argues independently against the identification of knowledge and *aisthesis*.[11] The upshot is that he thinks that he has disposed of both of his targets. But, as we shall see (sec. 2), it is the rejection of the Protagorean contention that plays a somewhat more important role in the discussion from 187 onward.

Now let us turn briefly to the account of *aisthesis*, expounded from 152 to 157. Unlike the identification of knowledge with *aisthesis*, and the Protagorean view, this account is not refuted or explicitly rejected in the *Theaetetus*. This fact is crucial, whether or not one believes that the account of *aisthesis* was actually accepted by Plato.[12] The account is indeed introduced in order to support the identification of knowledge and *aisthesis*, and thus also the Protagorean contention, but it turns out that Plato does not show signs of thinking that the account itself actually entails either of them. If Plato had thought that it did, then one would expect him to point out that if they are false, then it must be false too, but because he does not think that it entails them, nothing in his arguments against them may be seen as grounds for rejecting the account of *aisthesis*. In fact, the very most that the account of *aisthesis* could entail is that every *perceptual* judgment is true (or "true for" the person making it),[13] but it could not entail that every true judgment is a perceptual judgment, nor that every case of knowledge is a case of the exercise of *aisthesis* and nothing else. For the account of *aisthesis* is merely an account of how *perceptual* judgments are arrived at and contains nothing whatever to show that those are the only judgments that there are. Moreover, Plato shows his recognition of this fact, in 179c1-d1, when he says that perhaps all *aistheseis* are true and goes on to show, in 184-186, that *even if* this were so, it would still not be demonstrated that knowledge is *aisthesis*.[14] This being the case, the account of *aisthesis* turns out not to entail anything that is refuted, and thus does not have to be repudiated by Plato. This is not to say that he must himself accept it; perhaps he does and perhaps he does not.[15] The main point, however, is that he is not, for the purposes of his argument, required to count it false.

The importance of this fact emerges when we consider the last of the four points that I shall take up in discussing the first part of the dialogue, namely the view that everything is somehow in constant change, or what is often called "the doctrine of flux."[16] The puzzle arising from this doctrine is as follows. The account of *aisthesis* in 152-157 is supported, in part, by a claim that everything is constantly changing, and lo and behold in 181-183 there is a refutation of a claim that everything is constantly changing. But the two claims are different, the latter being considerably stronger than the former. For the doctrine of flux that figures in the account of *aisthesis* is to the effect that for any object and any two temporal points in its career, however close, the object undergoes a change in *some* respect in the interval between those two points. But the doctrine of flux that is refuted in 181-183 is to the effect that for any object and any two temporal points in its career, however close, the object undergoes a change in *every* respect in the interval between those two points. There is no need here to go into Plato's argument against the latter doctrine.[17] The important point is that the former doctrine is obviously weaker than the latter, and that by disproving the latter Plato has not *ipso facto* disproved the former.[18] It is accordingly important to realize that Plato has no need to refute the former, weaker, doctrine. The only motive that he would have had to do so would have been a desire to show that the account of *aisthesis* is false; but we have seen that showing this is not part of his program. If it had been, then he would have been guilty of a flagrantly invalid argument, because he would then have been treating the account of *aisthesis* as entailing (or containing as a part) the stronger doctrine of flux, which it does not do. If, on the other hand, we regard Plato as willing for his purposes to let the account of *aisthesis* stand, then he is free of this charge of paralogism. The argument of 181-183, then, can be seen as a sort of *obiter dictum*, of which we can perhaps guess the purpose,[19] attacking an absurdly strong doctrine of flux.

What emerges from the first part of the *Theaetetus* is, then, as follows. The Protagorean contention and the identification of knowledge and *aisthesis* have been argued against and rejected. The strong doctrine of flux has likewise been rebutted. The weak doctrine of flux and the account of *aisthesis* of which it is a component have been left aside, not attacked but not emphatically asserted either, since their survival goes unnoted at the end of the first part and for the rest of the dialogue. The really important results of this phase of the discussion are the rejection both of the identification of knowledge and *aisthesis*, and of the Protagorean contention. As we shall see immediately, it is in particular the rejection of the Protagorean contention that sets the stage for the next part of the dialogue and motivates the major portion of it.

2 The Problems of False Belief

The second part of the *Theaetetus* itself falls into two sections. The first, 187a-200c, consists of a largely unsuccessful attempt to explain

how false belief is possible; the second, running from 200c to the end
of the work, gives us some ill-fated efforts to say what knowledge is.
Both of these sections bear directly on topics that have been important
concerns of ours.

Once Plato has argued in the first part of the dialogue that not all
beliefs are true (or true for the believer), he is of course immediately
obliged to try to meet any further objections which may arise to saying
that some beliefs are false. And this is what he proceeds to do in
187-200. Without meeting such objections, of course, he would not be
in a position to maintain what he very strongly wishes to maintain,
that there are genuine disputes between people concerning states of
affairs in the world, and that in such disputes one party is correct and
the other is incorrect. It is for this reason that I have emphasized that
the Protagorean contention was a vital target for him to hit in the
earlier part of the work, and that its denial was something of which he
was going to make use. But it is also important that he has rejected the
identification of knowledge and sensation, because as will emerge
shortly, he thinks that it is concerning objects that cannot be sensed
but can only be thought about (195d6-9, e1-4, 196c4-8) that the problem of false belief becomes most severe. We have clear reasons, then,
to think of these two topics as the truly central ones in the first part of
the dialogue.[20]

Although most of *Theaetetus* 187-200 is concerned with such false
identity-beliefs and mistaken identifications (on this distinction see
sec. 3), there is a brief passage that introduces another difficulty for
the notion of false belief in general. In 188c9-189b9, it is suggested
that believing falsely is impossible, on the ground that it is "believing
what is not" (μὴ ὂν δοξάζειν, 189a10), which is taken to be tantamount
to "believing nothing" (οὐδὲν δοξάζειν), which in turn is said to
amount to not believing at all (12-13). From this it is concluded that
believing falsely is not "believing what is not" (b4-5), at least *if* there is
such a thing as false belief at all. In the *Sophist*, Plato returns to this
issue and argues that false belief, construed as "believing what is not,"
is indeed possible. In the *Theaetetus*, on the other hand, this notion of
"believing what is not" is touched on only in this brief passage and
plays no role in the rest of 187-200. We shall return to this issue when
we examine what the *Sophist* has to say about false belief (sec. 4). For
the moment, however, we should notice the following points. In the
first place, it is this problem about false belief that was raised and then
quickly shelved in the *Cratylus* (cf. Ch. VI, sec. 4, and *Crat.* 429c-d),
and not the other problems that take up the rest of 187-200.[21] Since

the time of the *Cratylus*, Plato has come to see additional difficulties. Secondly, however, Plato says nothing here about the relationship between this problem and those other problems, and we shall see that he may have been the victim of some confusion on this point (sec. 4). Bearing these facts in mind, let us temporarily ignore 188c-189b, and its notion of "believing what is not," and concentrate on the remaining dominant issues in this section.

One of the salient facts about the rest of the discussion of false belief is that although Plato does not highlight or explain the fact, its direct concern is exclusively with the question how it is possible to believe falsely that *X* is (identical with) *Y*.[22] Why is this?

One suggestion is that he is concentrating on the subclass of false beliefs which seem to him to raise difficulty and leaves others aside as not problematical. After all, if one cannot explain how it is possible falsely to believe, e.g., that Socrates is Theaetetus (188b7-10), then one cannot claim to give a fully general account of all of the false beliefs that would appear possible. And an account that made clear the possibility of only some of the false beliefs of whose existence we are convinced would be less than we would wish, particularly in a confrontation with Protagoreanism. Moreover, we could suppose that the concentration here upon misidentifications and false identity-beliefs also arises from the fact that mistakes of this sort could be involved in the kinds of conceptual confusions that Plato wished to ward off in the *Phaedrus* and the *Cratylus*. Thus, although we saw that the former work was not explicit about exactly how such confusions arose (Ch. V, sec. 1), Plato could have thought that conflations of the kind that was in view there could be manifested in false identity-beliefs; and this seems, though not spelled out, not an unreasonable idea. So there is a reason why such false beliefs might be particularly on his mind.

The other suggestion is more sweeping and more direct. It is to the effect that Plato at this point believed that every false belief, of whatever form, somehow involves a false identity-belief of some variety.[23] Thus, for example, he might suppose that someone who believes that Socrates is green must be falsely believing that some other attribute, which Socrates does have, is the attribute of being green. The *Phaedrus* contains at least one passage weighing in favor of this view. In 260b-c, a suggestion is apparently made that by mistaking the attribute of being an ass for the attribute of being a horse, one may fall into calling a horse something which is in fact an ass. Now Plato does not there say that this mistake over attributes (or Forms) is the only way in which one might come to call an ass a horse, but it is possible that he did hold this view. For in the present passage of the *Theaetetus*, at 188b3ff., the suggestion clearly seems to be that *anyone* believing falsely must be falsely believing one thing to be another, and the same idea is perhaps conveyed by 189b12-c4. Although it is not evident why Plato should have held this view,[24] nevertheless if he did hold it then we have a clear explanation of his emphasis here on this sort of false belief.

Now let us turn to the substance of Plato's difficulty over false identity-beliefs and see how it arises. At this point our exegesis, like Plato's argument itself, must become quite complex, so I must provide it with a brief introduction. Plato's difficulty rests on two assumptions which are closely intertwined. We must both keep them distinct in our minds and understand how they are connected. One assumption is that if one "knows" an object (or alternatively—cf. *infra*—if one "grasps it with one's mind" or "brings it into one's thoughts"), then one cannot mistake it for anything else or anything else for it. The other assumption is that if two singular terms refer to the same object (are codesignative or coreferential), then they must somehow *obviously* refer to the same object (be codesignative), and if two terms are not codesignative, then they must be somehow *obviously* not codesignative. We shall see eventually how the interplay between these two assumptions must be understood (sec. 3), but for the moment let us simply keep them in view and watch the progress of Plato's argument.

In 188a-c, Plato sets up the problem of false belief by urging that one must either "know" a given object or "not know" it, and then goes on to say that it is impossible to think that X is Y either when one knows neither of them, or one of them, or both. The basic outline of his problem is clear enough. He takes it on the one hand that if one does not "know X," then one cannot in the requisite way think about X or have X in one's thoughts (b9), so as to be able to believe that X is such-and-such (no matter what expression "such-and-such" may represent). On the other hand, he takes it that if one does "know X," then one is going to be unable to believe that X is identical with Y, where "Y" represents some term referring to something other than X. In 189b*sqq.*, the problem is stated in somewhat different but still analogous terms. Here the notion of "knowing X" is not initially used (it reappears in 191a8-b1 and afterward), but it is supposed, first, that if one "grasps X with one's mind" (ἐφαπτόμενος τῇ ψυχῇ in 190c6-7; cf. d9-10, 195d8, e5-6),[25] then one cannot believe that it is identical with Y if it is not, and second, that if one does not grasp X with one's mind, then it is not possible to claim that one believes that X is such-and-such (no matter what expression "such-and-such" may represent.)[26] This argument involves a retreat for the moment from the first argument, in that it does not presuppose a requirement that one must know X in order to have a belief about it; rather, one must only in some sense think about it or "have it in one's thoughts." But the form of the argument, and its upshot, are the same.

Note for future reference (in sec. 5) that this requirement on "thinking about" an object, and on "having a belief about it," is not restricted to this passage. For later on, in 209, Plato again betrays the view that if one cannot always distinguish Theaetetus from everything else, then there is no saying that one is really thinking about Theaetetus rather than about one or another of the objects with which he could be confused. This is indeed a strong requirement on what it is to think about a thing, and it has important repercussions which we shall examine shortly. The point now is simply that it is a crucial part of the argument in this passage against false-identity beliefs.

Thus far we have seen Plato operating with the first of the two assumptions set forth two paragraphs back. In 189e*sqq.*, however, he switches without warning to the other assumption (thus making it fairly clear that he is not keeping the two separate). Here Plato says that to make a judgment in accordance with one of one's beliefs is to affirm a sentence silently to oneself,[27] and he goes on to claim in effect (190b2-8) that no sentence that (so to speak) represents or expresses a false belief that X is Y would ever be affirmed by anyone to himself. Thus, if one's affirmation to oneself of "Socrates is Theaetetus" is to count as constituting the false belief that Socrates is Theaetetus, then—he must be arguing—this sentence could not in that circumstance be asserted by anyone. He does not say why it could not be asserted, but 190b2-8 is best taken to say simply that such a sentence could be too implausible to assert. Why? Why could there not be circumstances in which such a sentence might seem quite plausible? Moreover why—one rightly objects—should it be such obviously false sentences that must represent the belief that Socrates is Theaetetus? Why could the relevant mistaken belief not be expressed to oneself by the (false but not necessarily *obviously* false) sentence "The teacher of Plato is Theaetetus"? But let us postpone these questions (to sec. 3), and continue for now to watch Plato trying to evade his two assumptions, but being repeatedly caught by them.

In 191a-195d, the argument takes a new turn (which soon proves unsuccessful), and Plato claims to have found a way in which some false identity-beliefs are indeed possible, in cases which involve perception. Since the cases in which he allows such false beliefs are similar to each other in the crucial respect, we may concentrate on one of them. He presents a comparison of the mind to a wax tablet, and maintains that, e.g., if we have a memory-imprint of Theaetetus, and at the same time perceive Socrates, we can, by wrongly "fitting" the sensory impression of Socrates into our memory-imprint of Theaetetus, do something that he is willing to count as falsely believing that the thing that we are perceiving is Theaetetus. There is much to be said about this comparison of the mind to a wax tablet, and about the use that Plato makes of it,[28] but we need only take up here the feature of his treatment of this sort of case which seems to him to make the false belief possible.

In the imagined case, we can be supposed to "know" both Theaetetus and Socrates, but we only see Socrates, and we wrongly "fit" that sensory impression of Socrates to our memory-imprint of Theaetetus. Plato stipulates that for this sort of mistake to occur, something must have gone wrong in either our sensory impression or our memory-imprint. Although he does not say precisely what may have gone wrong, he suggests that the sensory impression of Socrates may not in some sense "match" the memory-imprint of Socrates (τὴν δὲ γνῶσιν τοῦ ἑτέρου μὴ κατὰ τὴν αἴσθησιν ἔχω in 193d6-7; cf. c1-2, e1, 194a1-2) better than or as well as it "matches" the memory-imprint of Theaetetus. Now he *seems* willing to count the "mis-fitting" of the impression and the imprint as *itself* the believing that Socrates is Theaetetus, but this would run counter to his claim that believing is asserting a sentence to oneself, so we can suppose that some sentence ought, in consistency, to be involved in this case. What is the sentence? It would appear to be something such as "That person whom I see is Theaetetus," and it would appear that Plato is counting the asserting of this sentence to oneself as believing that the person whom one sees is Theaetetus. Now a plethora of problems is raised by Plato's construal of belief as silent assertion of sentences,[29] but what is striking about *this* sentence is that it need not on the face of it be an implausible one to assert, and so what Plato has done is to allow a nonimplausible sentence to represent the belief that X is Y, even though X is not in fact Y. He has done this by allowing the two terms, represented by "X" and "Y," to be noncodesignative even while they are not taken to be *obviously* noncodesignative, so that the sentence represented by "X is Y," though false, is not *obviously* false, nor too implausible to assert to oneself.

How has this trick been turned? Simply by not requiring in effect that every term that refers to Socrates be *obviously* noncodesignative with every term that refers to something other than Socrates. For if we could not have produced a term such as "That person whom I see," which is not obviously noncodesignative with, e.g., "Theaetetus," then the requisite nonimplausible sentence could not have been constructed.

Although in saying that false belief has been found in "the fitting together of perception and thought" (195d1-2) Plato shows that he thinks that the move to vindicate this sort of false belief has crucially involved cases in which perception is operating, he is nevertheless mistaken. Rather, the crucial move has been to allow pairs of noncodesignative but not obviously noncodesignative terms. If he had seen this, then he would have explored thoroughly the idea that such pairs might be constructed even for cases in which perception is not involved. For while "that person whom I see" and "Theaetetus" may on occasion not be obviously noncodesignative, the same might also in some circumstances be true of the pair of terms "the teacher of Plato" and "Theaetetus," so that a person could find "The teacher of Plato is Theaetetus" a not implausible sentence to assert to himself.

In 195d*sqq.* Plato immediately objects to the solution offered by the wax-tablet model that it will not help to vindicate the possibility of false belief in cases involving objects that we cannot perceive by sense (195d8-9, e1-2, 6-7).[30] The problematical case concerns a person who miscalculates and ostensibly believes that the sum of seven and five is eleven. Plato's attempt to accomodate this case invokes a comparison of the mind to an aviary, a comparison whose details we do not here have to treat, since the important point about it is that Plato simply allows the old problem to reinstate itself. For by the same kind of reasoning that introduced the difficulty in 188a-c and 189b-d, Plato refuses to allow the possibility of mistaking one's "knowledge of twelve" for one's "knowledge of eleven," and hence rejects the possibility of believing that the sum of seven and five is eleven; and the new features that the aviary model introduces do not substantially alter the nature of his difficulty. Once he has left perception out of the picture, he no longer sees how to allow a belief to be represented by a false but not obviously false identity-sentence or how to allow one to have two distinct things in mind in such a way that they are not obviously distinct. Accordingly, he holds that one cannot in the requisite way think about a non-sensible object without being able in all circumstances to distinguish it from every other non-sensible object.

Thus, his effort to vindicate across the board the possibility of false belief ends in failure. Plato says that the failure is due to his having tried to explain false belief without having an account of knowledge (200c8-d2). This diagnosis, however, is slightly off the mark, because the problem is equally precipitated by his requirements for thinking or having a belief about an object (cf. *supra* on 189b*sqq*.). Moreover in 192a6, 7-8, he denies that we can (as it were) believe that one object that we sense is another object that we sense, in cases in which we "know" neither of them. Plainly, in this latter case there is no threat that if false belief is to be possible then we might have to admit to knowing and not knowing the same thing, and what this fact shows is that it is not Plato's refusal to make such an admission that lies at the root of his difficulty. It is rather that he does not allow that two distinct things can be brought "into one's beliefs," whether as a matter of knowledge *or not*, except by being referred to by terms that are obviously not codesignative.

3 False Belief and False Identification

It is now time to return to the assumptions that we have seen working in Plato's argument. They were (1) that if one "knows" an object (or "brings it into one's thoughts"),[31] then one cannot mistake it for anything else or anything else for it, and (2) that if two singular terms are codesignative then they must be obviously codesignative, and if they are not codesignative, then they must be obviously not codesignative. We must see how these assumptions are related to each other, and how Plato's use of them is connected with his earlier reflections.

Clearly, the assumption that dominates Plato's cogitations is the former. Not only does it echo earlier ideas more plainly, but it is more prominent in 187-200. For even when in 189b*sqq*. Plato switches to using the latter assumption and says that to hold a belief is to affirm a sentence silently to oneself, he quickly returns to manners of speaking more suggestive of the former assumption (e.g., 193d6-7, and repeatedly in the aviary passage in 197c*sqq*.). Thus, although there is no reason to think that he explicitly distinguished the two assumptions, there is reason to regard the former as the more prominent in his thoughts. Moreover, if we are to connect the two in a substantial way, we may try to reduce, as it were, the one to the other and to show that it was by making the former assumption that Plato fell equally into making the latter. And it is precisely this move that we shall be helped to make by what we have seen in Plato's earlier works, and particularly in the *Cratylus*. Thus, let us see how the former assumption stimulated acceptance of the latter.

But first let us see what motivated the acceptance of the former assumption itself. Why can one not think about an object and nevertheless mistake it for something else? One crucial point, as many have seen,[32] is that Plato regards the relevant sort of thinking as analogous to having an object in one's visual field and gazing at it. We have seen this picture of thinking employed many times, from the earliest works onward, and particularly in the *Republic* and the *Phaedrus* (Ch. IV, sec. 2; Ch. V, introd.). But what is equally crucial is that Plato regards thinking about *two* nonidentical things simultaneously as analogous to having two distinct objects presented in one's visual field, *in such a way that* they are somehow *obviously* nonidentical. When he asks you to suppose that a person is thinking about (or seeing) two different objects and then claims that it is absurd to imagine that the person can be confusing them (192a1-4, 7-8, e.g.), what he is requiring you to suppose is that there are two objects in the person's visual field which are distinguished by him from each other, but that *at the same time* he fails to distinguish them from each other. Plainly, such a supposition is very difficult to make, and so it is not surprising that by employing this picture of what it is to think about two distinct objects, Plato sees no way for mistaken identification to arise.[33]

It is an intricate matter to say just what produces the difficulty, on this picture, of saying that misidentification might take place, and I shall pursue the issue only very briefly. It seems to me that of the following two statements only the latter runs a chance of expressing something like an impossibility, and that Plato has mistakenly moved from the former to the latter and thus thought that a confusion of two things about which you are thinking could be ruled out. The first statement is "S has two objects in his visual field and believes one of them to be the other." The second statement is "S has two objects in his visual field and distinguishes them and believes one of them to be the other." Now if I am correct, and if it is possible to have two things in your visual field and yet believe one to be the other, then Plato could have had the picture he does of what it is to think about two distinct objects and *still* have made a place for a sort of mistaken identification. But since it would take us too far out of our way to argue the question, I leave it to the reader to settle the issue. But even if I am incorrect, notice that what gives rise to the assumption under discussion is not simply the idea that thinking about an object is a sort of mental seeing of it, but more especially the idea that thinking about two *different* objects simultaneously is like having two *discriminated* objects within one's visual field.

Let us then suppose the former assumption was accepted by Plato and go on to ask how its acceptance might have led to the latter. Here we are asking, in effect, why he thinks that when you affirm an identity-sentence to yourself, you must be thinking about the object or objects referred to by the terms of the sentence, in that particular sense of "thinking about" that figures in the former assumption.[34]

One answer, in which there is much truth, is that from the beginning Plato had conceived of the understanding of a term as a matter of apprehending the Form to which the term in some sense corresponded (cf. Ch. I, sec. 1). But because this apprehension seems plausibly construed as a kind of mental seeing, it would appear that Plato's earliest views about the understanding of terms led him into a position in which he could not resist what we have been labeling the former assumption (cf. Ch. IV, sec. 1). On this account, then Plato's difficulty over false identity-beliefs is a difficulty built into his theory of Forms.

But this account goes too far in blaming the earlier theory, since that theory will not by itself produce the difficulty, but only when supplemented by what we have seen to be the developments of the *Cratylus*. For while earlier in his career Plato did regard the ability to apprehend a Form in some way as requisite for an understanding of the corresponding term (Ch. III, sec. 5), there is no reason to believe that the ability or the apprehension envisioned was such that a mistaken identification of the Form would automatically count as a failure to understand the corresponding term. Say if you like that he had not yet seen the obstacle to such mistakes which his theory implicitly contained. But it seems more judicious to say that, so far, the theory as he had formulated it did not yet fully raise the obstacle.

Where, then, does the obstacle arise? As I have said, it first becomes wholly visible in the *Cratylus*. There, in his effort to explain namehood and the correspondence between terms and Forms, and having rejected the conventionalism of Hermogenes and the naturalism of Cratylus, Plato arrives at the view that for a name to do its job properly, it must make one in some sense think of an object and ought to be said to name what the speaker is thinking of as he uses it. Now suppose that someone utters a sentence containing the two names "Socrates" and "Theaetetus." It follows from Plato's view that the speaker must be thinking of objects that are the nominata of these names, and if the speaker is using the names as names of two distinct things, then he must at the same time be thinking of two distinct things. But given Plato's notion of what it is to think about two distinct things simultaneously, it follows that the speaker must be thinking about these objects—having them before his mind—in such a way that it is obvious to him that they are distinct. But this consequence is precisely the other assumption that we have been discussing. So we have seen how that first assumption, along with both the results of the *Cratylus* and Plato's longstanding view of what it is to think about an object, lead him into the second assumption. The same point, of course, applies *mutatis mutandis* when—as Plato thinks must be the case for us to be using fully genuine names (Ch. VI, sec. 4)—we are dealing with Forms rather than sensibles. The upshot is that for him, particularly in the important cases in which we are speaking about Forms, both assumptions hold. In his view, we cannot, properly speaking, think about two distinct Forms without their being obviously distinct, and thus we cannot refer to two distinct Forms unless the terms employed are patently and obviously not codesignative.

To complete our picture, we need to fill in one gap. I have earlier alluded to a distinction between false identity-beliefs and mistaken identifications, while deferring explanation of just what that distinction amounts to (Ch. VI, sec. 1, and Ch. VII, sec. 2, *init.*). This distinction is closely related to philosophical issues which we cannot explore fully here, but for our purposes it comes to something along the following lines.[35] A false identity-belief, as *we* might think of it, can be entertained even when the objects that it concerns are not confronting one, or when one is not observing them. Just what this "confronting" and "observing" amount to is of course a severe problem, but let us here take the notions for granted. A mistaken identification, on the other hand, takes place in a situation in which the object that is mistaken *is* observed or confronted. Now I take it that both identity-belief and identifications (false or true, mistaken or not) can be in some sense "expressed" by sentences of the form "*X* is identical with *Y*" (even if these sentences are not thought of as "running through the mind of" the person holding the belief or making the identification, and even though the notion of "expressing" here is intensely problematical). But I take it that there is a difference between the types of sentence involved in the two cases. In the case of what I am calling an identification, one of the terms represented by "*X*" or "*Y*" may be one that indicates that the speaker means to be treating of some object that he is, in our vaguely explained sense, observing or confronting. Thus, for example, the term may be a demonstrative such as "that" or "this," or it may be some such term as "the thing at which I am staring" or the like.[36] In a nonidentificatory identity-belief, on the other hand, neither term will be of this character and will typically be some such expression as "Socrates" or "the eighth largest city in Greece." (On this account, an identification is a species of identity-belief, but I shall sometimes speak tersely of an "identity-belief" when precision would require "non-identificatory identity-belief".) Let us take the distinction to be explained clearly enough for our purposes.

It is evident that Plato's objections to the possibility of false belief must be taken, at least as far as non-sensible objects are concerned, to touch both false identity-beliefs and mistaken identifications. But the reason why it touches both is notable. It is that on Plato's view of what it is to refer to and think about such an object, the distinction between the two collapses, and in fact all identity-beliefs become mistaken identifications. For by Plato's lights, a sentence expressing an identity-belief must contain a term referring to an object that the believer is, whether by sense or otherwise, confronting. For to be thinking about the thing, and thus (by the result of the *Cratylus*) to be naming it, it must be "before one's mind" in the manner earlier described. For Plato, there is no holding a belief about an object that one is not in this way confronting.[37]

4 The *Sophist* on False Belief

The *Sophist* contains a long and involved effort to show that false belief is, after all, possible. In effect, it takes up the issue where it was left in *Theaetetus* 200. Although there is much in the *Sophist* that I shall not treat, it is instructive to see just how much progress Plato is able to make on the puzzle. In fact, although Plato believes at the end of that dialogue that he has solved the problem, he is mistaken, and indeed he does not even manage to confront directly the main obstacle which the *Theaetetus* had raised.[38]

We saw that the *Theaetetus* raises, and then quickly drops, the suggestion that believing falsely is "believing what is not," a suggestion that was first advanced in the *Cratylus* (*Theaetetus* 188c-189b, *Cratylus* 429c-d; cf. sec. 2 and Ch. VI, sec. 3). It is this suggestion that the *Sophist* follows up, trying to show that "believing what is not," and therefore also believing falsely, are possible. According to the *Sophist*, the difficulty in the notion of false belief, construed as believing what is not, arises from a more basic problem in the notion of false statement, construed in turn as "saying what is not," and Plato consequently thinks that if the latter notion can be shown to make sense, then so can the former. Most of the *Sophist*, therefore, is given over to explaining how false statements are possible. This explanation is involved and difficult, and the subject of much exegetical controversy. Fortunately, we can avoid much of this controversy here, since it turns out that whatever precisely the explanation comes to, it fails to solve the major part of the problem of false belief.

In *Sophist* 260a-263d, having shown to his satisfaction that the notion of "what is not" (τὸ μὴ ὄν) can be so construed as to be coherent, Plato argues that the notion of "saying what is not" is also coherent. Having done this, he returns to the claim, already familiar from *Theaetetus* 189e*sqq*., that to make a judgment in accordance with one of one's beliefs is to assert a sentence silently to oneself (263e3-264b3). He then thinks that it is a simple matter to redeem the notion of false belief, merely by pointing out that since there can be false statements, it ought therefore to be possible to hold false beliefs simply by asserting false statements to oneself; and thus the problem of false belief is dismissed.

It is easy to see that this will not do. For even if it should be thought to disarm the problem of "believing what is not" in *Theaetetus* 188c-189b, it cannot by itself touch the problem of false identity-beliefs which Plato set for himself.[39] For we saw that that problem was generated not by any doubts about the possibility of there being false statements which one could assert to oneself, but rather by Plato's view that the sentence whose assertion would constitute false belief would have to be implausible and obviously false, and thus would not be asserted by anyone to himself. Showing that there are false statements or sentences does nothing to alleviate *that* problem.

The situation is in fact even worse if we adopt one possible interpretation of Plato's account of what it is for a statement to be false. I have said that Plato may have been inclined to the view that any false belief, of whatever form, rests on a mistaken identification (cf. sec. 2). For example, he may at certain points have thought that a person who falsely believes that the thing that he is seeing is a horse when it is in fact an ass may be doing so because he mistakes the attribute of being an ass for the attribute of being a horse. If the *Sophist* endorses this view, then it will be unable to show how any false belief is possible unless it can show how false identity-belief is possible. But it may be that this very view is endorsed, in effect, in the discussion of false statements in 260a-263d. There Plato considers the case of the false sentence "Theaetetus is flying" and the true sentence "Theaetetus is sitting," and it may be that in 263b he is supposing tacitly that a person holding a belief expressed by the former must be mistaking the attribute of flying for the attribute of sitting.[40] *If* he is, then as I have just said, his whole account of false belief in 263e-264b is infected by his failure to show how, contrary to the arguments of the *Theaetetus*, a person can hold a false identity-belief. On the other hand, this very fact makes it unattractive to suppose that he does here think that all false beliefs rest on false identity-beliefs, because the neglect of the problem of false identity-beliefs would then be so gross an oversight that we might well not want to attribute it to him. Moreover, there are arguments that can be advanced, on behalf of other interpretations of 260a-263d, for thinking that he is here trying to avoid the view that raises the problem and is trying to show that false beliefs do *not* in general arise from false identity beliefs.[41] If this is so, then he has still failed to solve the problem of false identity-beliefs, but at least that failure would not affect what he says about other sorts of false belief.

How can we account for Plato's neglect in the *Sophist* of the problem concerning false identity-beliefs? I think that the explanation emerges when we look back at the structure of the argument against false belief in *Theaetetus* 187-200. There, in 188c-d and 189b-c respectively, Plato talks as though he had two alternative *accounts* of false belief to use in combating his difficulties, the former saying that believing falsely is believing what is not, and the latter saying that it is the mistaking of one thing for another (ἀλλοδοξία).[42] In the *Sophist*, he decided that false belief could be redeemed if it were construed according to the former account. What he did not see was that he does *not* simply have two alternative accounts of false belief, and one argument against each of them. Rather, the argument against the second account is an argument against a certain sort of false belief, namely false identity-belief, and this argument is, unless disarmed, still an obstacle to the notion of false identity-belief *even if* the argument against the former account is rebutted. For even if he can make sense of the notion of "believing what is not," he has not thereby removed the narrower argument against false identity-belief. Not realizing this fact, however, Plato mistakenly thought that if the former account could be vindicated, then objections to the latter could be ignored.

5 Knowledge and Definition

In *Theaetetus* 200c, Plato turns from false belief back to the main issue of the dialogue, the question what knowledge is, and this question occupies him explicitly until the end of the work. He does not find an answer to it, but this very fact itself, and the reasons for it, reopen many issues which, although they have been lying dormant, are central to his enterprise.

He begins by taking up a suggestion made earlier by Theaetetus, that knowledge is true belief (200e4-6; cf. 187b4-6). He disposes of it quickly, citing a case of a jury and an eyewitness, and claiming that although the members of the jury may have true belief about an event because of the testimony of the eyewitness, only the eyewitness himself can be said to have knowledge.[43] Other features aside, this claim is interesting not only because it gives voice to Plato's longstanding distrust of hearsay, but also because it suggests what Plato has oftentimes earlier denied, that there can be knowledge about matters in the sensible world. Some have argued that this is not what Plato means to maintain, but there is also other evidence in the *Theaetetus* that supports the suggestion.[44] Nevertheless, even if Plato does now think that there can be knowledge of sensible matters, it is hard to see how this can be a point that he wants to stress here. This passage, like the rest of *Theaetetus* 200-210, is plainly an attempt to say what knowledge is, *quite apart from* the question what sort of objects it may be concerned with.[45] Whereas this in itself is something of a departure from his earlier view, Plato is not *primarily* aiming here to say that we can know about sensible objects or that we cannot. He is after a more general account of knowledge, *whatever* its subject matter be.

His previous suggestion having foundered, Theaetetus is then made to propose that knowledge be taken to be true belief "with an account (λόγος)" (201c9-d1). This proposal immediately suggests to some modern minds an account of knowledge that goes back, in one form or another, at least to Descartes.[46] This account attempts to explain what it is to know that *p*, where "*p*" stands in for some sentence or proposition, and says that for a person to know that *p* it is necessary and sufficient that *p* be true, that the person believe that *p*, and that the person be in some sense or other justified in believing that *p*. It is easy to feel that in using the term "*logos*," Plato is thinking of something like the notion of justification and the role that it plays in this account.[47] But this impression is misleading. For when Plato comes to explain what knowledge is, he has in view, in the first instance, a notion of knowledge which figures, not in statements of the form "*S* knows that *p*," but in statements of the form "*S* knows *X*," where "*X*" does *not* stand in for a sentence or proposition.[48] That is to say, he wants to elucidate the notion of knowledge which he had used in urging us to "know" Forms (even though, as we have seen, he is here remaining neutral on the question what sorts of objects we can "know" in this sense). This is not to say that sentences or propositions have no place whatever in his account of knowledge. They do (cf. Ch. VIII, sec. 4). But it is to say that he takes as his official definiendum here something different from what the modern account would suggest.

Having made the proposal that knowledge is true belief "with a *logos*," Plato spends the rest of the dialogue examining three interpretations of "*logos*," in the hope that one of them will make the proposal turn out to be a satisfactory definition of knowledge. All of them eventually fail. But before these interpretations are proffered, he takes up a dream which Socrates says he has had, according to which the contents of the world can be divided into atoms and compounds somehow made up of those atoms.[49] The dream goes on to say that only the compounds are knowable whereas the atoms are not, on the ground that a *logos* can be given only of the former (202a-b), whereas the latter can only be "named" (ὀνομάζειν). The interpretation of Socrates' dream has been the focus of much exegetical effort, and contains much that is obscure.[50] In order to judge its purpose, it must be read in conjunction with what follows it, and particularly with the second of the three interpretations of "*logos*" which are given subsequently. According to this interpretation of "*logos*" (206e-207a), to have a *logos* of a thing is to be able to give on demand an enumeration of the "parts" of the thing. This interpretation of "*logos*" is so obviously linked with Socrates' dream that we should try, at least, to show how the dream might be connected with it.

It was in the *Cratylus* that Plato had proposed dividing things into atoms and compounds (see Ch. VI, sec. 3). The proposal was made there quite apart from any connection with the notion of knowledge, but merely as a part of the "naturalist" view of naming, and it is fairly plain that Plato is here trying to see whether the proposal can be of any use in determining what knowledge is. His answer is that it cannot.

We shall put Socrates' dream in its proper perspective if we keep firmly in mind that the whole of *Theaetetus* 200-210 is primarily concerned with the question what it is to "know" a thing. The upshot of Socrates' dream serves to point up this fact. That upshot is that it must be incorrect to think that a compound can be known whereas its atoms cannot. This conclusion is reached in two stages. First, it is argued quite generally that it is absurd to suppose that a compound can be known when its constituent atoms are unknown (202d6-205e8). Second, Theaetetus is made to admit on the basis of his own learning of syllables and letters (taken here as paradigms of compounds and atoms respectively; see 202e3-7) that one knows letters before one knows syllables (206a1-b12).[51] (It will soon become important that by this he clearly means that it is possible to recognize and identify individual letters before one can recognize the syllables of which they are composed.)[52] On the basis of this two-stage argument, then, two contentions emerge: one is that compounds could not be known if atoms could not be, and the other is that atoms can be known.

Now let us turn to the second interpretation of "*logos*," and the argument of 206e-208b. This argument is supposed to show that knowing a thing cannot consist in being able to enumerate its atoms. It is clear that this has in fact already been shown, since the dream-passage has demonstrated that things that do not have constituent atoms to be enumerated can nevertheless be known. But 206e-208b does more than merely repeat what the dream-passage said. For it shows that even if we restrict ourselves to knowledge *of a compound*, we cannot say that knowledge of such a thing is the ability to enumerate its atoms, on the ground that one may be able to enumerate the constituent atoms of a thing without knowing the thing itself. The strategy of the argument is complicated, and has often been misjudged.[53] Socrates is made to suppose that a person is able on demand to enumerate the letters in the name "Theaetetus." But he then argues that the person might still not know the name, on the ground that he might not in the requisite way know its initial syllable. (He is here relying on a result of the dream-passage, which argued not merely that one who knows a compound must know its *atoms*, but quite generally that one who knows a compound must know its *parts*, whether atoms or not; see 205b8-10, d1-10.) The person would be said not to know the syllable if he could spell it correctly in the name "Theaetetus" but not in the name "Theodorus," e.g., if he could correctly spell "Theaetetus" but wrongly spelled "Theodorus" as "Teodorus."

The result is that the ability to enumerate the atoms of a thing is neither a necessary nor a sufficient condition of knowing that thing. It is not a necessary condition because, as the dream-passage has argued, atoms can be known. And it is not a sufficient condition because, as 206e-208b contends, one can know—and even be able to enumerate—the atoms of a thing without knowing the thing itself.

Two important facts emerge from Plato's argument to this point. One is that the partitioning of the world into atoms and compounds does not, after all, aid in saying what knowledge is, and this is the joint lesson of Socrates' dream and the discussion of the second interpretation of "*logos*." This conclusion (along with what I have said in Ch. VI, sec. 3) should serve as a caution against attaching too much importance to Plato's talk of atoms and compounds.[54] This talk certainly embodies a suggestion that he thought had to be taken seriously, but it was not used by him to any lasting effect. This is not to say that he would have denied that some things are, in some sense, components of others, or that some things have no components at all. Rather, it is merely to say that he found that he could not make use of this fact in this crucial phase of his epistemological cogitations. This conclusion is strengthened, moreover, by the final pages of the present dialogue, in which a third interpretation of "*logos*" turns out to fail to redeem Theaetetus' proposal that knowledge is true belief with a *logos*. For this interpretation has nothing whatever to do with the idea that the *logos* of a thing must treat of its constituents.

The second fact that emerges from Plato's argument so far has been touched on only lightly but will be pressed shortly. It is that in his discussion of knowledge before 208b, Plato has shown more than a passing concern (though of course not an exclusive one) with the notion of *recognition*, and the ability to recognize a given sort of object when it presents itself.[55] This concern shows itself in 206a5-8, where Plato speaks of the need to recognize, and particularly *distinguish*, the different letters. It is not an accident that the word used here, "διαγιγνώσκειν," has before been employed to convey the necessity of distinguishing among different Forms and of recognizing which is which.[56] In 206a10-b3, likewise, the aim is to be able to recognize and classify musical notes.

Keeping this point in mind, let us proceed to the third interpretation of "*logos*," which is for our purposes by far the most crucial. (The first is quickly disposed of, and we can ignore it; it is to the effect that to know is to believe and to be able to express one's belief in words.) To be able to give a *logos* of a thing, according to it, is to be able to "utter a sign by which the thing asked about differs from all other things" (208c7-8, τὸ ἔχειν τι σημεῖον εἰπεῖν ᾧ τῶν ἀπάντων διαφέρει τὸ ἐρωτηθέν). Someone who knows a thing, then, is someone who can give a description that applies uniquely to that thing; and thus to attempt to know a thing is to attempt to acquire the ability to give such a description.

This notion ought to sound very familiar. Plato's quest for definitions has from the beginning involved an effort to give some such description and to be able to say wherein the object whose definition was sought differs from other objects.[57] Although I have said that Plato is not exclusively concerned with Forms, it is plain that he here has on his mind the notion of definitions with which his views about Forms had been so closely associated. What he is doing is to ask one of the questions that I have pressed in the foregoing pages (esp. Ch. I, sec. 4; Ch. II, sec. 5), namely the question how obtaining a definition is supposed to be able to help us in gaining knowledge of a Form. And he is not raising the question simply to reaffirm old doctrine. For he finds that he cannot give an answer to it.

The objection to the account of knowledge generated by the third interpretation of "*logos*" is, in its basic outline, relatively straightforward. The proposed account of knowledge is that a person knows a thing just in case he has true opinion about it, along with a *logos* of the sort just described. Plato's objection is that (unless the account is to be altered so as to be circular—see 209e6-210a1) the ability to say wherein an object is distinct from all others must be possessed even by the person who holds merely a true belief about the object, and that being able to give a *logos* of the object amounts to nothing over and above having a true belief about it (209d4-e4). The reasoning behind this objection is expounded in 209a1-c9. It is that a person who cannot give a description applying uniquely to the object of which he is purported to be thinking, but can only give descriptions that also are true of other objects, cannot be said to be thinking about *that* object any more than he is thinking of all of the other things of which the descriptions are true. If you initially try to suppose, for example, that I am thinking about Theaetetus, but then I turn out to be able merely to give descriptions that apply equally to Socrates, then you cannot say after all that I am thinking just about Theaetetus. On the other hand, if I do satisfy the condition for thinking about Theaetetus, then according to the present account I must already know him.[58]

The ramifications of this argument are numerous; they extend both backward and forward in time. Let us begin by considering a link with the *Cratylus*. Plainly, the ideas that were working there are working here as well: to use a term so as to refer to a given object is to be thinking, in some sense, about that object (Ch. VI, sec. 2). Plato now adds the idea that if one is thinking about just that object, as opposed to all others, then one must be able to give some specification of it which will apply to it alone; so that if one cannot give such a specification, then one is not thinking of *that* object. But if one is in a position to think of it, then what progress beyond this point is the ability to give a *logos* which was suggested to be required for knowledge? Cast in the terms by which we described the *Cratylus*, the point is this. To use a term to name a certain thing is, roughly, to use that term while thinking about the thing or having it before one's mind. But likewise, to use the *logos* to refer to that thing is, simply, to use it while having the thing before one's mind. This being so, there appears so far to be no advantage whatever in having the *logos* over simply having the corresponding term. If you have the thing before your mind, then the only difference would be in what words you are whispering to yourself as you think about it. And Plato has no apparatus to enable him to say what difference *that* difference would make (cf. n. VII-61).

Another way to see the point is to notice that if the *Cratylus* had come out differently on the question what namehood amounts to, then the difficulty over the third account of *logos* could not arise. For on neither the naturalist nor the conventionalist account of naming would it be the case that naming an object required having it before one's mind or being able to distinguish it from everything else. For on the naturalist account, to name a thing is simply to come out with the "natural" name of it; and on the conventionalist account, to name a thing is to come out with an expression that has been linked to the object, so to speak, by a convention already made either by oneself or by one's group. On both of those views, one can in principle use a term to refer to or name an object, and *then* go on to bring the object into one's ken, or to discover some description applying to it alone. (*How* one may do this is another question; the point is that these accounts of namehood do not by themselves rule out the possibility.)

But this concatenation of events is not permitted by the view of namehood that the *Cratylus* chose, and that is at work here at the end of the *Theaetetus*.

But we can make a connection even further back, with the paradox of inquiry in the *Meno* (Ch. II, sec. 4).[59] There, Plato's difficulty was fundamentally that he found it hard to see how a person could be capable of recognizing the completion of an inquiry without thereby having already attained it, and he therefore was unable to see—short of the supposition that we recollect—what cognitive progress could be made by someone already in possession of a specification whereby his inquiry is framed. The problem in the *Theaetetus* is very much the same, except that it now rests on a considered account of naming. For because of the view of naming developed in the *Cratylus*, the genuine use of a name is thought to require the apprehension of its nominatum, in a way excluding any confusion of it with other things, and it thus becomes difficult to see what cognitive progress could be made by someone already possessing a name which picks out the object concerning which he seeks knowledge; and in particular it becomes difficult to see what progress it would be to gain a *logos* that distinguishes the object from all others, since confusion is already ruled out, on the view now adopted, by the possession of the name itself. Put in a slightly different way, the new problem could be said to rest on an assimilation—a mistaken one, by most lights nowadays—of possessing the name of an object, and having the object itself within one's ken in such a way as to be unable to confuse it with something else, so that again it becomes difficult to see what cognitive progress there is to be made by the person already possessing the name.

The paradox of the *Meno* has come home to roost, but it is now perched even more firmly than before on a theory about naming and a view about what it is to have something in mind that excludes the possibility of confusion. If we begin by naming the object of our search, then is there anything further to be done? The *Theaetetus* ends by suggesting that there may not be. But what if, when you begin, you are *not* capable of naming it? Then what is there that you can do? Plato had earlier shelved these questions, thinking that he could dismiss them simply by briskly appealing to the notion of recollection. He must see by now that to say that we recollect will not, by itself, solve this problem (Ch. II, sec. 6), since while the notion of recollection is alluded to toward the end of the dialogue, it is not even hinted to be the final answer to the question what knowledge is. Instead, as the dialogue closes with echoes of earlier works, Plato realizes that he is, in certain important respects, very nearly back where he had started long before.[60]

Let us remind ourselves what some of the problems then confronting him were. Broadly described, they concerned the nature and goals of the enterprise of gaining knowledge, and the starting point from which it began. There was to be an effort to establish definitions, and an effort to apprehend what later came to seem to him the only genuine objects of knowledge, Forms. One thing to be made clear was the relationship between these two projects (Ch. I, sec. 4), and the paradox of inquiry depended to some extent on not elucidating it (Ch. II, sec. 4). More generally, there was the need for an account of the way in which investigations were to be launched, that is, of how their aims were to be described so as to be recognizable, and of the legitimate means for attaining them. Plato showed a strong disinclination to use ordinary usage or common opinions as data or measuring-rods of success (Ch. I, sec. 3), but there was no presentation of a clear alternative. For a time, it looked as though the method of hypothesis might at least provide a starting-point for inquiry (Ch. III, sec. 7, and Ch. IV, sec. 4); but in the *Republic* the effort to use the Form of the Good to achieve something more than merely provisional hypotheses was unable to cope with the problems that arose within that work itself and was put aside in the *Phaedrus* when those problems came to prominence (Ch. IV, sec. 4; Ch. V, sec. 1). When the *Theaetetus* is over, these problems remain. For Plato has now asked himself more fully and explicitly than ever before what knowledge is and has not seen his way to an answer. In particular, he has been unable to establish that his old apparatus of definitions could be made to provide the service that he had hoped to receive from it.

Plato concludes that the search for an account of knowledge has ended in failure and seems satisfied that no further explanation of "*logos*" will vindicate the suggestion that knowledge is true belief with a *logos*. It has often been asked why he is moved to give up this suggestion by the failure of a mere three explanations of "*logos*," when there might be others that would fill the bill.[61] The answer is that although his conclusion is indeed not validly drawn, it was the last account of "*logos*" that was crucial to Plato, because it was it that represented the way in which he had all along thought of definitions. Once it went by the board, then there was a grave threat to the whole idea that knowledge of a thing might involve getting a definition of it. And that there is such a threat is Plato's message at the end of the *Theaetetus*. This is *not* to say, as some have, that he no longer thought that a necessary condition of knowledge was the ability to give a *logos*. Without any doubt, he had a strong inclination to think that.[62] What he did not see was *how* he could uphold the view, however strongly inclined he might have been toward it, and this is the impasse around which he must now try to see his way.[63]

Notes

1. See for example Cornford **1**, pp. 7, 28, 83, and *passim*, Cherniss **1**, pp. 6-8, and Bluck **3**. All hold the view that Plato is deliberately leaving the Forms out of the picture in order to show that a satisfactory account of knowledge cannot be reached without them. (The same broad type of interpretation can be found in Jackson, pp. 265ff., in that Jackson likewise sees something being left out so that it will be missed; see also Gulley **2**, pp. 83-91, 106). For arguments against this view, see Robinson **4**, McDowell **1**, pp. 257-259.

2. See Runciman, pp. 28, 55. For arguments for such a change of view in the *Tht.*, see esp. Owen **1**, pp. 323-325, 327; McDowell **2**, pp. 114, 139-140, 184; and Cooper (though at the end of his paper Cooper expresses some views that I find doubtful about Plato's notion of knowledge in the *Rep.*). Another interpretation according to which the *Tht.* revises earlier epistemological doctrine is advanced by Prauss, esp. pp. 139ff., but though his account and mine have some common features, they diverge so widely (particularly with regard to Plato's earlier views) that I cannot treat his views in full detail here (for some comments, however, see nn. *infra*.).

3. See, e.g., Owen **1** and **8**, Cherniss **7**, Vlastos **2**, and Strang—to mention only a few of the pertinent works. My neutrality here on these issues means that there is no necessity for us to decide whether the *Tht.* comes before or after the *Parm.* On this question, see for example Campbell, pp. 155-156; Diès, pp. 122-123; Ross **2**, pp. 6-9; and McDowell **2**, p. 113 and nn. there cited. I am inclined to believe, however, that the *Parm.* must be the later (cf. n. VII-16).

4. For various suggestions to the effect that Plato returns in the *Tht.* to old issues, see: Stenzel, pp. 66-67, Hicken **1**, and A. O. Rorty; cf. n. VII-60.

5. This identification, although not always kept distinct from the Protagorean contention, (1) (cf. McDowell **2**, pp. 120-121), is kept separate at the crucial junctures, as we shall see. (For other occasional conflations, see McDowell **2**, *ad* 157e5, 163a7-8.)

6. On some of the problems arising out of the ambiguity, both for Greek philosophers and their interpreters, see Cooper, pp. 130ff., and Hamlyn **2**, Ch. I.

7. See also Robinson **4**, p. 61.

8. For an argument that in the *Protag.* he did, see Vlastos **3**.

9. By contrast, the identification of knowledge and *aisthesis* is, from a certain point of view, less important to Plato to rebut. For although the claim that

all knowledge is of sensibles (which would follow from this identification) would not sit well at all with what he has believed, I take it to be even more important to him to deny that no belief can be preferred to any other on the score of truth or reliability. For a somewhat similar view, see Grote, vol. II, pp. 325-335, esp. pp. 334-335.

10. For considerations in favor of viewing (2) as supported by something like (1), see McDowell, pp. 119-121. It is doubtful that Plato thought of (1) as being supported by (2), or particularly as being entailed by it. For (2) is refuted in 184-186, *after* the refutation of (1) in 169-179—which would have been an odd procedure, since if (2) entailed (1), then the refutation of the latter would be all he needed for the refutation of the former. The reason why (2) does not entail (1) is as follows. If (2), namely the identification of knowledge and *aisthesis*, is true, then every case of knowledge is a case of *aisthesis* and vice versa, and so perhaps it follows that every *perceptual* (*aisthesis*) belief is true. But even if this does follow, it still does *not* follow that every *belief* is true—which is what (1) asserts (leaving aside the filler "for X," for convenience). But there is still a worry about Plato's procedure, pressed by McDowell 2, pp. 179-185. It is that although in 169-179 Plato has shown that not every case of knowledge can be a case of *aisthesis*, he nevertheless in 184b5-7 seems to regard (2) as still requiring refutation. So do we not still have Plato refuting a thesis, and then independently and superfluously refuting something which entails that thesis? The best response to this problem is to acknowledge it, and then to explain why Plato proceeded as he did. The explanation, I think, is that in 169-179, what Plato was consciously intent on refuting was not a consequence of the identification that he goes on to attack. What he is intent on refuting in 169-179 is the claim that every belief that a person has is true (for him), i.e., (1). So he concentrates on producing cases of beliefs that are false for those who hold them (see esp. 178e2-3, 179a1-3, b7-8), Perhaps he is thereby *also* producing cases of knowledge that are not cases of *aisthesis* (though he does not explicitly say so), but if he is, then he is not attending to *that* feature of them, and he thus believes that the identification of knowledge and *aisthesis* still remains to be disposed of. (I remark also that in 151e8-152a5 Plato does not seem to me to be assimilating (1) and (2), since he carefully qualifies himself there with "κινδυνεύει" and "τρόπον τινά"; rather, I think he is trying—misguidedly—to avoid complications at the start of his discussion.)

11. The interpretation of this argument that I adopt is close to that of McDowell, pp. 185-193, which is close to the former of the two suggested by Cooper, pp. 138-144 (not the one that Cooper actually adopts). But mine diverges from theirs in the following manner. When Plato says that *aisthesis* does not "attain truth" because it does not "attain being" (186c-d), he is indeed saying this on the ground that *aisthesis* is not capable of operating with the notion of "being" (*ousia*; see 185e-186a). But there is no reason to think, as Cooper and McDowell both seem to, that according to Plato, *every* manifestation of knowledge involves the notion of "being." Plato can perfectly well say

that some of them do and some of them do not, and in 186d4 and e4-5, he only commits himself to saying that knowledge *can* deal with "being," not that it *always* does so. But this is enough to distinguish knowledge from *aisthesis*, which he thinks *never* treats of that notion. (As Cooper recognizes, there is no reason to say that "being" here is "existence"; but there is equally no warrant for restricting the notion here to the sort of "being" that is involved in statements of "what a thing is," as McDowell 2, pp. 192-193, suggests.)

12. On this question see Burnet 2, pp. 242ff.; Jackson, pp. 250ff.; Cornford 1, pp. 49f.; but for arguments against assimilating the account to the theory of perception in *Tim*. 45b-46c, 67c-68d, see McDowell 2, pp. 139-140. Note that the account of *aisthesis* in the *Tht*. is not carried out with utter consistency (McDowell, pp. 130-131).

13. McDowell, pp. 119-120, makes substantially the same point. There are problems over just what the term "perceptual" here ought to cover; cf. *ibid*., pp. 117-118, 137-138.

14. Cf. n. VII-12, and notice that even if the account of *aisthesis* is not meant by Plato to be a repetition of what he had said in the *Tim*., it would not be in the least surprising if he borrowed what seemed to him plausible elements of the *Tim*. theory to help prop up the opposing Protagorean position.

15. For two alternative accounts of the way in which Plato might be trying to demonstrate the nonidentity, see Cooper, pp. 138-144; Cooper inclines toward one and McDowell (pp. 188ff.), toward the other, though McDowell develops it somewhat differently from the way in which Cooper does. McDowell suggests (pp. 192-193) that Plato "comes near to making the claim that the verb 'know' requires a propositional construction; which would involve confining his attention to that use of the verb in which its French equivalent is *savoir* as opposed to connaître." But McDowell rightly observes that Plato does not seem clear about this implication of what he is saying. Moreover, it is not certain that it *is* an implication anyway. McDowell's view of Plato's argument makes his crucial premise—that knowledge does, whereas *aisthesis* does not, "grasp *ousia*"—amount to a claim that knowing a thing requires knowing "what it is," which in turn requires a thought involving the notion of "being," which is a notion with which *aisthesis* is not, Plato argues, capable of dealing. But there is an objection. The evidence for this interpretation is not clearly evidence that in Plato's view, the *only* judgments expressing knowledge of a thing are those of the form "*S* knows that *X* is . . . ," where ". . ." represents an expression telling "what *X* is." The evidence seems to me equally (well or badly) to support the view that according to Plato, to have knowledge in which *X* figures (so to speak) requires that one know "what *X* is." But if this is what Plato means, then there is no reason to picture him as close to making the syntactic point that McDowell would have him approaching. It also seems doubtful to me that the text contains any indication of a general insistence on the employment of the verb "to be" in knowledge claims, or *even* (as I suggested above) a general insistence that the objects "figuring" in knowledge-claims must have been the subject of prior knowledge-claims involving that verb. If Cooper's interpretation is not

correct (and I am not sure that it is not), then what Plato is saying, I think, is that *some* knowledge-claims (though *not* necessarily all) involve the use of the verb "to be," while no *aisthesis*-claims do (for the reason for this, see Cooper, pp. 138-141). Now this is enough to get his conclusion that knowledge and *aisthesis* are distinct, which is all that he really needs. It does not *prove*, what Plato clearly believes, that there are cases of knowledge that do not involve the notion of being or the verb "to be." But why should Plato need to prove this here? And moreover, once the identification of knowledge and *aisthesis* had been defeated, then why would anyone demand a proof that there are such cases?

16. I cannot here treat adequately the exact role of the doctrine of flux in the account of *aistheseis*. The matter has been extensively discussed by McDowell in his commentary, but there are several points on which I disagree with him. Rather than detail them, however, let me simply indicate briefly two reasons why I think that the doctrine is employed in the account. (1) In claiming that the *aisthesis* of an object is in a certain sense private to the person who has it, the account tries to ensure that there will be no way in which anyone else can dispute him about what it is like (though there are problems here). But the account must likewise ensure that the person himself will not be able to check, by memory, on his own previous *aisthesis* and open the possibility that they were somehow incorrect. To this end, Plato draws on the idea that any change in any object amounts—to speak roughly—to the going-out-of-existence of what existed before and the coming-into-existence of a new object. (See 154a6-b6, 158e5-160b3, and my **1**, pp. 190-191.) The point of this move is to say that instead of having an *aisthesis* and a memory belonging to the same person, we actually have two different objects, the person's earlier and later selves—to speak roughly again; so that I cannot have a hope of checking my earlier *aisthesis*, because they are not, now, *mine*. What the hypothesis of flux does is to guarantee that one and the same percipient will not persist for any stretch of time, however small (159e-160a). (2) The other reason why flux is introduced is as follows. The account of *aisthesis* is supposed to be consistent with the Protagorean doctrine, which has the effect of claiming that, as it were, there are no matters of fact which are not relative to some percipient, but which simply obtain in some "objective" manner (cf. McDowell, pp. 142-143). But plainly the account of *aisthesis* itself certainly looks like a claim about "objective" matters of fact (*ibid.*), and appears to be contending that the world *is*, irrespective of percipients, as the account describes it. I suspect that Plato wanted to allow the account to avoid, at least at this stage, the impression of making such a contention, and that it is for this reason that he made it claim that all of the objects with which it dealt merely "become" (γίγνεσθαι) rather than "are" (εἶναι). This is not to say that this expedient is successful (cf. McDowell, pp. 151, 153-154), but it provides a satisfactory motive for its presence in the account. It is also compatible with the not impossible suggestion of Zeller (**2**, p. 1370, n. 4) that the reason why an "objective" theory of perception was provided at all was that otherwise

men's opinions would have to be said to be "about nothing." (The "table-turning" argument in 169-171 might be construed to touch indirectly on this point, though Plato does not take note of the fact. If there were evidence that he was aware of it, however, then we would have grounds for saying—contrary to what I have claimed—that he does not mean to let the account of *aisthesis* stand. But I suspect that prior to the *Parm.* and *Phileb.*, at any rate [cf. Owen 1, p. 322, n. 2, and pp. 324-325, though note that I am here supposing that the *Parm.* is later than the *Tht.*—see n. VII-3], Plato would have thought that the expedient was successful in any case.)

17. See esp. Robinson, pp. 47-48 and Owen 1, pp. 323-325, *vs.* Cherniss 7, pp. 355-360, and 3, pp. 217ff.

18. It is true that in 156a4-5 the former doctrine is announced in such a way as to make it appear about as strong as it could be (τὸ πᾶν κίνησις ἦν καὶ ἄλλο παρὰ τοῦτο οὐδέν). But the exposition of the latter doctrine pointedly corrects the earlier one in a manner that shows that the two are not being assimilated. For at 156a5-7, there are said to be two kinds of change (κίνησις), one active and one passive. At 181c3-4, however, it is said that whereas on the earlier view there is only one kind of change, in fact there are two, which are then said to be qualitative change and locomotion. The point is that, as Plato sees, the former doctrine had not taken account of the two kinds of change which are so crucial in the refutation of the latter (esp. 182c*sqq.*), and thus, through this oversight, failed to be as thoroughgoing a doctrine of flux as the latter one turns out to be.

19. The likeliest answer, I believe, is that of Owen 1, that Plato is criticizing his own earlier views.

20. This account gives better sense to the line of argument, and to the connection between the two halves of the work, than those of Prauss, pp. 139ff.; McDowell 2, p. 194; and Ryle 1, p. 137. Cornford 1, p. 110, is closer to the truth, as is perhaps Campbell, p. 167. (Clearly it will not do to say simply that 187-200 is a digression.)

21. We see bits of both problems in *Euthyd.* 277c and 284a, 286a, but nothing much is done with them there.

22. See Ackrill 1, esp. p. 385; and McDowell 2, p. 195, along with McDowell 1.

23. Cf. Ackrill 1, p. 385, and McDowell 2, pp. 195, 203-204.

24. See McDowell 2, pp. 195, 202-204. As he observes, it may be that Plato held 1) that if a person believes falsely that *a* is beautiful when *a* is in fact ugly, that person must in some manner have beauty figuring in his belief instead of ugliness, and 2) that a person who does this must be believing, falsely, that ugliness is beauty (at least I think that these are the steps that McDowell has in view). This view *could* be—though it *need* not be—supplemented by the view that such a false believer was apprehending *a*'s ugliness and somehow mistaking it for beauty. One is tempted to say that step 2) is plainly mistaken, quite apart from step 1). But to say this alone is not enough, because there is a difficulty in understanding what it means to say that someone has beauty

figuring in his belief "instead of" ugliness. For this way of putting the matter makes it appear as though the believer's believing falsely is the result of the fact that ugliness is, in some way, *the* notion that should have figured in his belief instead of beauty (cf. McDowell, p. 204). But suppose for the sake of example that *a* is green. Then if greenness had figured in the believer's belief instead of beauty, that belief would have been true. So it does not appear that there is such a thing as *the* notion that should have figured in the belief instead of beauty. It is not clear to what extent Plato may have been under the impression that there was, for each false predicative belief, such a thing as *the* notion that should have been there instead of the one that was. One may perhaps argue that such passages in the *Soph.* as 257b3-c3 are later efforts to retract this idea, but the matter is uncertain.

25. Cf. earlier such passages as *Phdo.* 65d11-12; *Rep.* 490b3-4, 484b3-4, 534c5-6; *Phdr.* 253a2-3.

26. This point is made by Ackrill **1**, p. 388. McDowell **1**, p. 182, attributes to Plato the use of a principle that "if something is to figure in one's judgment at all, then one must know it." Of the passages that he cites, 188b8-c1 supports the attribution, but 190d7-10 does not, since it does not require knowledge of what figures in one's judgment. For what it does require, see sec. 3.

27. See also *Soph.* 263e-264b and sec. 4, with Cornford **1**, p. 118, and Robinson **4**, p. 64. The same idea is perhaps suggested by *Tim.* 37b5-6; see also *Phileb.* 38d, 39a. (On the notion of judgment here, see McDowell, **2**, *ad* (189e4-190a7.)

28. On the way in which Plato's use of the comparison differs from that of empiricists, see McDowell **2**, pp. 209-210, vs. Cornford **1**, pp. 129-130.

29. Cf. e.g., Wittgenstein **2**, pp. 3ff.

30. Notice that although this move does not require us to say that Forms are lurking behind the argument in any substantial way (cf. Cooper, *op. cit.*, and McDowell, pp. 218-219), it does show plainly that Plato is still willing to countenance the notion of objects that cannot be apprehended by sensation. We shall see (secs. 3 and 5) that whether or not Plato means to back up this notion by any substantial part of the metaphysics of previous works, there is an important way in which he is still dealing with problems which that theory raised (cf. Ch. VII, introd.). (This is not to say, however, that he now believes that sensible objects can be apprehended, in some sense, *only* by sensation, or that there is no knowledge concerning them; cf. Cooper and n. VII-11 .)

31. Not that these two are equivalent, but rather that Plato uses both; cf. sec. 3, n. VII-26, and Ackrill **1**, p. 388.

32. Though some, having observed it, have attempted to explain it away; cf. n. IV-9). For recent observations of the fact, see Robinson **4**, p. 66; McDowell **2**, pp. 217-218; and McDowell **1**, *passim*. We have of course seen the idea at work since Plato's earliest works (cf. Ch. I, sec. 1, and Ch. IV, sec. 2).

33. We must here take up an objection to this account, based on the view that the claim of the impossibility of misidentification is actually traceable to a quite different source in Plato's theory of Forms, namely the idea that in that

theory each Form is taken to be, in a strong sense, an indivisible unit. (For related lines of thought, see Oehler and Prauss, as well as Bluck **2**, p. 38.)

This claim can be supported as follows. As we saw (Ch. VII, secs. 2-3), Plato's argument in *Tht.* 187-200, and particularly at 195d*sqq*., depended on the tacit supposition that when two distinct objects apprehended "by thought" are designated, they must be designated by expressions that are obviously noncodesignative. This supposition was explained in turn by citing Plato's tendency to regard thinking about an object as similar to a kind of mental viewing of the object, and—more crucial in this connection—to regard thinking about two distinct objects as similar to a mental viewing of the two of them at distinct places in one's "mental visual field." But the suggestion that we must now consider is that both of these ideas are explained when we recall that, for Plato, Forms were always meant to be "one" or "unitary" in a very strong sense, reminiscent of the sense in which Parmenides had applied the term "one" to his monad. For our purposes, the relevant sense could be expressed by this principle: any two designations of a given Form are obviously codesignative.

How would the acceptance of this principle by Plato help to explain his supposition that any two designations of *distinct* Forms must be obviously *non*codesignative? For plainly the former does not entail the latter, since even if all of the ways of designating the Form of *F* should be obviously codesignative, why should there not be a designation of the Form of *G* that seemed to refer to the same thing as they? To get the entailment of the latter claim, we need an additional premise, though one that Plato might easily have accepted: that, in the present case, *some* of the ways of designating the Form of *G* be obviously noncodesignative with some way of designating the Form of *F*. For if this is so, then because by the initial principle all of the ways of designating the Form of *G* are obviously codesignative, and likewise for the Form of *F*, one can conclude with only a little further ado that each designation of the Form of *F* is obviously noncodesignative with each designation of the Form of *G*. So if Plato had accepted the principle and the plausible additional premise, it would have been entirely natural for him to accept the supposition governing the argument in *Tht.* 195d*sqq.* But in addition—it can be urged—Plato's claims to the effect that each Form is strongly unitary (esp. at *Phdo.* 78d5-8 with c1-4, 80b2-3, e.g., or *Symp.* 211b1, e4) show that he would indeed have accepted the principle. So the explanation would be complete.

In spite of its attractiveness, this account will not do. For in the first place, though Plato did believe that each Form is unitary in some quite strong sense, there is no reason to think that he held that the Forms were unitary in the sense that the account requires, or even formulated that sense to himself before or in *Tht.* 187-200. One might well see it in Socrates' dream 201d*sqq.*, in the talk of atoms and compounds, and then suppose that some such idea as this is already working in 187-200. The fact is, however, that there is no support for the reading-back of the notion of atoms from the dream into the previous pages. (Strictly read, in fact, the dream does not make the requisite claim of unity, because nothing in its text precludes the possibility that an atom might have more than one ὄνομα. An analogous point applies to the thesis of the "late-learners" at *Soph*. 251b*sqq*., whose claim was rather that one cannot call a thing by the ὄνομα of something else.) In the first place, the dream introduces the notion of an atom as though it had previously not been in play at all (201d8ff.). In the second place, it is decisive that in the argument in 195d*sqq*. against false identity beliefs about objects of thought, there is neither the faintest hint that the argument applies only to atoms and not to compounds, nor indeed any way at all of linking the argument to the notion of an atom in the manner that the principle in question would necessitate. Finally (cf. sec. 5), when Plato in 208c*sqq*. gives an argument closely allied to the one against false belief, to show that knowledge is not true belief with a *logos* in the third sense, he turns completely away from the contrast between atoms and compounds. Nor does the *Soph*. corroborate the proposed interpretation—though a full-scale demonstration of this claim would require a full-scale examination of that dialogue. The chief point to notice is that (in spite of what some have believed) the *Soph*. does not direct its attention to the problem of false identity-beliefs as such (Ch. VII, sec. 4). It might be thought that the concern in 251a*sqq*. to show that a thing can be designated by "many names" is an effort to get to the bottom of that problem, by showing that the same thing may be designated in ways which are not obviously codesignative. But that is not the case. Rather, that passage has strictly to do with the distinct problem arising out of the construal of false belief as "believing what is not" (see *ibid*.).

34. As for the philosophical question in its own right, one thinks naturally of Wittgenstein, e.g., in the early parts of **3** and in **2**.

35. The issues have to do with the distinction between referential and opaque contexts, and between *de re* and *de dicto* knowledge, which were touched upon in n. II-8. In the present context we have to do instead with the contrast between *de re* and *de dicto* belief. Just as we saw there that Plato does not heed the *de re/de dicto* distinction with regard to knowledge, so too there is no reason to believe that he makes the distinction with regard to belief, and we shall see *infra* that he fully obliterates it. Indeed, it is possible to trace his problem over false belief precisely to this neglect of the distinction; see n. VII-37.

36. I say "may be" because a person can perhaps be making an identification by means of such a sentence as "the teacher of Plato is the husband of Xanthippe" in a situation in which he is face to face with the husband of Xanthippe and knows that he is but nevertheless does not formulate what he intends as an identification of the person in front of him by using the sort of term which is the usual hallmark of an identification in my sense. Indeed, as we shall quickly see, Plato's cases of identification are usually of this inexplicitly identificatory sort.

37. Cf. n. VII-35, and Robinson, p. 65. By many standards, Plato would therefore be said to be obliterating the distinction between *de re* and *de dicto* belief-statements and in effect making all belief-statements out to be of the

former sort. The way in which we could then explain his problem over false belief by his failure to heed the distinction is to imagine the following line of reasoning. Suppose, to use one of Plato's examples, that we take it to be clear that (A) "Twelve is (identical with) eleven" is a totally implausible thing for anyone to assert to himself, whereas (B) "The sum of seven and five is eleven" is not. Now we might, using the *de dicto* notion of belief, say that a person believes that the sum of seven and five is eleven, but we would not thereby have to infer, in the *de dicto* sense, that he believes that twelve is eleven. (Thus, we might say that the person might, under suitable circumstances, assent to (A).) But using the *de re* notion of belief twice, we can infer, from the claim that he believes *concerning* the sum of seven and five that it is twelve, the claim that he believes *concerning* twelve that it is eleven. Now if Plato had confused these two notions of belief, we could easily imagine that he would fall into trouble, and thus we might attribute his embarrassment over false belief to just this confusion. For he would then think as follows. He would wrongly suppose that believing that the sum of seven and five is eleven is tantamount to believing concerning the sum of seven and five that it is twelve; he would then correctly suppose that one who believes concerning the sum of seven and five that it is eleven therefore believes concerning twelve that it is eleven; and he would then wrongly suppose that believing concerning twelve that it is eleven is tantamount to believing that twelve is eleven. He would accordingly think that one who believes that the sum of seven and five is eleven must believe that twelve is eleven and reject the possibility of the former belief on grounds of the impossibility of the latter. (It is true that on some accounts— e.g., that of Kaplan—"Theaetetus believes that the sum of seven and five is eleven" [nearly] entails "Theaetetus believes, concerning the sum of seven and five, that it is eleven;" but even on his view one cannot take the last step of the reasoning explained above, from "Theaetetus believes, concerning twelve that it is eleven" to "Theaetetus believes that twelve is eleven.")

This is not, indeed, a bad way of diagnosing Plato's problem, apart from anachronism. For his insistence that a false identity-belief must often be represented by an implausible identity-sentence could certainly be brought on by a failure to make the distinction in question. Another way of putting the point is this. If you replace a singular term in a sentence "representing" a belief of mine by another codesignative singular term, then you may no longer have a sentence that "represents" any belief of mine. Thus, "The sum of seven and five is eleven" might represent a belief of mine even while "Twelve is eleven" did not. But Plato is not much alive to this fact, and it would be extremely difficult for him to be, given his view of naming.

The reader will note that this diagnosis is very similar to McDowell's in his 1 since both turn on a distinction between opaque and transparent occurrences of singular terms and use the distinction in much the same way. Notice also that Plato's notion of what it is to think about a thing can be viewed as another case of a confusion between meaning and reference, which we earlier saw leading to certain of his other views, including "self-predication" (Ch. I, sec. 1; Ch. III, introd.). Briefly, the point is that what matters to Plato in an identity-statement is just the references, and not the meanings, of the singular terms involved. This point, including the connection with self-predication, is discussed by McDowell **1** esp. n. 22.

38. Thus too McDowell, p. 226, and Hicken **1**, p. 188.

39. Robinson, pp. 68-73, seems to me to exaggerate the extent to which the *Soph.* answers the *Tht.* problem over false identity-belief, since although the *Soph.* makes false belief a matter of believing a false sentence (263d-264b), there is no explicit substitute for the *Tht.* view of what it is to think about an object, and thus no specific solution of the problem of false *identity*-belief. The same comment seems to me to hold for *Phileb.* 38ff., which presents a picture that is somewhat more elaborate than that of the *Soph.*, though directed at many of the same points. (Cf. by contrast, Runciman, pp. 36, 119ff., who holds that both of these dialogues effectively disarm the problem.) I do not deny that one can draw from these later works the *materials* for a solution of the problem; what I seriously doubt is that Plato had worked up these materials in any complete manner.

40. Or mistaking for the attribute of flying some one of the other attributes that Theaetetus possesses, on the interpretation that says that for Plato here, "Theaetetus is not flying" amounts to "Flying is different from all of the attributes possessed by Theaetetus"; cf. Owen **11** pp. 237-238.

41. I have in mind especially those interpretations under which Plato in the passage in question uses "ἕτερον" in the sense of "contrary" *vel sim.*

42. Some would say that there are three accounts, on the view that the account in 189b-c is importantly different from the earlier account in 188a-c. But see n. VII-26 with the text to which it is appended.

43. As many have recognized, this claim is reminiscent of the example in *Meno* 97asqq., in which the man who has been to Larissa *knows* the road there whereas the man who has only heard of it merely has *belief*.

44. With 201b7-8, compare Cooper on 184-186, and the wax-tablet passage, *passim* (e.g., 192d3, 193a1). See also McDowell **2**, pp. 227-228, *vs.*, e.g., Cornford, pp. 141-142. Compare also Ch. III, sec. 1, and notice that on this view Plato has to some extent broken out of the confusion noted there, which was to think that because sensing and thinking were different activities, they must therefore have to do with disjoint sets of objects. See further Hardie, pp. 21-23. On this point my interpretation is somewhat akin to those of Robinson and Hicken, particularly to the latter. But I disagree with Hicken's view (pp. 188-189, 195-197), shared by Cornford (p. 151), that Plato aims to show that knowledge cannot be of sensibles; cf. n. VII-52.

45. On the fact that in the dream-passage the atoms there spoken of are said to be sensible (αἰσθητά, 202b6), see n. VII-52.

46. Though not explicit, something very like this account can be extracted from, e.g., Descartes' Second Meditation, vol. VII, pp. 19, 25-26.

47. See Chisholm, pp. 6-7.

48. In support of this claim see the considerations advanced by McDowell **2**, p. 252, and Hicken **2**, pp. 128-129. The reader will notice, however, that my account of the general line of thought in 200-210 differs considerably from McDowell's, which is derived from that of Ryle **1**, esp. pp. 136-141. Although the reasons for my disagreement with his interpretation are too detailed to be discussed fully here, a couple of points can be made. First, as he admits (pp. 252-253), his interpretation can make little sense of the relation between the dream-passage and the second account of *"logos,"* whereas mine accords them coordinated roles. Second and more important, unless Plato is being more than usually cryptic, there is no call to believe, as McDowell does (p. 248; cf. pp. 231-237), that "the dream theory is an attempt to capture the complexity of propositional constructions." For although one of the sorts of compounding that must concern Plato (especially given the views which we have seen in the *Crat.*—cf. Ch. VI, sec. 3, on Plato's troubles there over falsity) is the sort that engenders propositions, it seems doubtful that this could be his primary concern in the present passage. For his interest in *logoi* here is not developed for its own sake (in fact, it is not developed for its own sake even in the *Crat.*, as we have seen), but for its bearing on the notion of knowledge. So if one wishes to mount an interpretation of McDowell's sort, it seems to me that one must do more than he does to show just how that interpretation casts light on the official concern of the *Tht.* with knowledge. Moreover, his account suffers from the fact that (as we saw him agreeing, p. 52; cf. n. VII-11, and Runciman, pp. 11ff.), Plato does not seem overridingly concerned with knowledge that *p*, or "propositional" knowledge. (Note that Plato's δόξα and δοξάζειν can involve both propositional and non-propositional sorts of things: see *Tht.* 190a3-5, 200e-201c—though with the usual nonpropositional grammatical structure—*vs.* 209b2-3, a2-3, 208e4-5, with *Rep.* 475esqq.) Finally, there is evidence against McDowell's interpretation in the fact that (as he also agrees, **2**, pp. 233, 240), Plato's examples of compounds, syllables and persons, are "unpromising" as illustrations of the complexity of propositions. If Plato had wanted to bring this sort of complexity to the fore, he could surely have exemplified it by the way in which sentences are formed from words, or for that matter from letters or syllables. (And that this example is at his disposal is put beyond all doubt by the fact that he employs it in the *Crat.*; cf. Ch. VI, sec. 3.) But this is not to deny that the ideas in play stimulate, in the *Soph.*, further ideas that *do* have to do with the makeup of propositions.

49. Plato is not very clear on the nature of the compounding; cf. n. V-17. McDowell **2**, pp. 243-245, 249, and Burnyeat, pp. 118-119, 109-110. Burnyeat, however, exaggerates in depicting the dream-theory as so heavily dependent for its intelligibility on the illustration provided by letters and syllables (p. 109), though he is quite correct that Socrates does not offer to produce any genuine atoms. The ideas involved are not difficult to grasp in a rough way (which is all that is needed for Plato's purposes), and moreover the

general notion of an atom was by this time hardly novel and had been illus-trated by means of the alphabet in the writings of the atomists themselves. For evidence, see Ar., *Met*. 985b5-20, and *De Gen. et Corr*. 315b7-15, noting 1) that line 5 of the former passage certainly need not mean that Leucippus and Democritus themselves used the term "στοιχεῖον," and thus does not conflict with the report of Eudemus *ap*. Simplicius in *Phys*., 7, 10-14, which is cited by Burnyeat, p. 110; 2) that Alexander, *in Met., ad loc.*, knows nothing of an Atomist use of the term; and 3) Burnyeat's argument on p. 110 is therefore weakened, though without damage to his case for dismissing Antisthenes from the discussion (cf. n. VII-56). There is accordingly less reason for reject-ing the view of Cornford (**1**, pp. 143-144) and Hicken (**2**, pp. 139ff.), that the dream theory was suggested by some unnamed contemporary of Plato's, than Burnyeat (p. 108) might seem to suggest. There is indeed no reason why the whole idea could not have been one that was developed in conversation in the Academy by no one particular person (cf. Hicken). It is difficult to see why Burnyeat thinks (*ibid*.) that this suggestion is rendered less plausible by the consideration that the dream-theory is firmly rooted in the area of Plato's own philosophical concerns.

50. For some discussion, see Oehler, Runciman, pp. 39ff., Prauss, pp. 162ff., Morrow, and Burnyeat. Little needs to be said, I think, about the suggestion that the dream represents the views of Antisthenes. The evidence was already weak and it is disarmed by Hicken **2**, pp. 133-139, and Burnyeat (though on one doubtful point see n. VII-49). Moreover, even if it be still suspected that Antisthenes might in some way have had to do with some of the ideas in the dream (and Burnyeat does not remove all grounds whatever for such suspicions), the important point holds firm: that the introduction of his name into the discussion of the dream provides, as things stand, no help in interpreting it.

51. This fact is seen by Robinson, pp. 52ff., but he draws from it the unwarranted conclusion that according to Plato there must therefore be knowledge of things that have no *logos* (p. 54). But even if an atom has no *logos* in the sense of a tallying of its elements (the second interpretation of "*logos*," which we are about to treat), it does not follow that an atom has no *logos* at all. For it *could* have a *logos* in the third sense offered by Plato, which, as pointed out *infra*, has nothing to do with elements. (This point fits with, though it is different from, that of Burnyeat, pp. 119-120.) It is equally incorrect to be-lieve with Stenzel, p. 73, that Plato's only point is that compounds are un-knowable if their atoms are. Nor is there reason to think, with Hicken **2**, p. 190, that Plato thought that letters must be knowable in a sense different from that applicable to syllables. For while someone might want to say that the senses involved are different, Plato shows no sign of doing so (cf. n. VII-56). In particular, he does not mark such a difference by a contrast between "ἐπίστασθαι" and "γιγνώσκειν," in spite of valiant efforts to show that he does by Hamlyn and Lesher. Cf. *contra* Bluck **3**, and notice that the fact that the two

verbs have somewhat different syntactic roles in Greek (the former tending to be more like "connaître" whereas the latter behaves more like "*savoir*"—though this difference is hardly invariable) does not show that Plato made anything of the fact, let alone that he saw in it a sign of difference of sense. Runciman's way of taking the passage, though it agrees that Plato argues for the knowability of atoms, does so for the wrong reasons (pp. 41-44). See also n. VII-62.

52. Note esp. 206a5-8, with "διαγιγνώσκειν" in a6, and cf. *infra*. The aim in view is to *distinguish* among letters so as to be able to say which a given letter is. Given this fact, and the fact noted earlier that Plato wishes to carry out his discussion of knowledge without highlighting any particular assumption about what the "objects of knowledge" are, we can see an explanation of the fact that in 202b6 the atoms of the dream theory are said to be sensible. The reason is that in what Plato thought of as the best illustration of his contentions, the atoms are letters, which Plato takes to be discriminable by sight or by hearing (ἔν τε τῇ ὄψει . . . καὶ ἐν τῇ ἀκοῇ, 206a6). But although Plato here wishes to preserve the parallel between the dream theory and its illustration, there is no reason to think that he viewed its moral as restricted to a particular sort of object. (I thus see no reason to adopt the view, suggested but rejected by Hicken, that "αἰσθητά" in 202b6 means "directly cognized"; see her **2**, p. 130.

53. An especially curious misinterpretation is to be found in both Cornford **1**, pp. 157-158, and in Morrow, pp. 309-310. The argument does not depend on supposing that one spells "Theaetetus" correctly on one occasion and incorrectly on the next. Rather, the claim is that even though one can spell "Theaetetus" as consistently as one likes, one might still not "know" it. Why? Because one did not know its initial syllable. How not? Because one did not realize that it is the first syllable in the name "Theodorus." Further see McDowell **2**, pp. 253-254.

54. As is done by many commentators, e.g., Ryle **1**, pp. 137ff., and Prauss, pp. 139ff. (on Ryle's sort of interpretation, cf. nn. VII-48 and VII-51). See also McDowell, p. 246. In spite of their arguments, I see no reason to think that Plato ever fully intended his Forms to be simples in the strong sense required for their view (Prauss, *passim*, and Ryle, p. 139). For considerations against this interpretation, see Hicken **1**, pp. 190-194 (though I do not understand her positive conclusions), and n. VII-33. For mention of other views about the possible target(s) of the latter part of the *Tht.*, see Prauss, pp. 139-140.

55. This concern is commented upon by Hicken **1**, p. 195, and McDowell, pp. 239-240, 247-248. Some of the other cognitive achievements that Plato discusses also involve recognition. For example, the person who misspells words (207d-208b) is a person who would mistakenly take the concatenation of letters "T-e-o-d-o-r-u-s" to be an instance of the name "Theodorus". (To say only this much is to oversimplify, but the point holds under elaboration.)

56. See *Rep.* 522c5-6; *Phdr.* 262a11 (cf. "διειδέναι" in a7); and after the *Tht.*

see *Soph.* 225c2 (a propos of division), 267d9 (likewise). See also reff. in Ch. V, sec. 1, *passim*.

57. See Ch. 1, secs. 2,4, and observe that a similar note is struck at the beginning of the *Tht.*, in 147d8-e1, 151e2-3.

58. Observe that as McDowell points out (pp. 256-257), Plato's argument does not depend on supposing that for a given object one particular description applying uniquely to it is somehow privileged over others as far as knowledge of that object is concerned. Observe too that on this account the problem confronting Plato here is far more severe than it would be on the interpretation of Cherniss 1, pp. 6-8, who believes that Plato's aim here is simply to show that true belief cannot be an "essential element" in knowledge.

59. The nature of the connection is seen by Hicken 1, p. 188. Like Hicken and Crombie, pp. 146-147, McDowell sees that the end of *Tht.* seems to criticize the use of the theory of recollection as an answer to the paradox of inquiry (see *infra*), though McDowell points particularly to 199c-d (pp. 222-223). For a different view of the connection with the *Meno*, see Prauss, pp. 157ff.

60. Many have seen that the *Tht.* contains allusions to earlier works (cf. n. VII-4). Plainly, 210c3-4 harks back to such places as *Meno* 84a-c and 86b-c, whereas 210d1-4 is a plain allusion to earlier *mises-en-scène* (contrast the endings of the *Phdr.* and the *Crat.*). Against the view that recollection is at work in the *Tht.*, see Robinson, pp. 39-41.

61. I have already rejected Cornford's claim that Plato had a fourth sense of *"logos"* up his sleeve; cf. n. VII-1. For the asking of the question, see, e.g., McDowell, p. 257. It may be suggested that Plato could still have seen a use for a *logos* that was more than simply a "mark" distinguishing a thing from everything else but explained what the thing was in a somehow special way. But the *Tht.* does not hint at such an idea, and moreover the results of the *Crat.* leave no room for it. In the *Crat.* (Ch. VI, sec. 2), the aim is to come to know things, and the way in which language is suggested to be able to help us to know things is simply by enabling us to distinguish one from another. No further possible elucidatory power of language is mentioned. (Cf. n. VII-58.)

62. Cf. n. VII-51. The point is that even if we cannot conclude with Robinson that Plato thought that there are knowable things without *logoi*, we equally cannot conclude that he thought that there are *logoi* of simples (if he thought that there are simples—cf. n. VII-54). At one point, he would have said that if you know a thing you must be able to say what it is (Ch. I, sec. 2; n. IV-62), but now the whole question at issue is whether he can retain some such view as that.

63. It is perhaps tempting to try to find some link between the difficulties over knowledge in the *Tht.* and the puzzle posed at *Parm.* 133b-134e, but such a line of interpretation would be fanciful, especially since the problem in the *Parm.* has to do explicitly with Forms in a way which that in the *Tht.* does not (cf. *supra*, sec. 5, *init.*).

CHAPTER VIII

The Seventh Letter: The Final Attempt

Between the *Theaetetus* and the Seventh Letter there intervene a number of works by Plato. Several of them—I think especially of the *Sophist*, the *Statesman*, and the *Philebus*—treat of matters that bear some relationship to our main topics.[1] But the relationship is not direct enough to place those dialogues in our line of march. In particular, although they employ and develop ideas concerning the method of collection and division (cf. n. 40), and also certain vital metaphysical issues arising from the theory of Forms, nevertheless they primarily discuss problems that are distinct from our main interests here. Thus we have already seen how the *Sophist* moves away from the problem that centrally concerned us in the *Theaetetus* and attempts to meet the difficulty over false belief in rather different terms (Ch. VII, sec. 4). As I have emphasized, Plato has issues on his mind in addition to the ones that we have been following, and like most philosophers he works on fronts where he sees the possibility of progress. It is perhaps significant in this connection that after the logical, epistemological and metaphysical interests of the *Theaetetus*, the *Parmenides*, and the *Sophist* (the last of which solves some, though by no means all, of the puzzles raised in the former two), the *Statesman*, the *Philebus*, and the *Laws* show an increasing shift of Plato's attention toward political philosophy, ethics, and the theory of value. At any rate, our problems are not substantially dealt with in these later works and are not significantly affected or answered by what they say.

1 The Question of Authenticity

Inevitably, the first issue that arises to meet someone discussing the Seventh Letter is the question of its Platonicity, which is disputed. Because I am going to claim that the letter is probably by Plato, or at least by someone who is following his line of thought in a coherent manner, it will be necessary to say something in defense of this claim. But not wishing to stray too far from our primary epistemological topics, I shall keep the discussion of this matter brief and emphasize the aspects of it that are relevant to our main concerns.[2] This means, in effect, that I shall be concentrating on the part of the letter known as the "philosophical digression," which runs from 341b (or, perhaps more properly, 342a) to 344d. In concentrating on it, I shall be attempting to show how it can be seen as continuing from Plato's epistemological views as we have observed them hitherto. But this concentration is also pertinent to the issue of the genuineness of the letter. For I believe—and this belief is to some extent shared by many of those who believe that the letter is spurious[3]—that the main obstacle to declaring the letter genuine without doubt lies in that digression, and in the possibility that it will not fit with the rest of what we know of Plato's philosophizing. If we can succeed, then, in making the letter square with the rest of Plato's philosophical work, then there is little else that would make most commentators reject it. I shall therefore take up, here at the start, only a few of the problems not directly associated with the digression.[4]

One of them has to do with the fact that the letter shows Plato interested in putting various views about political philosophy into practice and fearing the charge that if he does not, then his ideas will seem to be "mere words" (328c). It has been claimed against the genuineness of the letter that Plato's true interests lay in intellectual contemplation, in a way that could not be reconciled with a lively concern for political events.[5] Now there is evidence aside from the letter that Plato was interested in political affairs, and certainly that the Academy was, so this argument seems weak from the start.[6] Still, two facts are worthy of notice. First, we have seen some evidence that in the *Theaetus* Plato was at least willing to entertain the idea that there might be knowledge about sensible objects (Ch. VII, sec. 5). If this is so, then obviously there would be little reason to suppose that he must have rejected all concern with events in the sensible world. But in any case this point is outbid by another, which is that even in earlier dialogues, where Plato regarded Forms as the sole objects of know-ledge (Ch. IV, sec. 1), he still did not regard them as the sole proper objects of the philosopher's concern and was thoroughly anxious that the sensible world be improved—made to resemble the Forms, in effect—as much as possible.[7] One notable case of this concern, already remarked upon (Ch. III, sec. 4), was his belief that inhabitants of cities ought to model them as closely as possible on the Forms. And of course this is precisely what shows itself in the Seventh Letter.

Another point that is sometimes made against the letter is that in recounting some of the events that it covers, later authors who rely to some extent on its testimony nevertheless diverge from him on certain points and show sympathies that are not entirely the same as his own.[8] Why this fact should cast doubt on the genuineness of the letter is not clear. For to acknowledge that it is by Plato is not necessarily to believe everything that it says.[9]

A slightly more difficult problem is raised by the advocacy in the letter of the idea of ἰσονομία, i.e., of—in some sense—equality of laws (326d, 336d). It has been urged that this word is suggestive of democratic ideals, and thus not appropriate to Plato's own political views.[10] To this argument there is the reply that although Plato disapproved of democracy, and thus of equality of laws in the sense tied to *that* notion, there was nevertheless another sort of political equality that he was willing to accept, at least at a later stage of his life (the *Laws* 757a-d, 694a, 695d).[11] It can be asked why he had not, before the letter, used the term "ἰσονομία" in its hygienic sense, and thus requires the reader suddenly in 326d to take it non-pejoratively without explanation.[12] But I think that the context makes clear to the reader what Plato is doing, since he explicitly contrasts "just constitution with equal laws" as d5 (δικαίου καὶ ἰσονόμου πολιτείας) with, in d4 just preceding, "tyrannies and oligarchies *and democracies.*"[13] So the reader is clearly told not to take the equality in question to be of the democratic sort. Likewise in 336d4 the way is well enough prepared for the favorable manner in which "ἰσονομία" is used. Not that Plato here explains what sort of non-democratic equality of laws he has in mind (cf. the *Laws* 757a-d). In this respect, as in others, the letter is understandably brief and compressed.

2 The Philosophical Position

Let us leave aside now the question of authenticity and pass on to the philosophical matters in the digression, recognizing that the better we can integrate them into Plato's thought, the greater the likelihood that the work is genuine. I shall henceforth use the name "Plato" for the author of the letter, hoping that by the end of the chapter at least, the reader will acquiesce.[14] Before we begin, however, we must be careful to observe that integration need not necessarily mean a demonstration that the letter contains precisely the same doctrine as that of some Platonic dialogue or other.[15] What will emerge is not that the Seventh Letter echoes the sentiments of the *Republic* or of the *Theaetetus*. Rather, we shall see that the letter shows further work being done on some of the epistemological problems that have troubled Plato from the start, and which the investigations of the *Theaetetus* have brought to a head.

To indicate first the direction in which we shall be going: in the Seventh Letter, Plato expresses certain views, particularly about an alleged defectiveness of language, and about the sort of knowledge for which a philosopher should strive, which have struck many commentators as uncharacteristic of the Plato of the dialogues.[16] Sometimes, for example, the point is put by saying that the Seventh Letter is "mystical" in a way in which the dialogues are not, and it is also suggested that the letter is in that way more akin to Neoplatonism than to Platonism proper.[17] Alternatively, it has been thought—by those who believe that the letter is indeed by Plato—that it hints at a doctrine in certain ways different from that of the works that we know, i.e., as an esoteric doctrine of some kind, which Plato did not publish.[18] I shall claim, on the contrary, that although the letter does not show signs of having reached firm conclusions on the epistemological points which it treats and may hint of discussions in the Academy which are not recorded in dialogues, nevertheless its views about knowledge and language are an intelligible reaction to the difficulties over definitions and Forms which had been pressing in on Plato's theory. To say that the reaction is intelligible is not to defend it, and I shall make objections to it in due course (sec. 3; cf. Ch. IX). But I think that there is no difficulty in seeing why, given the problems that he had to face, Plato might easily have adopted the measures that are at work—though they are not elaborated—in the letter. There is thus no self-contained esoteric doctrine (though there can have been further discussion within Plato's Academy), and there need be no author of the letter other than Plato.

In the first place, the attitude of the letter toward language, and particularly written language, is of a piece with what we have already seen in the *Phaedrus* and the *Cratylus*. It has the same basic preoccupation with the possibility of confusion about Forms, and particularly with the difficulty of knowing which Form corresponds to which expression or term.[19] In common with those dialogues, the letter holds that there is something inadequate about language,[20] in that it is not irrevocably and eternally fixed, when one hears a term used, which Form one is to think of in order to understand what is being said.[21] Thus, when a speaker uses an expression, the hearer must face the task of identifying the object to which the speaker means the expression to correspond.[22] Given what we have seen in the *Cratylus*, it is perfectly clear why Plato should be worried about this problem. For that dialogue brought to prominence the idea that the purpose of language is to help speakers put hearers in mind of the objects they wish to. And the objects in question, in both works, are primarily Forms. Moreover, a corollary is developed at 343c-e: the idea that in judging what a person's beliefs are, or assessing his claims to knowledge, one must employ more evidence than that of his merely linguistic behavior. Once again, the idea is that because words may be misleading or deceptive, one must examine far more of what a person does than simply his utterances, in order to determine what he does or does not have on his mind.[23]

The attitude of the letter toward writing is also similar to that of the *Phaedrus*. As in that dialogue, the problem is not simply one affecting written language alone. It is rather a difficulty afflicting language in general, for the reasons described, but which is intensified when language is written down (note esp. "γράφειν ἢ λέγειν" in 343d6; cf. d7, 341d2-3, and "ῥητόν" at 341c5), for reasons that the *Phaedrus* has already expounded (Ch. V, sec. 2). It is therefore misguided to see in the letter any claim that an orally promulgated doctrine could be free of the difficulties encumbering written work. Both are to some extent suspect, on grounds that are in principle the same. And both have their uses, as we shall see. There is therefore no good reason to think that the letter repudiates the doctrines or arguments of the dialogues, or on that score either to brand the letter spurious, or to see in it a hint of an esoteric doctrine at variance with the rest of the Platonic corpus.

Thus, from a superficial point of view, the stance of the letter jibes with that of the dialogues which treat of related matters, and they have the same concerns in common. But the letter introduces a new idea of a way in which the difficulties plaguing language can somehow be overcome or circumvented. The crucial suggestion is that gaining knowledge of the Forms, of the sort at which we are aiming,[24] is like a sort of illumination, or the leaping up of a flame (344b5-c1, 341c7-d1). Although Plato has used this image or something like it before, in the *Symposium* and the *Republic*, it is only in the letter that he applies it to the problems concerning language.[25] We cannot understand what the letter is driving at, or how its concerns are related to those of the dialogues, until we determine what Plato means by this suggestion, and how he thinks it can solve the philosophical problems that he is facing. But to understand these things in turn, we must look further into his discussion of language, beginning with his treatment of the notion of *logos*.

3 Language, Definition, and Illumination

So far we have neglected Plato's treatment of *logos* in the letter, and its part in his account of the deficiencies of language. By *"logos"* in this connection, he means "definition": thus he speaks of the *logos* of Circle (342b6-c1), which he gives as "that of which the distance from the edge to the middle is everywhere the same," and later on of the need to know "what" (τί) a thing is (343c1).[26] He has already said that when a name is used (ὄνομα), one has difficulty being sure what it is to be taken as naming. But, he says, because a *logos* is made up of names (as well as ῥήματα, 342b6, 343b4-5),[27] the same difficulty afflicting names also afflicts *logoi* (343b4-6). That is, if there is a problem in telling what a term names or corresponds to, there is equally going to be a problem in telling what a definition corresponds to. Thus, if one is in the dark as to what the expression *N* is supposed to name in a given situation, then there is no reason in principle why getting a definition for *N* will necessarily do any good. For if we are in general sceptical of our ability to identify the Forms to which terms correspond, then we should be just as sceptical of our ability to identify the Forms to which their definitions correspond, since the definitions are themselves made up of terms. If I hesitate in general to say that I know what you mean by your words, and thus what you mean by "circle" (cf. 342b), my hesitation will not be ended if you give me some further words to explain what you mean.

All of this should sound very familiar, and in fact what Plato is doing is to continue to dwell on the difficulties over definitions which have come to the surface since the *Cratylus* and the *Theaetetus*. At the end of our discussion of the *Cratylus*, it was remarked that determining which terms correspond to which Forms was bound to lead to difficulties over definitions as well (Ch. VI, sec. 4). That dialogue did not dwell on the point, but the letter brings it to the forefront. In so doing, it also develops a difficulty over definitions which the *Theaetetus* made explicit. The question raised there was how the getting of a definition could represent any sort of cognitive progress over the position in which one simply had a term to designate an object that one had in mind (Ch. VII, sec. 5). Plato did not there answer this question, and he indicated plainly that he did not see his way to a solution of the problem. In the letter, he has gone a step further and suggested that in a certain sense the problem is intractable. If there is an object that you wish to have in mind but do not, then there is no reason in principle why one sort of expression will necessarily help you more than another.[28]

So far, we know that there is a problem, which the letter recognizes, about how *logoi* are to be used in fixing one's mind on Forms, but as yet we have drawn no conclusions from the existence of this problem. At this point, however, Plato's line of thought takes an important turn. He does not say that definitions are of no use at all. Indeed, he actually presents one (the definition of Circle, already mentioned, at 342b7-8), and he suggests that discussions in which definitions figure are an important means toward gaining knowledge of Forms (343c*sqq*.). The idea must be that whereas there is no *guarantee* that giving a definition will put a hearer in mind of the right object, it may nevertheless help him to do so, or jog his mind, as it were, in the right direction. But as we noted, the actual discovery—the coming to view Forms—is described as though it were a sort of illumination, as though a light were kindled (341c7-d1, 344b7-c1). Let us again ask what Plato might mean by this, and how he can think of it as a response to his difficulties.

There are two answers to this question, one attributing to Plato a clearer understanding of his predicament than the other. Let us consider first the one attributing less understanding.

The idea of illumination seems to be called in, as I have said, to solve a difficulty created, as Plato sees the matter, by the inadequacies of language. Crudely put, the idea would be that because there is no definite way of answering the question which Form a given term corresponds to, there must be some sort of illumination that will provide us with the answer to the question. The suggestion supposes that Plato is still anxious to pursue efforts to apprehend particular Forms specified in advance, such as (thus put) "Justice," but is trying to find some way around the fact that according to the views that were developed in the *Cratylus* and the *Theaetetus*, anyone who is actually using such a term as a name must already apprehend an object to which he is then applying it; whereas a person who is *not* thus using it cannot be picking out any object that he is aiming to apprehend (see Ch. VII, sec. 5). The way around this fact, it is suggested, would be to say that for someone beginning *without* naming or apprehending some object, the successful conclusion of his effort to apprehend Justice could be viewed as some sort of illumination.

But this idea is confused. If we abide by the views of the *Cratylus* and the *Theaetetus*, then there is no way for a person beginning in the envisioned position to be regarded as in fact undertaking, at the start, to apprehend *any particular* Form. For the view of those dialogues leaves no way for a person to be aiming to apprehend a particular Form without already apprehending it; that is the crucial epistemological consequence of their view of naming, recognized at the end of the *Theaetetus* (*ibid.*). But if one is not aiming to apprehend any particular thing, Form or otherwise, then there is obviously no way in which any illumination can bring it about that one apprehend what one was attempting to apprehend, because there simply is no such thing. A search that begins with no goal obviously cannot be said to have reached its goal, and no subsequent illumination, however welcome, can make up for the fact that it had no goal to begin with.[29]

The paradox of inquiry in the *Meno* raised much the same difficulty (Ch. II, sec. 4), and we saw that Plato's solution failed to diagnose it but attempted to use recollection to evade it in much the manner that the present suggestion would have him use illumination (Ch. II, sec. 5). Should we not therefore see him as continuing as before, but this time using illumination rather than recollection? The idea is dubious, partly because the change would be unmotivated. If he were still misdiagnosing the problem, then why should he not have retained the solution involving recollection? (We saw, in Ch. VII, sec. 5, that he shows no sign of doing so.) Moreover, the *Theaetetus* looks to be a more considered treatment of the whole issue than the *Meno* had been, and therefore one is tempted to suppose that Plato has a better appreciation of what is at stake than he earlier had.

But there is another construal that makes Plato out to be far more alive to the nature of his situation and indeed to be diagnosing it with considerable accuracy. The problem arising out of the *Theaetetus* was that on the view presented there, it seemed to be impossible to name an object without already apprehending it. But Plato has no way of explaining how one might be able to frame a search for a *particular* object without actually naming it and therefore apprehending it.[30] Thus, the idea is precluded that one might somehow have a particular thing that is the object of one's search, which one could then go out and apprehend and *recognize* as the object of one's search. The interpretation suggested just now claimed that the notion of illumination could some-how rescue this possibility, but the suggestion was mistaken. The present suggestion, however, is that in the Seventh Letter, Plato is abandoning this sort of project altogether.

The point would be now that what one is trying to do is *simply* to apprehend the Forms, to bring them to mind, without any thought to being able to *recognize* them as particular things for which one had been searching.[31] It would be simply a matter of enjoying the spectacle, as it were—like gazing at an unidentified landscape, as opposed to seeing and recognizing places which one has sought.[32] We know that the spectacle of the Forms is one that Plato has always believed that the mind must enjoy, even when he has been concerned that we recognize those which we are viewing.[33] It would be a natural enough response to the problems engendered by the *Cratylus* and *Theaetetus* to suppose that the effort to recognize must give way.[34]

Where in the Seventh Letter should we see such a decision at work? Possibly in the very idea of illumination which has troubled us. There is now no such thing as specifying some object to be apprehended and then apprehending it and recognizing it as what one was after. Rather, the only contrast that there can be is between one's apprehending the object and one's not apprehending it, between its being in view and its not being in view—where there is no question of its being *recognized* in any sense at all. And the only cognitive progress that one could make is from not apprehending it to apprehending it. It would be tempting, and not entirely inappropriate, to compare this sort of transition to the illumination of a light, and perhaps this is what Plato meant by that manner of speaking in the letter. You are apprehending something that you were not apprehending before, as though a light had illuminated the darkness. But it must not be thought that you *recognize* the particular things which you see, or that you know them to be something which you have sought.[35]

If we see Plato as making this point, then certain other important facts fall into place. Consider his claim that philosophical doctrine cannot be expressed in language (esp. 341c5-6). Looking back at his philosophical career, note what a large and important part of a finished philosophical doctrine would have looked like. It would have consisted of definitions, along with an exposition of various logical relationships among them and other sorts of statements—the fruits, that is, of dialectic as advocated in the *Republic*, or of the later use of collection and division. The dialogues are in many cases efforts to gain such definitions, but they are not the definitions themselves. (This is a part of the meaning of the passage, 341c4-5, which says that there is no treatise, σύγγραμμα, by Plato on the subject of the philosophical digression.) But the point of such definitions, as playing the central role which Plato had accorded them, has been thrown into doubt by the end of the *Theaetetus*, and the move that the Seventh Letter now makes would be a step further. It would be an acknowledgment that because there is no fixed correspondence between words and Forms, and whereas definitions (being themselves composed of words) are of no help in establishing one, the use of language in expressing doctrine is severely limited (cf. sec. 4). All that one can do is to hope that a person will finally be able to bring the Forms into his ken (341c6-d2). Moreover, this same point would apply to any positive remarks which Plato has attempted to make about particular Forms. On this view they drop out as, in a certain sense, useless. What remains is simply the effort to apprehend the Forms.[36]

4 Language and "Mysticism" in the Letter

Whether in an effort to defend or to attack the genuineness of the letter, it has for obvious reasons been tempting to characterize the views appearing in it as "mystical." This characterization is lacking in clarity, and there are many different sorts of features that one might attempt to indicate by applying or withholding it. Still, there is some point in observing that in one important sense what the letter says is not mystical at all.[37] If I am right about its purport, its view rests on Plato's life-long examination of epistemological problems and on a full series of philosophical arguments and discussions. It was, that is to say, neither a flight of fancy nor some sort of quasi-religious conversion. Rather, it was a calculated response to certain quite well-defined philosophical problems which Plato found himself unable to avoid in any other way, but which were firmly planted in the work that preceded it.

For this reason, it is wrong to think of the letter as throwing aside the results and doctrines of the dialogues, and this is so even though the letter casts doubt on the legitimacy of using language as the dialogues had done—and even as the letter itself was doing (cf. n. 36). The philosophical discussions of the dialogues still stand, and indeed the justification of the position that the letter takes would be totally lacking without them, since it is they that set up the problems that the letter is a last attempt to meet. Indeed, Plato signals this fact plainly enough when he maintains, in 343b*sqq.*, that dialectic and philosophical discussion are essential to the sort of knowledge at which he thinks we should aim.[38] Thus, we need see in the letter neither the meanderings of an incompetent forger, nor hints of a secret or esoteric Platonic dogma, nor the repudiation of his earlier work by a cantankerous old man.

Nor must the epistemological worries, intensifying in the period from the *Theaetetus* and the letter, have discouraged Plato from expounding and developing other aspects of his philosophical position, and the evidence to the contrary is obvious. The *Sophist*, the *Statesman*, and the *Philebus* take up numerous topics of various sorts and develop them intensively.[39] Some of these topics are directly at the center of the theory of Forms, and some of them are connected with the issues that we have been discussing.[40] But that fact is not in conflict with the supposition of a lingering and even increasing puzzlement on Plato's part concerning how language can be used to make sense, and how definitions, in particular, can be of any aid at all in gaining knowledge of the sort that he has in view. For he can perfectly well hold that he may legitimately use language to develop his philosophical view, even while that view itself declares language to be in certain ways problematical.

A philosophical conundrum, to be sure, is posed by this contention. For if language is suspect for the reason that Plato gives, then he must himself have doubts about the intelligibility and usefulness of what he had written, both in the dialogues and, as I just remarked, in the letter itself. Certainly there is something peculiar, at least, in the position in which he finds himself. But it is by no means an unheard-of or impossible position to attribute to a philosopher. Since Plato's time other philosophers have been in analogous predicaments, and even in his own time his was not unprecedented. Thus, it would appear that Parmenides had adopted a view raising similar problems, and certainly the *Theaetetus* accuses Protagoras of doing likewise.[41] From philosophy after Plato, we may compare the position of certain sceptics, who worried that they might have to take a sceptical view of their own position, or that of the early Wittgenstein, who declares his own work senseless and compares it to a ladder which one must discard once one has mounted it.[42] This is not to pass judgment on the tenability of such positions. It is only to point out that Plato's is reminiscent of them. But in an important way his situation is less uncomfortable and more defensible than theirs. For he need not declare his own position false (as he accuses Protagoras of having to do), or meaningless (as Wittgenstein does, and Parmenides may be required to do), or subject to doubt (as certain sceptics must). He must only say, at worst, that his hearers or readers may not understand the words that he utters or writes. That is an unfortunate predicament to be in, described as he describes it, but it is arguably less self-defeating than the analogues of it which I have mentioned.[43]

Notes

1. My own belief is that the *Parm.* probably follows the *Tht.* too, but for present purposes the point is unimportant. These two works are now generally agreed to precede the *Soph.*, *Polit.*, *Phileb.*, and *Legg.*, which are usually thought to have come in that order. The *Tim.* I place in the period of the *Rep.* and *Symp.*, on grounds separate from my concerns here (cf. nn. IV-3 and 7), about which it says nothing of significance.

2. The most recent complete discission of the authenticity of the letter is by Edelstein, who cites previous literature extensively and gives a brief history of the debate (pp. 1-2, 119-120). For bibliography see also Friedländer, vol. I, pp. 236-246, 377-380, and (with references to ancient sources) Morrow **1**, esp. pp. 3-16, 44-81. Although it perhaps is true that the question of authenticity of one Platonic letter is not independent of the question of authenticity of others (see Edelstein, Ch. III), I see no reason why *Ep.* II, and others, should not be rejected even while *Ep.* VII is kept (cf. Morrow, pp. 13ff.). About the other letters nothing need be said here.

3. Thus see Edelstein, pp. 3, 69, 167, who also observes (p. 2) that there is no external evidence against authenticity.

4. For further problems, which I shall not be able to take account of here, see esp. Edelstein. For a reply to him, see Parente, pp. 103-111; and for another recent defense of the letter, see von Fritz **2**. One further point about Edelstein's view deserves brief mention here. On his view, it is a difficulty (observed by him) that the forger, while trying to follow Plato's doctrine quite faithfully, bungled the job as Edelstein thinks he did (see pp. 24-39, esp. 27, n. 63); and the reply to this point given by Edelstein (p. 38, n. 91, and pp. 67-69) seems insufficient.

5. See Edelstein, pp. 17ff., 109.

6. In different veins see Shorey **5**, vol. I, pp. xlii-xlv, and von Fritz **3**, esp. pp. 29-30, as well as Parente, pp. 171-204.

7. See also Shorey, *loc. cit.*

8. This issue is developed by Edelstein, pp. 39ff. He admits, however, that Plato had his detractors and Dionysius II had his admirers (pp. 60ff.; cf.

Morrow **1**, pp. 44ff., 61-62), and there is no reason why Plutarch would have resisted all influence from them.

9. Thus, we are not necessarily forced into the choice, on which even some defenders of the letter insist (e.g., Morrow, pp. 12-13), between the spuriousness of the letter and the inaccuracy of conflicting tradition. After all, if Plato wrote the letter, then he was a firsthand source, but he was not necessarily a disinterested one.

10. See esp. Edelstein, pp. 12-13, and Vlastos **6**, esp. pp. 202-203.

11. Thus see Vlastos, p. 202, and Parente, pp. 108-109.

12. This question is pressed by Vlastos, *ibid*.

13. For a further argument see Ostwald, pp. 180-182.

14. Of course, much of the evidence for authenticity that the following pages will provide, being evidence that the ideas in the letter fit intelligibly with those of the dialogues, is equally compatible with the hypothesis that the letter was written by someone other than Plato but carrying on his line of thought (thus Edelstein, pp. 71, 111ff., 168, and Cherniss **3**, p. 244, n. 150). But as is argued by evidence given by Edelstein himself (pp. 114ff.), it is hard to see who else it could be beside Plato; see also von Fritz **2**, pp. 134-135.

15. The opposite assumption is often made, both by attackers and by defenders of the genuineness of the letter. On the former side see, e.g., Edelstein, *passim*, Boas, pp. 454-457; Crombie, pp. 124-127 (who on pp. 122-124, however, does try to connect *Ep.* VII with the *Tht.* in a manner not too very different from mine). On the latter side, compare for example (noting his attempt to link the letter to the views of the *Rep.* about geometry) Taylor **1**.

16. See the citations *ap*. Edelstein and von Fritz.

17. See variously Porphyry, *Vita Plotini* 23; von Fritz, **2**, p. 121; Taylor **5**, pp. 149-154; and Edelstein, pp. 100ff., 106, nn. 80 and 81. Edelstein also observes, however (pp. 114ff.), that there is no reason to ascribe the letter to any other particular figure.

18. For a brief discussion of a recent version of this view, see Krämer. For a critique of the same sort of position, see Vlastos **5**, and also von Fritz **2**, esp. pp. 135-153. (Notice, however, that the view that Plato held some views not contained in the dialogues need not be tied, as some do, to the idea that the dialogues do not contain his "true" doctrine and could not do so because they are in written form; for a different sort of account, see e.g., Ross **2**, Ch. IX. For an attack on all such views, see Cherniss **4**.

19. See Morrow **1**, p. 69, vs. Taylor **1**, p. 361. Edelstein, pp. 82-85, sees differences between the attitude of the letter and that of the *Phdr.* toward language, but the differences, such as they are, are adequately accounted for by what we have seen of the intervening developments in the *Crat.* Furthermore, the difficulties seen by Edelstein in squaring the letter with *Parm.* 135a are taken care of if we observe, first, that that dialogue may not have reached the degree of scepticism about language shown in the letter (even if the *Parm.* was written after the *Tht.*), and—more important—it is trying at that point not

merely to show difficulties in the theory of Forms, but also the motivation for accepting it.

20. See esp. Ch. V, secs. 1-2, and Ch. VI, secs. 2,4.

21. Ch. V, secs. 2, 4, and 343a9-c5. The point must be that there is a problem of identification. For when Plato says that the meanings of "straight" and "curved" (i.e., the Forms to which these terms correspond) might be reversed, he is presenting this fact as a bar to our perfect understanding of what these terms mean ("ἀσαφές", b7), and knowledge of the things to which they correspond (c1, 6). So he must intend that the fact that they *could* be reversed be taken as a reason for one's not being fully confident about what their meaning actually is. Likewise in 343d2-3, it is said that a person is trying to "answer and show" a Form (τὸ πέμπτον ἀποκρίνεσθαι καὶ δηλοῦν), i.e., to indicate in answer to questions which Form one means, and to induce the interlocutor to fix his mind on it. For a similar use of "δηλοῦν" and cognates, see *Soph.* 261e1, 5, 262a3; cf. also "ἐνδείξεως" in *Ep.* VII, in 341e3, with "ἐπιδείξωμεν" at *Soph.* 265a1. See further *infra*, sec. 3.

22. For the idea that the link between term and Form is not unshakable, see Ch. VI, secs. 2 and 4, and Ch. III, sec. 5, along with 343a9-b3. For the idea that terms can be applied strictly to Forms alone, see Ch. VI, sec. 4, and Ch. IV, sec. 2, along with 343a4-9. (There is little to be said for Edelstein's claim, pp. 97ff., that the letter holds that Forms are somehow "in the mind"—a claim that is supposed [p. 99] to explain certain facts which are easily explained otherwise.)

23. The point is glanced at by Morrow **1**, p. 78. In *Ep.* VII, the same point is apparently at work at 343c5-344c1, esp. 343c5-7 (how dilligently knowledge is pursued is more than a matter simply of what a person says), e1-3, 344a3, b2-3. There is no harm in connecting this need for more than mere talk with the idea of a complete philosophical regimen and way of life (cf. Taylor **1**, p. 354), or in connecting this idea in turn with Pythagorean notions (see, e.g., *Rep.* 600a-b); but still, Plato's use of the idea is based firmly in the philosophical problems with which he himself is dealing. It is of course related, in a roundabout manner, to the importance that Socrates placed on the role of an interlocutor in philosophical thought, and to the fact that he did not write (see, e.g., Jaeger, vol. II, pp. 60-62).

It is not clear how close a connection Plato held to exist between the intellectual activity of a soul and the behavior of its associated body, and some will see a problem here about one's ever being able to tell, on his view, whether or not someone else is or is not apprehending the same thing as oneself. A verificationist, of course, will conclude that there is no sense in such claims. But there is no reason to think that Plato was ever tempted by any sort of verificationism (cf. Robinson **1**, pp. 110-111). Moreover, there is an important fact about his psychological theory that would probably have prevented him from facing this issue explicitly. As he looked at the matter, when a person is "viewing" a Form, it is his soul or mind (ψυχή) that is doing the viewing. But he certainly thought that there are in principle other ways of telling what a soul is doing than looking at the behavior of the body which it inhabits. In fact, he plainly believes that at least sometimes the actions and state of a soul are easier to determine when it is disembodied (*Gorg.* 523a*sqq.*; *Rep.* 611b-612). On the other hand, he does not say anything directly about whether or not disembodied souls communicate with and observe each other, aside from passages that are so metaphorical or embedded in myth that one hesitates to place much weight on them, and we are best off if we recognize that Plato does not address himself to these issues in any sustained way.

24. Note that the letter vacillates regarding the use of the term "knowledge" (compare 342c7-d1 with e1-2); cf. von Fritz, pp. 123-124.

25. At *Rep.* 527e1, "ἀναζωπυρεῖται" can thus be taken, though it is used in a context rather different from the one in which it figures both in the *Symp.* and in *Ep.* VII, in that it is not here used of the culmination or completion of an investigation. The relevant passage of the *Symp.* is 210e-212a, esp. 210e3-6, 211b6-7, d-e. This passage, however, contains only the notion of "seeing" or "viewing" the Form of the Beautiful (cf. Ch. IV, sec. 1, for this image in the *Rep.*), along with the idea that that Form is overwhelmingly beautiful. The images of 341c7-d1 and 344b7 are quite different (and different—*nota bene*—from each other). More importantly, the *Symp.* passage has nothing to do with any problem about language or its inadequacy and is thus not attacking the same problem as the letter. (211a2-5 might be thought to require concern—though it does not actually express it—about whether the term "beautiful" can be properly applied, without qualification, to sensibles; but the problem in view in the letter obviously goes further than that. In 211a7, "οὐδέ τις λόγος οὐδέ τις ἐπιστήμη" is irrelevant; see Bury *ad loc.*)

26. This is also the force of "ὄν" in 343a1, b8; cf. *Rep.* 480a11, 484d6, and *infra*, n. VIII-35. Notice that the contrast here between τί (or ὄν) and ποῖον (342e3, 343b8) is the same as the contrast between τί and ποῖον in the *Meno*; cf. Ch. II, sec. 1. To know "what" a thing is, is to know how to find and recognize it, and this is what language is unable, Plato thinks, to convey. On the other hand, he seems to suppose that the terms can be true of Forms (i.e., say "what sort of thing" they are), without serving uniquely to identify any of them. This supposition is perhaps made in order to allow him to avoid the problem mentioned in n. VIII-35, *infra*. Alternatively (or, in addition—the two ideas are compatible), the notion of "ποῖον" here could be derived from a similar contrast in the *Crat.*; cf. n. VI-22.

27. The contrast between ὀνόματα and ῥήματα here ought certainly to be the same as that of the *Soph.* rather than that of the *Crat.* (cf. Ch. VI, sec. 3). Thus, for instance, in the same *logos* in 342b7-8, "ἀπέχον" would be a ῥῆμα.

28. In this comparison to the end of the *Tht.*, we have the answer to a question that has puzzled commentators and induced some to think the letter spurious; why does 342c4-5 assimilate ἐπιστήμη (and νοῦς) with ἀληθὴς δόξα? Is this not unplatonic? Not if one realizes that the letter is picking up where

the *Tht.* left off. And where the *Tht.* left off, no distinction has been established between thinking about a thing, or referring to it, and having knowledge of it (Ch. VII, sec. 5).

29. It will be objected that we might still have a way of specifying, in a particular case, which Form is the object of an inquiry. For instead of using the word "Justice," one might use "the Form to which such-and-such a speaker at such-and-such a time is employing the word 'Justice' to correspond." Thus, on a particular occasion, my injunction to you to "think about Justice" would come, in effect, to this: "Think about what I am thinking about." Unfortunately, the view of naming in the *Crat.* and *Tht.* is equally fatal to this suggestion (recall that Plato offers no distinction between, say, names and definite descriptions such as might be used to advance this suggestion. Moreover, there is no trace of this idea in the letter.

30. This fact, of course, was a crucial factor in the emergence of the paradox of inquiry; cf. Ch. II, sec. 4, and also Ch. I, sec. 4, and Ch. IX, sec. 2. Plainly, the letter is not putting any stock in the ability of recollection to solve its problems. Memory is implied to be helpful (344a2-b1, esp. a7-8) but is said to be insufficient by itself, and no stress is put upon it.

31. It is perhaps something such as this idea that some commentators have attributed to Plato in saying that he regards knowledge as a kind of "direct acquaintance." As I have said, however, this notion has been so meagerly explained in accounts of Plato as to have been practically useless. Cf. Ch. I, sec. 1, and Ch. IX, sec. 2, esp. n. IX-14.

32. In support of this interpretation one might cite the claim in 344b1-2, that one must at the same time learn what is true and false about all of οὐσία, the idea perhaps being that there is no use in making statements about individual Forms in an attempt to identify them individually. (I refrain here from speculating on whether or not this idea is connected with views standardly attributed to Speusippus; cf. Aristotle, *An. Post.* II, 97a6ff., with Ross *ad loc.*)

33. See, e.g., *Phdr.* 249dsqq., with Ch. V, introd.

34. Obviously, we have here to do with ideas that are also at work occasionally in Aristotle, e.g., at *Met.* 1051b17ff. (cf. 1027b15ff.). It is noteworthy, however, that there is relatively little in Aristotle that is really directly pertinent to this issue, or to related issues concerning the use of language (exceptions are *De Int.*, *passim*, esp. 1, 2, 4; *An. Post.* 92b21-22, 32-34; *Met.* IV.4, *passim*, esp. 1006a18ff.). One of the reasons is Aristotle's relative lack of interest in the relevant sort of epistemological worry (cf. introd.). Another is his rather uninquiring and down-to-earth attitude toward the question how language is linked to the world (see esp. *De Int.*, *ibid.*).

35. Cf. n. VIII-26, and note that by his claims about ποῖον, Plato seems to be trying to leave a way open for making *general* statements about Forms (e.g., that they are Forms, perhaps, or that they are eternal, and the like) without thereby allowing identifying references to particular Forms. Whether doing so is legitimate may be debated.

36. This, then, is the import of the remark in 344d9-e2, that there is not

much to forget of Plato's view once one has learned it. Why "once one has learned it"? Because Plato supposes that to see the meaning and point of the claim that his doctrine is so brief, one must work through a great deal of philosophical argument; cf. sec. 4.

Notice that there are plenty of indications that the author of the letter knows that much of his use of language in the letter itself must be suspect. Thus, e.g., the use of "λόγος" at 342a3 and 343b4-6, which is too obvious to be a mere inadvertance, and the use of "εἰπεῖν," "λεχθέντων," etc., at 342a2-6, contrasting with "ῥητόν" at 341c5.

37. In another connection, Oehler, p. 114, denies that Plato's notion of *"Einsicht"* is "mystical," but his approach differs appreciably from mine in important ways. See also Morrow, pp. 77, 78-79.

38. It is not, then, that dialectic is in some vague and amorphous manner a "propaideutic" to the illumination that Plato promises. The whole *need* for the notion of illumination cannot be explained without the arguments and discussions that Plato has set forth.

39. So, of course, does the *Parm.*—if it was produced after the *Tht.*; cf. nn. VII-3 and VII-16.

40. To mention only one, the method of division is treated, and used, extensively, esp. in the *Soph.* and the *Polit.* See also *Legg.* 895d, 897e, and esp. 962-969, where philosophical discussion is relied on in the manner that is pointed to (as just noted) by *Ep.* 343b*sqq.*

41. For remarks on the relevant difficulties in Parmenides' position, see Owen **4**, and Furth. For the accusation against Protagoras, see *Tht.* 169-171. In the *Euthyd.* too, Socrates is quick to accuse his opponents of holding self-defeating doctrines (286c, 288a, 303d-e). (Diog. Laert. III.35 is hardly a reliable source on this matter, and it is not even certain that its point is of the same character.)

42. For Wittgenstein, see **1**, sec. 6.54. For expression of the sceptics' worries, see e.g., Sext. Emp., *Outlines of Pyrrhonism* I.13-15; Diog. Laert. IX.76.

43. I fully recognize that the contrary is also arguable, and that the issues are extremely complex (though they are generally little discussed). But to pursue these questions would be unfruitful here. (To keep matters clear, however, note the following. According to Plato here, what hinders understanding of spoken or written discourse is the difficulty of identifying the Forms that correspond to the words used in it. Accordingly, just how much of his letter would be subject to this problem depends on which of its words are those whose understanding requires identification of Forms. But this is a matter on which Plato does not plainly pronounce.)

CHAPTER IX

Philosophical Retrospect

As presented in his works, Plato's theory of knowledge is like the other parts of his thought in emerging piece by piece rather than in any very systematic exposition. Plato had his reasons for this procedure, and there are distortions that are inevitably engendered by the attempt to pull certain of his ideas out of the contexts in which he placed them and to string them together in a different exegetical arrangement. Having done this once already, however, I must now do it again, in a brief summary of the course of Plato's thoughts on the pertinent topics, as they have been presented in the foregoing account. This accomplished, I shall then explain—again, all too briefly—the major philosophical problems that I take Plato to have raised and attacked, and which ultimately provide the impetus for this book.

1 The Route So Far

As I began this account by saying, the overriding motivation of Plato's theory of knowledge is the firm belief, in opposition to various opposing intellectual currents of his time, in facts about the world which are in some vague and difficult but important sense independent of the judgments of any particular human beings or groups of human beings. This belief shows itself in a general distrust of hearsay and received opinion and in a determination to press for definitions of crucial and problematical concepts, in order to gain some degree of solidity for our judgments (Ch. I, introd. and secs. 1, 3).

The philosophical tools for attaining this end are developed only gradually. The Forms are introduced in an unobtrusive manner, on the basis of various considerations which are not always fully spelled out. Their epistemological function, though evidently important, is not laid out in any cut-and-dried manner, but slowly developed in the process of the discussions to which it is pertinent. For this reason, Plato's earlier works show a certain lack of clarity about what he thinks the starting point of our epistemological investigations should be taken to be. The establishment of definitions is one of the aims; another is a certain sort of knowledge of Forms which involves a kind of mental apprehension and recognition of them; but the way in which we proceed to these goals, as well as the point from which we are to begin our journey toward them, are left without much explanation, and the two goals themselves are not always clearly distinguished or related to each other (Ch. I, sec. 4). This state of affairs helps to foster the paradox of inquiry in the *Meno*, which is, however, put aside somewhat unsatisfactorily by the theory of recollection*(Ch. II, secs. 4, 5).

But in the meantime, Plato is beginning to develop a method for meeting some of these problems. The notion of a hypothesis is advanced in the *Meno*, and it constitutes, in undeveloped form, an answer to the problem of the starting point of investigations concerning Forms. The Forms themselves become more firmly and openly established in the *Phaedo* as the subject matter of our most reliable intellectual activity, and as the objects with which definitions are concerned (Ch. III, secs. 1, 2, 4). The method of hypothesis is developed too (Ch. III, sec. 7), still understood as a method for gaining provisional agreement, rather than as a means of reaching something somehow more solid, though Plato plainly still believes that there is something more to reach, which is a sort of judgment independent of what some adventitious community may happen to agree upon.

The *Republic*, though not claiming to exhibit a fully refined and finished epistemological doctrine, contains the most ambitious attack theretofore mounted by Plato against problems concerning knowledge. The theory of Forms is expounded in a more systematic and extended manner, and the method of hypothesis is claimed to be capable in principle of being supplemented by a way of establishing something more than the merely provisional conclusions allowed in the *Phaedo* (Ch. IV, secs. 4, 5). The crucial fact is that hypotheses are to be about Forms (sec. 3), and in particular the Form of the Good, which is apparently made into a sort of foundation of science (sec. 4). Although many problems and obscurities still remain, we now have the sketch of a way in which we might set out from starting points provided by hypotheses and somehow reach foundations which are more solid.

But this sketch is never filled in, and the reason is that problems arise to lead Plato into new preoccupations. The *Republic* shows worries about the fact that confusion can arise over Forms, and difficulties in keeping different Forms distinct from each other in our thoughts (Ch. IV, sec. 2). The *Phaedrus* develops these worries systematically and proposes the method of collection and division as a device for meeting them (Ch. V, sec. 1). This method overshadows or supersedes the method of hypothesis. As a result, little attention is given to possible ways in which the notion of a hypothesis might be refined and explained, and a clearer conception thereby attained of precisely what knowledge of Forms is, what the starting points of the search for it might be, and how the goal is reached, as well as a more complete account of the respective roles of definition, and of the apprehending of Forms in these proceedings. Attention is now concentrated instead on the way in which the quest for definitions may avoid mistaken conflations of distinct Forms.

This concern leads in turn to new worries about language. The *Phaedo* had treated the connection between terms and Forms as unproblematical, supposing that there was somehow a correspondence between each appropriate predicate and an associated Form. In the *Phaedrus* it becomes clear that this correspondence is not without its difficulties, expecially since Plato is now aware of the importance of ambiguity, and of the fact that one and the same term may apparently correspond, at least in our minds, to different Forms (Ch. V, secs. 1, 2). As a result, he comes to have certain doubts about the efficacy of language in philosophical investigation and exposition (sec. 2). The *Cratylus* then raises the whole question of the nature of the correspondence between "names" and objects. When it is over, Plato has emerged with the idea that only Forms can strictly be named(so that the relation of naming is in effect what we have been calling correspondence), and also with the contention that, in view of what the whole purpose of naming turns out to be, the naming of a thing is, roughly (Plato not being precise or detailed about the matter), the having in mind of an object in some sort of association with the use of the name. Actual languages are said to be unreliable as a means of causing other people to bring objects to mind, but the view is developed, not as an account of the workings of actual language, but as an explanation of what names ought to be expected to accomplish. It is therefore suggested that superior languages could serve as clearer indices of the objects of their users' thoughts, and thus as a more reliable means of communication (Ch. VI, secs. 2, 4).

Working under the influence of these developments, Plato turns explicitly in the *Theaetetus* to the question what knowledge can consist in, and how his long-held convictions about it can be vindicated. He attacks Protagoreanism and defends his view that there are matters of fact independent of our beliefs, to which any claim to knowledge must be true (Ch. VII, sec. 1). Since this view insists on the possibility of there being beliefs that are false, he then attempts to show how false belief is possible (Ch. VII, secs. 2, 3). Defeated in this attempt, he tries nonetheless to explain what knowledge is. The crucial move fails, for reasons which spring in large part from the account of naming in the *Cratylus*: because of the idea that naming involves having the nominatum in mind, in such a way as to preclude the possibility of confusing it with other things, Plato becomes unable to see how there can be room for any cognitive progress beyond simply the naming of a thing, and moreover the role of definitions in knowledge seems to slip away (Ch. VII, sec. 5). The Seventh Letter then shows signs of a last and valiant effort to salvage the situation by appealing to some means of explaining knowledge which will be free of the troubles arising from language and naming, as they are construed in the *Cratylus*. But Plato maintains the conviction that there is a reality of which we may gain knowledge, however paradoxically and tantalizingly shrouded it may seem from our attempts to describe it and communicate our thoughts of it.

This is, then, a thumbnail sketch, much simplified, of the course that Plato's thoughts on these matters have taken. Its purpose is to focus attention on the philosophical issues with which we shall now deal.

2   Plato's Epistemological Realism

In some sense that is as philosophically important as it is difficult to describe, Plato was a realist of as thoroughgoing a sort as has ever written.[1] Even if his views changed in certain respects during his life, he did not waver in his realist stance, and at the end of his career he was still carrying on the battle against the same antirealist, antiobjectivist tendencies that had aroused his opposition in earlier days.[2] But the main thrust of his realism does not come simply from his belief in Forms. As we saw (Ch. I), he was in fact a realist before his views about Forms were at all fully developed, and indeed it is possible to be a realist, in the epistemological sense which I have in mind, without believing in the existence of anything very much like Forms. As far as his epistemology is concerned, the Forms are in a certain way (though not in all ways) a means to an end. The end is that it be clear that there is a world, somewhere or other, which is in some radical manner independent of what anyone may happen to believe. The crucial difficulty in a view such as this is to understand the pertinent sense of the word "independent," but this is by no means easy to do. Perhaps the best way of starting is to mention one of the views with which Plato's is chiefly to be contrasted, since it is often easier to describe what a philosopher was trying *not* to have to say than to explain what he actually meant. One of Plato's chief targets, then, is what I have called Protagoreanism (Ch. VII, introd.), or the view that all that is required for true belief is belief, or that truth must be thought of as relative to the person doing the believing, and applied in this way to anything that he happens to believe. More generally, though, he is opposing any view that suggests that the fact that a proposition is believed is grounds for believing it. By contrast, he is convinced that somehow there is something hard outside of our minds against which our minds must push, and which will not yield.

To characterize his position further, we shall do best to describe a certain more modern view (which may or may not be a view of common sense), about the way in which we think about the world. We shall then see how Plato's view diverges from it.

It is easy for us nowadays to think of science and the language in which it is couched as ongoing projects, slowly but steadily changing to meet new evidence. It is not essential for my purposes that the evidence be thought of as sensory, though it typically is. What is important is that it be thought of as constantly bombarding minds which have not yet seen everything that there is to see, and whose opinions about things do not fit all of the evidence which comes in. Theories of the world therefore adjust. They may or may not be thought of as converging on or approaching some final ideal, as Peirce suggests. What is important here, however, is that even if they have not yet reached that ideal and are often found defective when faced with new evidence, they be thought of as usable, if imperfect, instruments for describing much, at least, of the evidence to date.

The terms of such theories are thought of as meaningful. Sometimes, of course, there are what are viewed as radical changes of theory which involve the introduction of new concepts for which terms do not yet exist in the language, or changes in the meaning of established expressions. (Whether this notion can really hold up under scrutiny is irrelevant to present exegetical concerns.) Nevertheless, as the picture usually is, the terms of the old theory are thought to have had their own meanings, even if the theory as a whole was not as adequate to the evidence as the one that resulted from the change. The terms with their old meanings were all right in their way; the only thing that spoiled them was the (presumably contingent) fact that new observations were made which the old theory would somehow not accommodate.

Now of course this picture contains difficulties. The most pressing questions to ask are: what justifies a change of theory, what it is for a theory to accommodate or not to accommodate evidence, what evidence in fact is, and so forth. But however great these difficulties may be, the picture is one that rightly exercises its spell. Science appears as a going concern, like Neurath's ship, which though it may need constant repair, nevertheless is always afloat and moving, perfectly satisfactory as a ship, even if it never reaches the final destination—if such there be—of a flawless and unimprovable theory.

With this point in mind, let us begin to approach Plato, considering first certain facts about the language of science as we think of it compared with the sort of expressions with which his epistemological theory is mainly concerned.

The crucial fact to notice is that Plato's attention is confined, on the whole, to a relatively simple and straightforward part of our language and scheme of concepts, a part that is one of the least subject to radical revision. For in constructing his theory of Forms, the predicates that chiefly concern him are those that are applied to concrete sensible objects, and generally to those that we observe quite regularly. His predicates are usually predicates such as—in this respect—"equal," "large," "triangular," "beautiful," and so forth. One of his first efforts is to find out how we can be more certain of our predications involving these terms that concern everyday objects (Ch. I, sec. 1), and it is his idea that these terms fail to apply "unqualifiedly" to those objects, even though they at first sight seem to apply to them, that prompts the first major elaboration of his metaphysical theory (Ch. III, introd. and secs. 1-2). For aside from terms applicable to Forms, to which I shall come in a moment, he pays little heed to predicates that might generally be applied only to unobservables, or at least are true only of such (e.g., "neutrino"), or to predicates of a—vaguely speaking—more "theoretical" character (e.g., "mass"). In fact, almost all of the predicates that ever occupy him explicitly are those whose qualified application to sensible objects is, according to him, made on the basis of a fairly direct use of the senses on the objects detectable by them.[3]

The factors leading to this propensity are, at a certain level, not especially obscure. One pertinent fact is that from the very beginning he had relatively little interest in how to explain the behavior of sensible objects, except by the invocation of Forms (*Phaedo* 96ff.), and thus he was not led very far (except in the *Timaeus*) toward postulating unobserved entities in the sensible world whose actions might account for what is done by the things we can perceive, or toward discussing what might be true of those objects (cf. n. IX-3). Closely connected with this fact (though probably independent of it) is the fact that he quickly came to the view that in a certain sense there is nothing "firm" to be said, or explained, about sensible objects anyway (Ch. III, secs. 2, 4; Ch. IV, sec. 1). A third, more imponderable factor is the likelihood that he took a less optimistic view of the possibility of developing far-reaching ways of expanding our empirical evidence about the sensible world and was inclined to think that ways of gathering information would go on roughly as they had been. For after all, now that we know that technology is constantly producing detection devices of all kinds, and that such things have generally turned up new facts, we are on the lookout for startling information in a way in which he was not.

But whatever the causes, Plato's tendencies led him to concentrate his gaze on that part of the sensible world that is in a sense fairly accessible to view, with its objects on open display, and consequently to think that insofar as we are concerned with the sensible world at all (cf. Ch. IV, sec. 1), our problem is simply to classify properly and with reasonable justification the objects that lie before us into their natural kinds (Ch. V, sec. 1). It is as though the task were to take the visible contents of a room and sort them (by the time of the *Phaedrus*, into genera and species) but not to develop any very elaborate theory about how they got into their particular states.[4]

The part of our language with which Plato is thus mainly dealing is a part that is relatively stable. In this respect it contrasts sharply with the part of language that figures in our picture sketched earlier, namely those more "theoretical" reaches which are more subject to change and adaptation. Of course the contrast between Plato's view and a more modern one is not just the result of a difference between the parts of language that they happen respectively to examine. It is primarily the fact that we are nowadays more accustomed to rapid and fundamental change in scientific theory than people were in Plato's time. But the point about language serves to focus our attention on the aspect of the matter closest to our concerns.

Accordingly, Plato does not have the view that whereas some languages can be used to couch more developed and refined theories of the world than others, scientifically less up-to-date languages nevertheless express concepts just as their more advanced brethren do. Thus, the theory of Forms is not constructed so as to make room for different worlds of Forms designed for languages of differing degrees of sophistication. (Indeed, Plato never seriously considers problems arising from the fact that there are languages of any different sorts.) For example, it is not as though there were room in one area for a Form corresponding to the concept of mass in Newtonian physics, and another for an Einsteinian variety. Rather, as Plato pictures matters without any suggestion of an alternative, there is *one* system of Forms. The *Cratylus* provides the most obvious demonstration of this fact, as it never hints that the establisher of a language might have a number of systems of Forms from which to choose; but Plato's other works are equally clear on the point. Although different expressions might be allowed, the system of which they are a part is, in its structure, unique.

Note that this claim holds in spite of the fact that one of the reasons for the introduction of Forms was an attempt to explain how expressions are meaningful or can be understood (Ch. I, sec. 1). For this fact does not mean that Plato is interested in the semantics of natural language, in the way in which linguists and certain contemporary philosophers might be. For him, language is in fact understood, and meaningful, only in so far as it succeeds in representing approximately, as it were, the actual structure and interrelationships that hold within the single system of Forms. To the extent that we understand a language, in his view, we link its terms to Forms, and the process of learning language, properly speaking, is not one of simply accommodating ourselves to the linguistic habits of our community, whatever they may happen to be; it is a matter of fitting words to Forms and seeing which Forms are exemplified, to one degree or another, within the sensible world, while at the same time trying principally to gain better knowledge of the Forms themselves (Ch. III, sec. 6).

My point thus far has been that Plato's Forms are independent of human beliefs in the sense that he envisions a unique system of Forms corresponding to a language of the unique correct structure to represent that system, so that various different languages, rather than each having its own system of concepts, can make their way only to the degree that they in some sense approximate that correct structure, and their terms correspond to the Forms in the unique system of reality that exists.[5]

My next point concerns a further sense in which Plato wishes to view the facts of the world, particularly about Forms, as independent of human beliefs and practices.

Consider again the idea of scientific theorizing as a going concern, changing as new evidence presents itself, and think now of one way (not the only way) of viewing this phenomenon. We think of ourselves at any one time as employing a theory of the world which, although we know that it will be found inadequate to observations that will be made (and indeed no doubt to observations that have already have been made), is nevertheless an essential tool for us to use in formulating and arguing for any future improvement on itself. This is a conception that Plato does not share, and the fact that he does not share it is important.

To one who has this conception, it may well seem that there is no alternative way to proceed, and that any intellectual endeavor, whether overtly concerned with sensory observation or not, must begin from some body of already accepted assumptions which, even if they are faulty, can be discarded in favor of others only if it can somehow be shown that the alternative is superior. Because the alternative may contradict some of the already accepted assumptions, and because a statement is generally not useful (aside from arguments by *reductio*) in an argument for its contradictory, one may think that somehow a part of one's body of assumptions may be usable to show that some other part is wrong and should be revised. But however this may be, the point is that no matter how remote one's theoretical destination may be from what one now assumes to be the truth, it is thought that one's present assumptions are somehow indispensable in reaching that destination. The point is not simply that one must have *some* assumptions *or others* to start with. That claim would be less controversial. Rather, the idea is that one must start with the beliefs that one actually has. One argument for this view is that unless one is simply to pick one's assumptions arbitrarily out of a hat, one must have reasons for one's choice, and no reasons are possible except on the basis of, and by the canons of argument accepted as a part of, what one already believes.[6]

Now it would be too much to say that Plato ever explicitly opposes this view, but nevertheless the whole thrust of his philosophizing is in a contrary direction, with the exception of only one aspect of his reflections, which he never fully developed. The exception is his method of hypothesis, particularly as it is sketched in the *Meno* and the *Phaedo* (Ch. III, sec. 7), which allows one to begin a philosophical discussion with a hypothesis that simply seems to one to be sturdy (*Phaedo* 100a4). This is of course not to say that we are to accept ordinary opinions or anything of that sort; we have seen that that is not Plato's intention. But the method does give one a starting point which one may accept for the time being. Nevertheless, Plato experiences difficulty with this method on two related fronts. In the first place, he aims to use hypotheses somehow to reach something more than the merely provisional agreement that they grant, and his efforts to do so by using the Form of the Good create considerable obscurity concerning exactly how the goal is to be reached (Ch. IV, sec. 4). The point is that although that Form was supposed to provide us with the subject matter for some genuinely fixed and unprovisional foundation for all judgments derived from it, it was unclear how that foundation would be reached and how it would be recognized. But in addition, we saw that the *Republic* already introduced problems concerning the possibility of confusions over Forms, whose solution seemed to him in the *Phaedrus* to require a new method, which put the method of hypothesis into obscurity and prevented its further elaboration and refinement (Ch. V, sec. 1).

Aside from the method of hypothesis, however, the general picture is somewhat different. In the first place, we saw that in their talk of the effort to establish definitions and apprehend Forms, the early dialogues show a lack of explicitness about how this effort is to be begun, which is only partly clarified by the method of hypothesis, whose own exact bearing on definitions is left without full explanation. Much more important, however, is the idea that Plato presents in the *Cratylus*, in a passage that we have thus far left aside, of the relationship between language and the reality that it is supposed to represent. For there he considers the idea that there might have been a name-giver who, before there was any language at all, so constructed names that they would perfectly fulfill their function (see Ch. VI, sec. 2), and he advocates in this spirit that we ourselves examine the Forms to see what actually are appropriate names for them (435e–439b). This idea is not different from what we would have expected from other passages, but it does show clearly the view that to Plato it is conceivable that language, along with the theory of the world of Forms which he thinks the correct language must embody, be capable of being constructed from the ground up, without any prior language or theory, on the basis simply of an accurate apprehension of reality. There is no suggestion whatever that to reach this ideal language and its embodied theory we must in principle begin with the language and the theory that we already have. Rather, what we already have is seen as an obstruction to our correct apprehension of the reality that we want language to represent.

This point has an important bearing on a notion that has figured in our exposition, the notion of inquiry (Ch. II, secs. 4, 5; Ch. VII, sec. 5), and on Plato's handling of it. Inquiry is not just the random acquisition of new items of knowledge; it is the deliberate and purposive attempt to gain particular new pieces of information in response to particular questions or felt gaps in the knowledge that one already has. As such, we have seen it requires that the project of inquiry be framed, with greater or lesser clarity, in advance. To make this observation is not to denigrate discoveries that do not answer to a previous search; it is just to point out that they are not the conclusions of inquiries in a reasonably strict sense of the term.

It is obvious that any treatment of the notion of inquiry is weakened by a view that tends to regard the ideal condition of language as one in which all of the facts are finally represented with maximum correctness and plays down the status of languages which are used in stages preliminary to the reaching of this goal. It is not that inquiries must necessarily lead to the denial of previously believed statements, since inquiries can simply add to the stock of knowledge by leading to the settling of questions that had been completely unanswered before. But the understanding of an inquiry requires the understanding of the way in which it is initially framed, and the manner in which, and the degree to which, subsequent discoveries actually answer it. This understanding in turn requires that clear enough meaning be accorded to the language in which the inquiry is framed for us to be able to tell, at least roughly, what responses are and are not germane to it. Moreover, because the language in which the inquiry is framed will typically involve some presuppositions about various facts, such as are required for the understanding of the terms involved, the undertaking of inquiries will require, in the overwhelming majority of cases, that some beliefs actually be held before the inquiry is completed. (In fact, the point is perhaps true universally, since it is difficult to see how the question whether an inquiry has been successfully completed could intelligibly be asked without some beliefs, however impoverished, about what counts as an answer to that sort of inquiry.)[7] Thus, a neglect of the preliminary stages of inquiry, including its first stage, will lead to difficulty in understanding the notion of inquiry itself.

We have seen that this notion causes puzzles for Plato, in part for precisely these reasons. For we have seen that in early works he is vague about what presuppositions we may legitimately bring to an attempt to gain knowledge, and that this vagueness helps to engender some of his difficulties with the paradox of the *Meno*; and we even saw him tempted, perhaps, by the idea that we may bring no presuppositions at all, not even enough to specify what it is that we are trying to find (Ch. I, sec. 4; Ch. II, secs. 4, 5). The somewhat analogous problems at the end of the *Theaetetus* are based on fairly well developed views about language which, however, work to much the same effect as the vagueness of the *Meno*. For the theory of language that is operating there leaves no room for the framing of an inquiry which can then in any substantial manner be answered by the sort of item that Plato regards as constituting additional knowledge (Ch. VII, sec. 5). It is no accident that this difficulty is fostered by a theory developed in the *Cratylus*, a dialogue which, as we have just seen, clearly envisions the possibility of constructing a language and a theory completely *de novo*. It is likewise no accident that the Seventh Letter finally either brings the notion of illumination in as part of a last-ditch effort to salvage the possibility of inquiry or simply abandons the notion of genuine inquiry altogether (Ch. VIII, secs. 2, 3).

We have now seen two ways in which Plato believes in a reality independent of our beliefs, and some of the difficulties that he has encountered, in part as a result of them. In the first place, we saw that he does not accord full meaningfulness to languages that are not perfect and final representations of reality. In the second place, we saw the closely related fact that he neither holds to the idea that the final and perfect theory must be developed and argued for by means of preliminary theorizing nor pays much respect to the idea of successful inquiry as the discovery of facts to answer questions that have been previously raised within an intelligible language, and on the basis of already accepted beliefs. The final and perfect theory in his view has no fully intelligible precursors, and needs none.

But there is additional importance in the fact that not only is the true theory of the knowable world, i.e., of the world of the Forms, without genuine precursors, but it is also without genuine alternatives. As we have seen, it is the only genuinely intelligible, genuinely comprehensible theory that there is. Strictly speaking, it is *the only* theory.[8]

Consider now Protagoreanism as it appeared in the *Cratylus* and the *Theaetetus* (Ch. VI, sec. 1; Ch. VII, sec. 1) and consider the contrast between it and Plato's realism. According to Protagoreanism, there is an indefinite number of intelligible and acceptable theories of the world, i.e., just the theories that are, or may be, held by believers. Each of them is "true for" its holder, there being no notion of "truth *simpliciter*" by which to pick out one or more as superior to the others (though Protagoras is represented as trying to hold that there are other sorts of grounds for preference). In the *Cratylus*, we saw Plato opposing linguistic conventionalism, on the ground that it entailed Protagoreanism (Ch. VI, sec. 1). The idea was that if a sentence expressing a truth in one language could express a falsehood in another, there would be no hard facts for any language to represent. In passing, I noted the reply that one could resort to the notion of "truth-in-*L*," rather than "truth," but I also noted that Plato would be unhappy with this suggestion. We can now see more clearly how this is so. For him, the existence of a unique true theory is guaranteed by the existence of a unique theory.

We ourselves are likely to regard linguistic conventionalism as something clearly less than Protagoreanism, at least as long as we think that we can draw the distinction between genuine disagreement on the one hand and saying the same thing in different ways on the other.[9] It does not matter to us if we have slight differences in pronunciation, and it equally does not matter if the sounds that we utter are quite thoroughly different, so long as we think that they are correctly intertranslated in such a way as to show us in agreement, even though we are speaking different languages. The real difficulties come when we think that translation shows us that we genuinely disagree. Protagoreanism aside, the attitude of common sense is that one of us must be right and the other wrong, so that we must somehow choose between real alternatives. The problem, then, especially when there may be a host of competing theories, is to pick a privileged one in which to believe.

Once again, the point is that in Plato's view there is in fact only one real, genuinely intelligible possibility. Other views may hold that there is indeed one ideal theory toward which science strives, even though we must at any one time cleave to the theory that we at that time believe, and which we hope to improve by adapting it to new evidence. But Plato's attention is not focused on such preliminary stages.

It is not difficult to see what is disturbing about the alternatives to the sort of view that Plato represents. For the ineluctable fact that Plato sees is that we *seem* to ourselves to be able to make a distinction between what is the case and what we believe to be the case. Now it is perhaps true, as I mentioned earlier, that we must start any inquiry with the beliefs that we have, thinking that our procedures of investigation will enable us to correct our errors. But we *seem* to be able to ask the question whether our procedures of investigation are correct and to raise the worry that they may, after all, lead us away from the truth rather than toward it. (Our procedures may change, of course, but the spirit of this view is that new procedures are discovered by relying somehow on old.) Philosophers may attempt in various ways to cut off these disquieting reflections. One way is to say that there is no such thing as truth over and above what is given to us by the standards of investigation of the day, and whatever they may lead to (which we shall discover when it appears).[10] This view, in effect, attempts to rebuff our idea of the distinction between what is the case and what we believe, or to relativize the distinction to the current state of investigation, whatever it may be. Another view is that, yes, we may be heading in the wrong direction, but there is nothing that we can do about it.

It is this latter sort of view that Plato might have been tempted to adopt at the time when he was working seriously on the method of hypothesis: we make our hypotheses, and we hope. But his ideas about thought and language led him in a different direction, to the view that we have, in our ability to apprehend Forms, an avenue to knowledge of them which is independent of language, and which we must take, in fact, before we know what the correct language is to adopt (*Cratylus* 435e-439b; cf. *supra*). It was this view, as we saw, that finally led him toward the abandonment of inquiry strictly so-called (Ch. VIII, secs. 2, 3). The reaction is a natural one. If our language and our theories may lead us in the wrong direction, and if all that we can do is to make hypotheses and hope, then why not just dispense with the hypotheses and simply hope? We simply hope to *happen on* what we can, without worrying about whether it answers to a previous inquiry, or how it would be described in the terms to which we are accustomed.

It is Plato's picture of the nature of intelligible reality that makes this last expedient one that he can contemplate. For he can think of the Forms as somehow lying plainly open to one's mental gaze, if one could only clear away the obstructions (Ch. IV, secs. 1, 2). This fact is related to the point noted earlier in this section, that the predicates with which Plato associates Forms make up, by the standards of contemporary science and mathematics, a fairly simple array, so that one could conceive of their corresponding Forms as somehow set before one on clear display. But the intelligible world is not what it used to be. For one thing, few would now accept Plato's reasons for thinking of the sensible world as importantly unfit for truly scientific investigation (Ch. III, secs. 1-2; Ch. IV, introd. and sec. 1). For another thing, the idea of an access to the more complex reaches of mathematics or physics that is independent of the tools of language, and particularly the tools of proof as it is carried out in language, seems nowadays more and more difficult to make sense of, and only the greatest latitude in the notion of mental "viewing" could be hoped to render it defensible. At any rate, however, we can see how Plato's belief in the comparative simplicity of the world of Forms encouraged some of the later developments in his thought.

We have now seen yet another way in which Plato thinks that reality is independent of our beliefs. Once the idea of inquiry itself is under pressure, from the *Cratylus* onward (though the final step is not taken before the Seventh Letter), it begins to seem as though language itself, and whatever beliefs may be embodied in it, is unnecessary, since he thinks that we can have access to the Forms without it.[11]

There may seem to be an irony in the fact that a theory of Forms that was developed in part to explain how terms could be meaningful could end up attaching so little importance to them (Ch. I, sec. 1). One reply is that the explanation of meaning was not the only consideration for the existence of Forms. The other reply is that even in the *Cratylus*, where it is said that we have an avenue to the Forms independent of language, language is still viewed as useful for communication. But a further irony enters in here, because of the fact that the Seventh Letter, following on the reflections of the *Phaedrus*, has little faith in language as a communicative instrument.[12] Here, the trouble comes also from another quarter, the fact that, as Plato sees the matter, our minds and their activities are not open to each others' inspection, being shielded by corporeal coverings.[13] Otherwise, Plato might conceivably have explored the possibility of a sort of mental pointing which would serve to help us tell others what Forms or concepts we had in mind (though it is not clear that a mind apprehending the Forms would have any interest in knowing what other minds were doing).[14]

In all of the time since Plato lived, no philosopher has represented the impulse to realism in the theory of knowledge in as pure and straightforward a form.[15] It is by seeing such single-minded pursuit of a philosophical goal that we can come to understand what is really at stake in the debates that have come down to us. For whatever lack of clarity Plato's exposition may sometimes show, the ultimate end that he has in view is always clear, and his striving for it shows us what philosophy is.

Notes

1. Cf. Shorey 2, p. 28: ". . . realism was for Plato not merely the only metaphysical alternative to Protagorean relativity; it was the only practicable way of affirming the validity of universals, and abstract thought . . ." (Cf. also pp. 52-53). In my opinion Shorey is correct, as I shall claim, but he has the emphasis wrong. It is rather that realism was not merely the only practicable

232 | *Plato on Knowledge and Reality*

way of affirming the "validity" of universals, it was the only alternative to Protagoreanism.

2. In this sense, though not in others, I agree with Shorey (e.g., *ibid.*, p. 88), that Plato is the sort of thinker whose philosophy "is fixed in early maturity." (Although I think that Plato did modify important parts of his doctrine, it is quite wrong—particularly with regard to most of his epistemological doctrines—to think of Plato as similar to Wittgenstein in having undergone a radical shift of viewpoint. Wittgenstein's change was fundamental, far more so than Plato's, which was largely a matter of alterations in the details of his metaphysics.)

3. This statement holds even for many predicates applied in the *Tim.* to some of the unobservable entities out of which he constructs the universe (e.g., the various minute geometric figures in 53ff.). A notable exception, however, is provided by what he says about the "receptacle" in 48ff., though he does not dwell on it long enough for it to affect his outlook.

4. Late in the *Phdr.*, Plato seems to admit the possibility of something roughly like an empirical science of rhetoric (269-273), but he does not pursue the matter far (even if the idea is to be connected with the hints in the *Tht.*—see nn. VII-43 and 44, and Ch. VII, sec. 5—that there may be knowledge concerning sensible objects). This does not mean that he utterly despairs of describing the sensible world (on the contrary, see Ch. III, sec. 4), but only that he does not indulge in it very systematically.

5. With Plato's idea one should compare the view in Wittgenstein **1**, that ordinary language is "in order as it is" (5.5563), in which the idea appears to be that even if logical form is not always perspicuous in a natural language, it is nevertheless there. It would seem that whereas Plato thinks that there is only one genuinely intelligible language, Wittgenstein at that time believed that there is only one possible form for a language. In fact, the parallel is almost certainly even closer, since Plato no doubt allowed what would by some standards count as a plurality of optimum languages, so long as their structure was in some sense the same (cf. n. IX-8). For some partly related ideas, see Gosling **2**, pp. 271-290, 302-310.

Though I shall not pursue the matter far here, there are many very striking parallels between Plato's views and those of the early Wittgenstein. For it seems to me correct to see the latter as in many ways simply following out what he thought to be the consequences of the insistently realistic tendencies of Frege. (See Hacker, esp. pp. 34-36, 44, 33.) But Frege is in more ways than one, whether consciously or not, Plato's disciple. Compare, for example, Frege's demand for "determinacy of sense" in linguistic expressions (Hacker, pp. 39-43) with Plato's insistence in the *Crat.* that in a proper language, each term ought to correspond unambiguously to a single, fixed object. See further nn. *infra*.

6. For a related line of thought, see Peirce **2**, esp. pp. 188-189.

7. One must not confuse inquiry with what a child does in learning about the

world. A child does not start with a project of inquiry or an attempt to answer questions. He simply encounters the world. When he learns a certain amount about it, *then* he begins to have questions.

8. As usual, standards for the individuation of languages and theories are obscure, but by saying that he allows only one theory, I mean to allow for a certain possible variation, since he may mean to allow for a plurality of optimum names of a given object. What is demanded, however, is a certain isomorphism among all allowable systems of speech.

9. Worries pressed in recent years by Quine obviously help to make this distinction problematical. Cf. Putnam and H. Field.

10. See for example Neurath p. 201, and Quine **8** pp. 3-5 and *passim*. In thinking about these matters, one must be careful not to make what may be a confusion between the notion of discovering truth and the notion of completing an inquiry. If we conceive of the effort to discover the truth about the world as an inquiry in the strict sense, then perhaps it is correct to adopt this sort of view. But the question then arises whether we should so conceive that effort.

11. Like Plato, Wittgenstein in the *Tractatus* (though not in later works) seems to suppose that one can adopt a standpoint "outside of language" from which one can compare it to the world in some way. Thus see Black, pp. 92-95, and Hacker, pp. 56-57.

12. Note that Plato is not one to be impressed by what are sometimes called "transcendental arguments." For if someone claimed that if a certain view were not accepted we would have to deny the possibility of intelligible communication, Plato might still be willing to say that we must find out whether the view is *true*, since if necessary he would be willing to take the consequences of denying it. I have already observed that he did not go so far as to deny the *intelligibility* of language (though some will disagree and will argue that the consequences of his position are worse than I have pictured them), but there is no clear reason to think that he would have insisted, no matter what, on stopping short of such a denial. Indeed, it is not fully clear that he would not at least *consider* the possibility that there are no Forms, even if that would "destroy the intelligibility of discourse" (*Parm*. 135c2 with Ch. I, sec. 1). For that the existence of the Forms is a "hypothesis" of a sort is strongly suggested in the *Phdo*. (100b*sqq*. with 76d-e) and the *Parm*. (135c*sqq*.) and is nowhere countered by a forthright claim that their existence is guaranteed against all possible doubt (cf. the remark of Taylor cited in n. I-32).

13. See n. VIII-23.

14. For hints of this idea see perhaps "ἐνδείξεως" at *Ep*. VII, 341e3 with 344e1-2, along with the observation in Ch. VIII, sec. 3, that Plato thought that language had *some* kind of pedagogical use, however unreliable. One might also conceivably cite the indications in the *Rep*. that those who are ignorant need to have their "mental gaze" somehow turned toward the Forms (nn. IV-11 and IV-19, with accompanying text), though the connection here is somewhat tenuous, since it is one thing to turn someone's gaze toward a collection of

234 / Plato on Knowledge and Reality

things (Forms), and another to point out individual members of the collection. Aside from these passages, there is little of the notion of ostension in Plato (cf. n. I-67). He is thus to be distinguished from those philosophers who have appealed to it as the ultimate source of our understanding of language: see, e.g., Schlick, esp. p. 57, as well as Wittgenstein 1, 3.263, *if* the term "*Er-läuterung*" there has to do with ostension, as is argued by Hacker, pp. 48ff. Plato's neglect of ostension is perhaps surprising, in the light of the fact that the Forms, as perfect samples of things to which predicates apply (Ch. III, sec. 2), might well seem natural things to point to in explaining terms. But Plato must recognize the difficulties involved in pointing to a Form, since he presumably holds that the pointing would have to be done by a soul for a soul, and is therefore precluded for those who are embodied (but cf. n. VIII-23). It is the obvious difficulty of pointing informatively to one's mental contents that renders unattractive the view suggested by, e.g., Schlick, p. 57.

This is a good place to remind the reader of my disinclination to rely in my exegesis on Russell's contrast between knowledge by acquaintance and knowledge by description, and allied distinctions (see his 5 and n. II-29), which seem to me different from the notions on which my account relies, namely apprehension and recognition.

15. One of the most forceful modern representatives of this point of view was Frege; see his 3, and *supra*, n. 5. For signs of recently renewed interest in this matter, see e.g., Putnam and Field.

List of Works Cited

Ackrill, J. L. **1**, "Plato on False Belief: *Theaetetus* 187-200," *Monist*, 50 (1966), 383-402.

2, "In Defence of Platonic Division," Wood and Pitcher, pp. 373-392.

Adam, J., ed., *The Republic of Plato* (Cambridge, England, 1902).

Adkins, A. W. H. **1**, *Merit and Responsibility* (Oxford, 1960).

2, *From the Many to the One* (Ithaca, 1970).

Allen, R. E. **1**, "*Anamnesis* in Plato's *Meno* and *Phaedo*," *Review of Metaphysics*, 13 (1959), 165-174.

2, "Participation and Predication in Plato's Middle Dialogues," *Philosophical Review*, 69 (1960), 147-164, reprinted in Allen **3**, pp. 43-60, and Vlastos **11**, pp. 167-183. (Pagination of Allen **3**.)

3, ed., *Studies in Plato's Metaphysics* (New York, 1965).

4, *Plato's "Euthyphro" and the Earlier Theory of Forms* (N. Y., 1970).

Anagnostopoulos, G., "The Significance of Plato's *Cratylus*," *Review of Metaphysics*, 27 (1973), 318-345.

Aristote et les problèmes de méthode: Symposium Aristotelicum, 1960 (Louvain and Paris, 1961).

Austin, J. L. **1**, *Philosophical Papers*, 2nd ed. (Oxford, 1970).

2, "Are There A Priori Concepts?" Austin **1**, pp. 32-54.

3, "Other Minds," Austin **1**, pp. 76-116.

4, *Sense and Sensibilia* (Oxford, 1962).

Ayer, A. J. **1**, *Language, Truth and Logic* (London, 1936).

2, ed., *Logical Positivism* (Glencoe, 1959).

Baldry, H. C. "Plato's Technical Terms." *Classical Quarterly*, 31 (1937), 141-150.

Bambrough, R., ed., *New Essays on Plato and Aristotle* (N.Y., 1965).

Benacerraf, P., "Mathematical Truth," *Journal of Philosophy*, 70 (1973), 661-679.

Bennett, D., "Essential Properties," *Journal of Philosophy*, 66 (1969), 487-499.

Berkeley, G., *A Treatise Concerning the Principles of Human Knowledge*.

Black, M., *A Companion to Wittgenstein's Tractatus* (Ithaca, 1964).

Bluck, R. S., **1**, *Plato's Phaedo* (London, 1955).

2, "*Logos* and Forms in Plato," *Mind*, N.S. 65 (1956), 522-529, reprinted in Allen **3**, pp. 33-41. (Latter pagination.)

3, " 'Knowledge by Acquaintance' in Plato's *Theaetetus*," *Mind*, N.S. 72 (1963), 259-263.

4, ed., *Plato's Meno* (Cambridge, England, 1964).

Boas, G., "Fact and Legend in the Biography of Plato," *Philosophical Review*, 57(1948), 439-457.

Bradley, F. H., *Appearance and Reality*, corr. ed. (Oxford, 1930).

Brentlinger, J., "Incomplete Predicates and the Two-World Theory of the *Phaedo*," *Phronesis*, 17 (1972), 61-79.

Brody, B. A., "Why Settle for Anything Less than Good Old-Fashioned Aristotelian Essentialism?" *Nous*, 7 (1973), 351-365.

Buchmann, K., *Die Stellung des Menon in der platonischen Philosophie* (Leipzig, 1936).

Burnet, J., **1**, ed., *Plato's Phaedo (Oxford, 1911)*.
  2, *Greek Philosophy:Thales to Plato* (London, 1914).
  3, ed., *Plato's Euthyphro, Apology of Socrates, and Crito* (Oxford, 1924).

Burnyeat, M. F., "The Material and Sources of Plato's Dream," *Phronesis*, 15 (1970), 101-122.

Bury, R. G., ed., *The Symposium of Plato*, 2nd ed. (Cambridge, England, 1932).

Butchvarov, P., *Resemblance and Identity* (Bloomington, 1966).

Calvert, B., "Forms and Flux in Plato's *Cratylus*," *Phronesis*, 15 (1970), 26-47.

Campbell, L., ed., *The Theaetetus of Plato*, 2nd ed. (Oxford, 1883).

Carnap, R., "Meaning and Synonymy in Natural Languages," *Philosophical Studies*, 6 (1955), 33-46.

Castañeda, H.N., "Plato's *Phaedo* Theory of Relations," *Journal of Philosophical Logic*, 1 (1972), 467-480.

Cherniss, H. F., **1**, "The Philosophical Economy of the Theory of Ideas," *American Journal of Philology*, 57 (1936), 445-456.
  2, review, *American Journal of Philology*, 58 (1937), 497-500
  3, *Aristotle's Criticism of Plato and the Academy*, vol. I (Baltimore, 1944).
  4, *The Riddle of the Early Academy* (Berkeley, 1945).
  5, review, *American Journal of Philology*, 68 (1947), 133-146.
  6, "Plato as Mathematician," *Review of Metaphysics*, 4 (1951), 395-425.
  7, "The Relation of the *Timaeus* to Plato's Later Dialogues," *American Journal of Philology*, 78 (1957), 225-266, reprinted in Allen **3**, pp. 339-378. (Latter pagination.)

Chisholm, R. M., *Theory of Knowledge* (Englewood Cliffs, 1966).

Church, A., "On Carnap's Analysis of Statements of Assertion and Belief," *Analysis*, 10 (1950), 97-99.

Cohen, S.M., "Socrates on the Definition of Piety," Vlastos **12**, pp. 158-176.

Cooper, J. M., "Plato on Sense-Perception and Knowledge (*Theaetetus* 184-186)," *Phronesis*, 15 (1970), 123-146.

Cornford, F.M., **1** *Plato's Theory of Knowledge* (London, 1935).

Cornford, F. M., **1** *Plato's Theory of Knowledge* (London, 1935).
  2, *Principium Sapientiae* (Cambridge, England, 1952).

Crombie, I. M., *An Examination of Plato's Doctrines*, Vol. 2 (London, 1962).

Cross, R. C., "Logos and Forms in Plato," *Mind*, N.S. 63 (1954), 433-450, reprinted in Allen **3**, pp. 13-31.
  and Woozley, A. D., *Plato's Republic: A Philosophical Commentary* (London, 1964).

Davidson, D., and Hintikka, J., eds., *Words and Objections: Essays on the Work of W.V. Quine* (Dordrecht, l969).

Descartes, R., *Oeuvres de Descartes*, ed. C. Adam and P. Tannery (Paris, 1957).

Diels, H. *Die Fragmente der Vorsokratiker*, 11th ed., ed. W. Kranz (Zürich, 1952).

Diès, A., ed., *Platon, Théétète* (Paris, 1924).

Dodds, E. R., ed., *Plato, Gorgias* (Oxford, 1959).

Donnellan, K., "Proper Names and Identifying Descriptions," *Synthese*, 21 (1970), 335-358.

Dover, K. J., "The Date of Plato's Symposium," *Phronesis*, 10 (1965), 2-20.

Düring, I. and Owen, G. E. L., eds., *Aristotle and Plato in the Mid-Fourth Century* (Göteborg, 1960).

Edelstein, L., *Plato's Seventh Letter* (Leiden, 1966).

Field, G. C., **1**, *Plato and his Contemporaries* (London, 1930).
   2, *The Philosophy of Plato* (London, 1949).

Field, H., "Quine and the Correspondence Theory," *Philosophical Review*, 83 (1974), 200-228.

Fogelin, R. J., "Three Platonic Analogies," *Philosophical Review*, 80 (1971), 371-382.

Foster, L., and Swanson, J. W., eds., *Experience and Theory* (Amherst, 1970).

Frede, M., *Prädikation und Existenzaussage, Hypomnemata*, 18 (Göttingen, 1967).

Frege, G., **1**, *Translations from the Philosophical Writings of Gottlob Frege*, trans. P. Geach and M. Black, 2nd ed. (Oxford, 1960).
   2, "On Sense and Reference," Frege **1**, pp. 56-78.
   3, "The Thought," trans. A. and M. Quinton, *Mind*, N.S. 65 (1956), 289-311.

Friedländer, P., *Plato, The Dialogues: The First Period*, trans. H. Meyerhoff (N. Y., 1964).

Furth, M., "Elements of Eleatic Ontology," *Journal of the History of Philosophy*, 6 (1968), 111-132.

Geach, P. T., **1**, "Good and Evil," *Analysis*, 17 (1956), 33-42.
   2, Plato's *Euthyphro*: An Analysis and Commentary," *Monist*, 50 (1966), 369-382.

Gillespie, C. M., "The Use of Εἶδος and Ἰδέα in Hippocrates," *Classical Quarterly*, 6 (1912), 179-203

Goodman, N., **1**, "On Likeness of Meaning," *Analysis*, 10 (1949), 1-7, reprinted in Linsky, pp. 67-74.
   2, "Seven Strictures on Similarity," Foster and Swanson, pp. 19-29.

Gosling, J. C. B., **1** "Δόξα and Δύναμις in Plato's Republic," *Phronesis*, 13 (1968), 119-130.
   2, *Plato* (London, 1973).

Gould, J., *The Development of Plato's Ethics* (Cambridge, England, 1955).

Grote, G., *Plato and the Other Companions of Socrates*, 2nd ed. (London, 1867).

Grube, G. M. A., *Plato's Thought* (London, 1935).

Gulley, N., **1**, "Plato's Theory of Recollection," *Classical Quarterly*, N.S. 4 (1954), 194-213.
   2, *Plato's Theory of Knowledge* (London, 1962).
   3, *The Philosophy of Socrates* (London, 1968).

Guthrie, W. K. C., *A History of Greek Philosophy*, vol. III (Cambridge, England, 1969).

Hacker, P. M. S., *Insight and Illusion* (Oxford, 1972).

Hackforth, R. M., **1**, *Plato's Examination of Pleasure* (Cambridge, England, 1945).
   2, *Plato's Phaedrus* (Cambridge, England, 1952).
   3, *Plato's Phaedo* (Cambridge, England, 1955).

Hamlyn, D. W., **1**, "Forms and Knowledge in Plato's *Theaetetus*: A Reply to Mr. Bluck," *Mind*, N.S., 66 (1957), 547.
   2, *Sensation and Perception* (London, 1961).

Hare, R. M., **1**, "Geach: Good and Evil," *Analysis*, 18 (1957), 103-112.
   2, "Plato and the Mathematicians," Bambrough, pp. 21-38.
   3, "Philosophical Discoveries," *Mind*, N.S. 69 (1960), 145-162.

Hicken, W., **1**, "Knowledge and Forms in Plato's *Theaetetus*," *Journal of Hellenic Studies*, 77 (1957), 48-53, reprinted in Allen **3**, pp. 185-198. (Latter pagination.)
   2, "The Character and Provenance of Socrates' "Dream" in the *Theaetetus*," *Phronesis*, 3 (1958), 126-145.

Hintikka, J., **1**, *Knowledge and Belief* (Ithaca, 1962).
   2, "Time, Truth, and Knowledge in Ancient Greek Philosophy," *American Philosophical Quarterly*, 4 (1967), 1-14.
   3, "Knowledge by Acquaintance—Individuation by Acquaintance," Pears, pp. 52-79.

Irwin, T., "Recollection and Plato's Moral Theory," *Review of Metaphysics*, 27 (1974), 752-772.

Jackson, H., "Plato's Later Theory of Ideas: the *Theaetetus*," *Journal of Philology*, 13 (1885), 242-272.

Jaeger, W., *Paedeia*, trans. G. Highet, vol. I (N. Y., 1939), vol. II (N. Y., 1943).

Joseph, H. W. B., *An Introduction to Logic*, 2nd ed. (Oxford, 1916).

Kahn, C., "Language and Ontology in the *Cratylus*," Lee *et al.*, pp. 152-176.

Kaplan, D., "Quantifying In," Davidson and Hintikka, pp. 178-214.

Kapp, E., review, *Gnomon*, 12 (1936), 71-72.

Krämer, H. J., "Die platonische Akademie und das Problem einer systematischen Interpretation der Philosophie Platons," *Kantstudien*, 55 (1964), 69-101.

Kretzmann, N., "Plato on the Correctness of Names," *American Philosophical Quarterly*, 8 (1971), 126-138.

Kühner, R., *Ausführliche Grammatik der griechischen Sprache*, 3rd ed., rev. B. Gerth, Teil II, Bd. 1 (Hanover and Leipzig, 1898).

Lacey, A. R., "Our Knowledge of Socrates," Vlastos **12**, pp. 22-49.

Langford, C. H., "The Notion of Analysis in Moore's Philosophy," Schilpp, pp. 321-342.

Lee, E. N., "On the Metaphysics of the Image in Plato's *Timaeus*," *Monist*, 50 (1966), 341-368.

Lee, E. N., Mourelatos, A. P. D., and Rorty, R. M., eds., *Exegesis and Argument: Studies in Greek Philosophy Presented to Gregory Vlastos* (Assen, 1973).

Lesher, J. H., "Γνῶσις and Ἐπιστήμη in Socrates' Dream in the *Theaetetus*," *Journal of Hellenic Studies*, 89 (1969), 72-78.

Linsky, L., ed., *Semantics and the Philosophy of Language* (Urbana, 1952).

Lorenz, K. and Mittelstrass, J., "On Rational Philosophy of Language," *Mind*, N.S. 76 (1967), 1-20.

Luce, J. V., **1**, "The Date of the 'Cratylus,' " *American Journal of Philology*, 85 (1964), 136-154.
   2, "Plato on Truth and Falsity in Names," *Classical Quarterly*, N.S. 19 (1969), 222-232.

Mabbott, J. D., "Is Plato's *Republic* Utilitarian?" *Mind*, N.S. 46 (1937), 386-393, revised and reprinted in Vlastos **13**, pp. 57-65. (Latter pagination.)

McDowell, J., **1**, "Identity Mistakes: Plato and the Logical Atomists," *Proceedings of the Aristotelian Society*, 70 (1969-70), 181-195.
   2, *Plato, Theaetetus* (Oxford, 1973).

Mau, J. and Schmidt, E. G., eds., *Isonomia: Studien zur Gleichheitsvorstellung im griechischen Denken*, (Berlin, 1964.)

Mill, J. S., *A System of Logic* (London, N. D.).

Mills, K. W., "Some Aspects of Plato's Theory of Forms: Timaeus 49cff.," *Phronesis*, 13 (1968), 145-170.

Moore, G. E., **1**, *Principia Ethica* (Cambridge, England, 1903).
   2, *Philosophical Studies* (London, 1922).
   3, "External and Internal Relations," Moore **2**, pp. 276-309.

Moravcsik, J. M. E., **1**, ed., *Aristotle: A Collection of Critical Essays* (New York, 1967).
   2, "Learning as Recollection," Vlastos **11**, pp. 53-69.
   3, "The Anatomy of Plato's Divisions," Lee *et al.*, pp. 324-348.

Morrow, G. R., **1**, *Plato's Epistles*, rev. ed. (Indianapolis, 1962).
   2, "Plato and the Mathematicians," *Philosophical Review*, 79 (1970), 309-333.

Mourelatos, A. P. D., ed., *The Pre-Socratics* (Garden City, 1974).

Nakhnikian, G., "Elenctic Definitions," Vlastos **12**, pp. 125-157.

Neurath, O., "Protokosätze," *Erkenntnis*, 3 (1932-33), 204-214, trans, in Ayer **2**, pp. 199-208. (Latter pagination.)

Oehler, K., *Die Lehre vom noetischen und dianoetischen Denken bei Platon und Aristoteles* (Munich, 1962).

Ostwald, M., *Nomos and the Beginnings of Athenian Democracy* (Oxford, 1969).

Owen, G. E. L., **1**, "The Place of the *Timaeus* in Plato's Dialogues," *Classical Quarterly*, N.S. 3 (1953), 79-95, reprinted in Allen **3**, pp. 313-338.

2, "A Proof in the Περὶ Ἰδεῶν," *Journal of Hellenic Studies*, (1957), pt. I, 103-111, reprinted in Allen **3**, pp. 293-312. (Latter pagination.)

3, "Logic and Metaphysics in Some Early Works of Aristotle," Düring and Owen, pp. 163-190.

4, "Eleatic Questions," *Classical Quarterly*, N.S. 10 (1960), 84-102.

5, Τιθέναι τὰ φαινόμενα, *Aristote et les problèmes de méthode*, pp. 83-103, reprinted in Moravcsik **1**, pp. 167-190. (Former pagination.)

6, "Aristotle on the Snares of Ontology," Bambrough, pp. 69-96.

7, "The Platonism of Aristotle," *Proceedings of the British Academy*, 51 (1965), 125-150.

8, "Plato and Parmenides on the Timeless Present," *Monist*, 50 (1966), 317-340.

9, ed., *Aristotle on Dialectic: The Topics* (Oxford, 1968).

10, "Dialectic and Eristic in the Treatment of the Forms," Owen **9**, pp. 103-125.

11, "Plato on Not-Being," Vlastos **11**, pp. 223-267.

Parente, M. Isnardi, *Filosofia e politica nelle lettere di Platone* (Naples, 1970).

Parsons, T., "Essentialism and Quantified Modal Logic," *Philosophical Review*, 78 (1969), 35-52.

Pears, D. F., ed., *Bertrand Russell: A Collection of Critical Essays* (Garden City, 1972).

Peirce, C. S., **1**, *Charles S. Peirce: Selected Writings*, ed. P. P. Wiener (N. Y., 1966).

2, "What Pragmatism Is," *Monist*, 15 (1905), 161-181, reprinted in Peirce **1**, pp. 180-202. (Latter pagination.)

Prauss, G., *Platon und der logische Eleatismus* (Berlin, 1966).

Price, H. H., *Thinking and Experience* (London, 1953).

Putnam, H., "The Refutation of Conventionalism," *Nous*, 7 (1974), 25-40.

Quine, W. V., **1**, *From A Logical Point of View*, 2nd ed. (Cambridge, Mass., 1960).

2, "On What There Is," Quine **1**, pp. 1-19.

3, "Two Dogmas of Empiricism," Quine **1**, pp. 20-46.

4, "Notes on the Theory of Reference," Quine **1**, pp. 130-138.

5, "Reference and Modality," Quine **1**, pp. 139-159.

6, "Meaning and Inference," Quine **1**, pp. 160-167.

7, "Carnap and Logical Truth," *Synthese*, 12 (1960), 350-374, reprinted in Quine **9**, pp. 100-125. (Latter pagination.)

8, *Word and Object* (Cambridge, Mass., 1960).

9, *The Ways of Paradox* (N. Y., 1966).

10, *Ontological Relativity and Other Essays* (N. Y., 1969).

11, "Natural Kinds," Quine **10**, pp. 114-138.

Raven, J. E., *Plato's Thought in the Making* (Cambridge, England, 1965).

Robin, L., **1**, ed., *Platon, Le Banquet* (Paris, 1929).

2, ed. *Platon, Phèdre* (Paris, 1933).

Robinson, R., **1**, *Plato's Earlier Dialectic*, 2nd ed. (Oxford, 1953).
  2, *Definition* (Oxford, 1954).
  3, *Essays in Greek Philosophy* (Oxford, 1969).
  4, "Forms and Error in Plato's *Theaetetus*," *Philosophical Review*, 59 (1950), 3-30, reprinted in Robinson **3**, pp. 39-73. (Latter pagination.)
  5, "The Theory of Names in Plato's *Cratylus*," *Revue Internationale de Philosophie*, 9 (1955), 221-236, reprinted in Robinson **3**, pp. 100-117. (Latter pagination.)
  6, "Criticism of Plato's *Cratylus*," *Philosophical Review*, 65 (1956), 324-341, reprinted in Robinson **3**, pp. 118-138. (Latter pagination.)
Robinson, T. M., *Plato's Psychology* (Toronto, 1970).
Rorty, A. O., "A Speculative Note on Some Dramatic Elements in the *Theaetetus*," *Phronesis*, 17 (1972), 27-38.
Ross, W. D., **1**, ed., *Aristotle's Metaphysics* (Oxford, 1924)
  2, *Plato's Theory of Ideas* (Oxford, 1953).
  3, ed., *Aristotelis Fragmenta Selecta* (Oxford, 1955).
  4, "The Date of Plato's *Cratylus*," *Revue Internationale de Philosophie*, 9 (1955), 187-196.
Runciman, W. G., *Plato's Later Epistemology* (Cambridge, England, 1962).
Russell, B., **1** *The Problems of Philosophy* (London, 1912); Galaxy edition (N. Y., 1959). (Latter pagination.)
  2, *Logic and Knowledge*, ed. R. C. Marsh (London, 1956).
  3, "On Denoting," *Mind*, 14 (1905), 479-493, reprinted in Russell **2**, pp. 41-56. (Latter pagination.)
  4, *Mysticism and Logic*, Doubleday Anchor ed. (N. Y., 1957).
  5, "Knowledge by Acquaintance and Knowledge by Description," *Proceedings of the Aristotelian Society*, 11 (1910-11), 108-128, reprinted in Russell **4**, pp. 202-224.
Ryle, G., **1**, "Plato's *Parmenides*," *Mind*, N.S. 48 (1939), 129-151, 302-325, reprinted in Allen **3**, pp. 97-147. (Latter pagination.)
  2, "Ordinary Language," *Philosophical Review*, 62 (1953), 167-186.
  3, *Plato's Progress* (Cambridge, England, 1966).
Sachs, D., "A Fallacy in Plato's *Republic*," *Philosophical Review*, 72 (1963), 141-158, reprinted in Vlastos **13**, pp. 35-51.
Santas, G., "The Socratic Fallacy," *Journal of the History of Philosophy*, 10 (1972), 127-141.
Scheibe, E., "Über Relativbegriffe in der Philosophie Platons," *Phronesis* 12 (1967), 28-49.
Schilpp, P. A., ed., *The Philosophy of G. E. Moore* (Evanston, 1942).
Schleiermacher, F., *Platons Werke, Einleitung,* Teil I, Band I (Berlin, 1804).
Schlick, M., "Die Wende der Philosophie," *Erkenntnis*, 1 (1930-31), 1-5, trans. in Ayer **2**, pp. 53-59. (Latter pagination.)
Sharvy, R., "*Euthyphro* 9d-11b: Analysis and Definition in Plato and Others," *Nous*, 6 (1972), 119-138.

Shorey, P., **1**, "The Idea of the Good in Plato's *Republic*," *University of Chicago Publications in Classical Philology*, 1 (1895), 188-239.
   2, *The Unity of Plato's Thought* (Chicago, 1903).
   3, "Note on *Philebus* 11b, c," *Classical Philology*, 3 (1908), 343-345.
   4, *What Plato Said* (Chicago, 1933).
   5, trans. and comm., *Plato, Republic*, vol. I, rev. ed. (London, 1937), vol II (London, 1935).
Sidgwick, H., **1**, "On a Passage in Plato, *Republic*, B. VI," *Journal of Philology*, 2 (1869), 96-103.
   2, *Outlines of the History of Ethics*, 6th ed. (London, 1931).
Skemp, J. B., *Plato's Statesman* (London, 1952).
Smyth, H. W., *Greek Grammar*, rev. ed. (Cambridge, Mass., 1956).
Snell, B., *The Discovery of the Mind*, trans. T. G. Rosenmeyer (Cambridge, Mass., 1953).
Sorabji, R., "Aristotle and Oxford Philosophy," *American Philosophical Quarterly*, 6 (1969), 127-135.
Staniland, H., *Universals* (N. Y., 1972).
Steiner, M., "Platonism and the Causal Theory of Knowledge," *Journal of Philosophy*, 70 (1973), 57-66.
Stenzel, J., *Plato's Method of Dialectic*, trans. D. J. Allan (London, 1940).
Stevenson, C. L., *Ethics and Language* (New Haven, 1943).
Strang, C., "Plato and the Third Man," *Proceedings of the Aristotelian Society*, supp. vol. 37 (1963), 147-176.
Taylor, A. E., **1**, "The Analysis of ΕΠΙΣΤΗΜΗ in Plato's Seventh Epistle," *Mind*, N.S. 21 (1912), 347-370.
   2, *A Commentary on Plato's* Timaeus (Oxford, 1928).
   3, *Plato: The Man and his Work*, 2nd ed. (N.Y., 1929).
   4, *Socrates* (London, 1933).
   5, *The Parmenides of Plato* (Oxford, 1934).
Thompson, E. S., ed., *The Meno of Plato* (London, 1901).
Tigner, S., "On the 'kinship' of 'all nature' in Plato's *Meno*," *Phronesis*, 15 (1970), 1-4.
Urmson, J. O., "Recognition," *Proceedings of the Aristotelian Society*, 65 (1955-56), 259-280.
Vlastos, G., **1**, "The Disorderly Motion in the *Timaeus*," *Classical Quarterly*, 33 (1939), 71-83, reprinted in Allen **3**, pp. 379-399. (Latter pagination.)
   2, "The Third Man Argument in the *Parmenides*," *Philosophical Review*, 63 (1954), 319-349, reprinted in Allen **3**, pp. 231-264. (Latter pagination.)
   3, introd. to *Plato's Protagoras*, trans. B. Jowett, rev. M. Ostwald (N. Y., 1956).
   4, "Socratic Knowledge and Platonic 'Pessimism,'" *Philosophical Review*, 66 (1957), 226-238.
   5, review, *Gnomon*, 41 (1963), 641-655, reprinted in Vlastos **14**, pp. 379-403. (Latter pagination.)

6, "Ἰσονομία Πολιτική" Mau and Schmidt, pp. 1-35, reprinted in Vlastos 14, pp. 164-203. (Latter pagination.)

7, "Creation in the *Timaeus*: Is it a Fiction?" Allen **3**, pp. 401-419.

8, "Degrees of Reality in Plato," Bambrough, pp. 1-18.

9, *"Anamnesis* in the *Meno," Dialogue*, 4 (1965), 143-167.

10, "Reasons and Causes in the *Phaedo*," *Philosophical Review*, 78 (1969), 291-325.

11, ed., *Plato I: A Collection of Critical Essays* (Garden City, 1970).

12, ed., *The Philosophy of Socrates* (New York, 1971).

13, ed., *Plato II: A Collection of Critical Essays* (Garden City, 1971).

14, *Platonic Studies* (Princeton, 1973).

von Arnim, J., *Platos Jugenddialoge und die Entstehungszeit des Phaidros* (Leipzig, 1914).

von Fritz, K., **1**, "Νοῦς, Νοεῖν, and their Derivatives in Pre-Socratic Philosophy," *Classical Philology*, 40 (1945), 223-242, and 41 (1946), 12-34, reprinted in Mourelatos, pp. 23-85.

2, "Die philosophische Stelle im siebten Brief und die Frage der 'esoterischen' Philosophie Platons," *Phronesis*, 11 (1966), 117-153.

3, *Platon in Sizilien und das Problem der Philosophenherrschaft* (Berlin, 1968).

Wallace, J., "Some Logical Roles of Adverbs," *Journal of Philosophy*, 68 (1971), 690-714.

Wedberg, A., *Plato's Philosophy of Mathematics* (Stockholm, 1955).

Weingartner, R. H., *The Unity of the Platonic Dialogue* (N. Y., 1973).

White, N. P., **1**, "Aristotle on Sameness and Oneness," *Philosophical Review*, 80 (1971), 177-197.

2, "Origins of Aristotle's Essentialism," *Review of Metaphysics*, 26 (1972), 57-85.

3, "Inquiry," *Review of Metaphysics*, 28 (1974), 289-310.

Wieland, W., *Die aristotelische Physik* (Göttingen, 1962).

Wittgenstein, L., **1**, *Logisch-Philosophische Abhandlung*, trans. D. F. Pears and B. F. McGuinness as *Tractatus Logico-Philosophicus*, corr. ed. (London, 1963).

2, *The Blue and Brown Books* (Oxford, 1958).

3, *Philosophical Investigations*, trans. G. E. M. Anscombe, 2nd ed. (Oxford, 1958).

Wood, O. P. and Pitcher, G., eds., *Ryle: A Collection of Critical Essays* (N. Y., 1970).

Zeller, E., **1**, *Die Philosophie der Griechen in ihrer geschichtlichen Entwicklung*, 6th ed., Teil I, Abteilung 2, rev. W. Nestle (Leipzig, 1920).

2, *Die Philosophie der Griechen in ihrer geschichtlichen Entwicklung*, , 5th ed., Teil II, Abteilung 1 (Leipzig, 1922).

Index of
Passages Referred To

Plato (Continued)

478-80	84, 85
479	23, 84, 85, 106, 107, 108
480	108, 213
VI	96
VI-VII	28, 33
484	106, 108, 127, 189, 213
485	59
487	112
488	23, 24
490	189
492	23, 24
493	23, 24
500	106
500-1	86
505	113
506	23, 78, 84, 113
507	87, 106
507-9	103, 112
508	106, 107
508-9	95, 112
509	78, 106, 107, 114
509-11	78, 84, 109, 110
510	109, 110, 111, 112
510-11	114
511	106, 109, 110, 111, 112
VII	94, 96
514-17	107, 108
514ff.	91, 107, 108
515	86, 109
515-16	107
517	112
518	91, 107
519	112
520	84
521	59, 84, 94
521ff.	94
522	59, 94, 196
522ff.	122
523-24	85
524	84, 94, 109, 123, 129, 152
525	94, 109

Plato (Continued)

525-26	111
526	106, 109, 111, 112
527	107, 109, 213
529	59, 106, 111
529-30	111
530-31	111
531	33, 87, 109
532	87, 103, 107, 109, 112, 114, 127
532-33	90
532-34	114
533	98, 109, 111, 112, 113
534	87, 94, 98, 102, 103, 104, 109, 110, 111, 112, 114, 189
534-35	109
538	23, 84
538-39	24
540	86, 106
541	24
555	95
562	95
575	79
592	84
X	84
596	27, 81, 86
596-97	84
597	81
598	84
600	212
602	84
603	84
611-12	213
Seventh Letter (*Epistle VII*),	55, 86, 149, 199-215 *passim*, 220, 228, 231
326	201
328	200
336	201
341	130, 200, 203, 205, 207, 208,

Index of
Proper Names